MART
CH

Christopher Catherwood, the editor of this book, is the
eldest grandchild of Martyn Lloyd-Jones. An editor
with Kingsway Publications, he has prepared for them
three of the Doctor's posthumous books: *Joy Unspeakable*
(1984), *Prove All Things* (1985) and *The Cross* (1986), as
well as *I Am Not Ashamed* (1986) for Hodder and
Stoughton. His own book, *Five Evangelical Leaders*, contains a chapter on Dr Lloyd-Jones, the only account of
the Doctor's entire life to have appeared to date.

Christopher Catherwood has been especially active in
the work of the International Fellowship of Evangelical
Students (IFES), of which the Doctor served as the first
chairman and later as president or vice-president until
his death in 1981.

Also by Christopher Catherwood
  Five Evangelical Leaders

Other Highland Books
by Paul Tournier
  The Adventure of Living
  Escape from Loneliness
  A Doctor's Casebook in the Light of the Bible
  Secrets
  Marriage Difficulties
  A Place for You
  The Strong and the Weak
  Learning to Grow Old
by Michael Green
  Evangelism in the Early Church
by Edith Schaeffer
  What is a Family?
by John L. Sherrill
  They Speak with other Tongues
by Phyllis Thompson
  Gladys Aylward: A London Sparrow
by Thomas à Kempis
  The Imitation of Christ (A Modern Reading)
by Oswald Sanders
  Prayer Power Unlimited
  What of Those Who Have Never Heard?
by Michael Harper
  Walk in the Spirit
by F. F. Bruce
  Paul and his Converts
edited by Edward England
  A Way with Words: A Handbook for Christian Writers
  David Watson: A Portrait by His Friends
by Jack R. Taylor
  The Hallelujah Factor
by Gordon MacDonald
  Ordering Your Private World
by Sabina Wurmbrand
  The Pastor's Wife
by Kenneth N. Taylor
  How to Grow—First Steps for New Christians

MARTYN LLOYD-JONES
CHOSEN BY GOD

Edited by
CHRISTOPHER CATHERWOOD

HIGHLAND BOOKS

Printed in Great Britain for
HIGHLAND BOOKS
1 Broadway House, The Broadway,
Crowborough, East Sussex TN6 1BY by
Richard Clay Ltd, Bungay, Suffolk

CONTENTS

FOREWORD

As I look back over the 54 years of our life together, one of the things for which I am most grateful is the rich and varied fellowship which we enjoyed with people all over the world. So it is a pleasure to me to be able to read these different contributions from men who shared my husband's joy in the Gospel and his desire to make known the unsearchable riches of Christ. And these are but representatives of the hundreds of others whom we knew and loved over the years.

I thank God upon every remembrance of our friends and am grateful too for all the love and support that I have received from so many since my husband went, as he said, 'to the glory.'

It is my hope that others may enjoy these varied glimpses of 'The Doctor' and that the Lord whom he loved and served may be glorified.

15 August 1985   *Bethan Lloyd-Jones*

INTRODUCTION

In a Welsh graveyard, near Newcastle Emlyn, lies a simple tomb. On it are inscribed the words:

Martyn Lloyd-Jones 1899–1981

'For I determined not to know
anything among you save Jesus
Christ and Him crucified.'

These words sum up what was most important about my maternal grandfather, Martyn Lloyd-Jones, known to thousands of Christians throughout the world by the affectionate title of 'The Doctor.'

Various tributes to him appeared shortly after his death on 1 March 1981. But none of the books that were planned ever materialised. So when my agent, Edward England, who had published my grandfather's classic work *Preaching and Preachers* for Hodder and Stoughton, asked if I would edit such a volume, I was naturally delighted to accept the offer. The family warmly agreed and this book is the result.

When my grandparents first moved to Wales their arrival aroused much interest, including that of the press. Up-and-coming Harley Street physicians seldom abandon fame and fortune to go to one of the poorer parts of Wales to preach the Gospel. My grandmother, besieged by reporters, refused to make a statement. So one of the more creative journalists, who had to write something, put in his story the words: '"My husband is a wonderful man," said Mrs Lloyd-Jones.'

My grandmother's reactions can be imagined, but the contributors to this book would not disagree—Martyn Lloyd-Jones was indeed a truly remarkable man, chosen by God for His service. He was a man of many talents, as reflected by the wide variety of contributions contained here. A family man, and very much a Welshman, he trained as a doctor but was called by God to preach in an unusually powerful style. He was an enthusiast, an encourager of others, loved throughout the world. (When he died, my grandmother received letters—including some from people who thought him still alive—from all over the USA and many other countries, paying tribute to all that his ministry had meant to them.) He had a profoundly theological mind, and was responsible for reintroducing Puritan thinking and doctrine into the mainstream of Christian life. His impact on Evangelicals, on both sides of the Atlantic, was enormous. Through his numerous books—adapted versions of his sermons—he influenced thousands of Christians who never heard him at Westminster Chapel. The aim of the chapters that follow is to reflect this exceptional diversity.

Some of the contributors to this book are themselves internationally known Evangelicals, household names in many countries. Others are highly respected on their own side of the Atlantic; others may be less illustrious. But each contribution is important in its own right. Many more people could have contributed. Some, like Douglas Johnson, were invited to do so but could not meet the deadline for publication.

Above all, each author knows the same living Jesus Christ that the Doctor preached. Every contributor has sought to maintain the perspective that the Doctor would have wished. We pay tribute to a great man, whose strength lay not in himself but in the fact that he had an infinitely great God.

Acknowledgments

I would first like to thank Edward England, who had the idea for this book. My parents, Frederick and Elizabeth Catherwood, have been both helpful and encouraging, as well as joining Edward in giving me advice. My grandmother, Mrs Bethan Lloyd-Jones, has given me her full support, as has her younger daughter, Mrs Ann Desmond. I would also wish to thank Honor Gilbert of Highland Books. I would like to convey special thanks to Wyn James and Brenda Lewis of the Evangelical Movement of Wales for their kind permission to reproduce the chapters by Frederick and Elizabeth Catherwood, which appeared originally as the Evangelical Press of Wales booklet, *Martyn Lloyd-Jones: The Man and His Books*. (This booklet also contains a bibliography and essay on Dr Lloyd-Jones' works up to 1983.) The chapter by Elwyn Davies first appeared in the EMW's *Evangelical Magazine of Wales* in 1981. I must also thank *Christianity Today* for their permission to reprint the Doctor's interview with Carl Henry, which first appeared in the issue of 8 February, 1980. Lastly, but by no means least, the individual contributors have been more than helpful, especially in meeting their deadlines, and any success that the book will have will be theirs.

Christopher Catherwood

Chapter One

HIS PLACE IN EVANGELICALISM

by

Robert Horn

Robert M. Horn is the editor of *Evangelicals Now*. A former pastor and staff member of the Universities and Colleges Christian Fellowship, he is now a trustee of the Martyn Lloyd-Jones Recordings Trust in Sussex, which houses the tapes of over a thousand of Dr Martyn Lloyd-Jones' sermons at Westminster Chapel.

One fact about the Doctor's place in evangelicalism is undeniable: he could never be ignored. Whether others agreed with him or not (and some at times did not), they had to take notice of him and what he said. This was not because he held offices or positions, for he held few. He cared nothing for status or its symbols. He had none of the trappings that usually signify 'influence.'

He started no movements; indeed, his views on them were more likely to lose him influence. He felt that the movements which had proliferated last century and since in evangelicalism were more bane than blessing. They each distorted the balance of truth, by each stressing their one truth. They ignored the church and often minimised or worked against it.

He published no paper—only the *Westminster Record* with an unadorned sermon of his every month. He initiated no campaigns, no crusades, no protests, no societies. Only after his retirement from Westminster Chapel did he publish many books. His influence rested on his own character and convictions, on what he was under God and how the Spirit filled him, on the mind and heart with which he served Christ; yet that influence was incalculable.

He led countless numbers to faith in Christ, from every

strata of society, wealth and education and from diverse ethnic origins. He powerfully influenced hundreds of men who became pastors or evangelists. He encouraged Christians all over the world, not least through his work in the International Fellowship of Evangelical Students. He sharpened the thinking and strengthened the Christian confidence of many who were battling with non-Christian approaches to life, whether in medicine and science, theology and philosophy, or the hard world of business. He put heart into many perplexed Christians, discouraged pastors and struggling churches, as he gave them his time, wisdom and love. His influence goes on, for he taught more than one generation how to teach others also. Today the preaching in many pulpits and the pastoral counsel in many homes clearly echoes the Doctor's example. He gave a distinctive lead to the whole of British evangelicalism—a lead that was potent, even though sometimes misunderstood and not always accepted.

Two problems are unavoidable in writing (as I have been asked to do) about 'the place that the Doctor held in British evangelicalism.' The first is that the subject invites comparisons. How did the Doctor compare with other luminaries on the British scene? Was he more or less influential? The Doctor's own example is the best solution of this difficulty. He was never interested in personalities or big names; to him it was the issues that mattered. He was concerned to do what was right, not to calculate effects. That was a large part of his influence. We shall try to base our assessment on the same approach.

The other difficulty is how to be objective. In many areas of his life there is much indisputable evidence. Published and recorded sermons give an objective basis for evaluating his preaching. Conference records and committee minutes show his role in the student world. Lectures to the Christian Medical Fellowship demonstrate his influence there. But how to determine with any precision his place in British

evangelicalism? The task is subjective and selective. Time
has not moved on enough to allow a totally detached view.
There is no answer to this problem, other than to be aware
of it, to invite the reader's understanding and to press on.

It is not difficult to describe his influence on one British
Evangelical (well, as British as he can be with an American
mother and a New Zealand father). I first heard the Doctor
at Westminster Chapel in my student days, when I occasionally played truant from my home church, and also at
student conferences. In my time on the Inter-Varsity
Fellowship (now UCCF) staff (1959–66) he was full of
patient wisdom when consulted about problems. To that
generation of students and staff Reformed doctrine was very
novel—intoxicating to some, unnerving to many. His
counsel was always towards persuasion rather than con-
frontation; he wanted us to understand those who differed
from us, to act with mind and heart engaged, to win people,
not arguments.

When I became a pastor I regularly attended the Westminster Fellowship. Like countless others, I sometimes
shared pastoral problems with him. On one such occasion I
outlined a case, the like of which had never entered my brief
pastoral experience before. It was not so much what he said,
for subsequent analysis showed that he had given rather
little direct advice. It was his method and his heart that
impressed. You felt that you were his only concern, that he
was giving his whole self to you. He was such a good listener
and such a good questioner. That was his method, though
to call it a method makes it sound much too mechanical.
Other elder statesmen would have recognised the problems
as 'number 342' and drawn the standard solution out of the
appropriate mental pigeon hole. Not the Doctor. He asked
questions: How did it arise? Who is affected? What is it
leading to? What Scriptures or principles have you turned
to? How do you think they bear on it? What would happen if
you did this ... or that?

When I left my eyes were watery with gratitude. I had no directive, no dictated solution, but simply the right questions to ask and the biblical basis on which to answer them and work things out. I had been taught to think and perceive at a moment when the problem seemed so big as to be beyond comprehension. I had not only been helped with one case, but given an approach to other pastoral problems. That was genuine in-service training, far better than anything I received in theological college.

The same applied when I consulted him from time to time concerning the *Evangelical Times*, the monthly paper I have edited since 1973. He never pushed a policy at the paper; he never interfered. He never niggled at details. He was concerned about the general direction, the overall thrust. He made you think about the big issues and trusted you to work out their detailed applications, saying always, 'keep on, keep on.'

His influence on this one individual was certainly one of encouragement. It was essentially the same in his role within British evangelicalism. His influence was founded on his long ministry at Westminster Chapel. That was his base. He showed there that the Word of God speaks powerfully today. He disliked talk of 'the relevance' of the Bible or of Christianity—you might as well talk of the relevance of petrol for a car. It was essential. Scripture was God-breathed, inerrant, authoritative, sufficient; his ministry showed that he believed that. He had no reservations about it and no new revelations to add to it. But his ministry also demonstrated what may be called a doctrine of the animation of Scripture. By the Holy Spirit the written word, ever true, came alive to his hearers as at the same time (in the vogue phrase) the 'now' Word of God. To him old and new were inseparable.

At a time when some Evangelicals were putting too much faith in academic qualifications, he showed that you did not need degrees to have discernment or think biblically. You did not need to be high-flown to reach students or simplistic to touch the less educated. He treated people as people, whoever they were. The child and the professor both understood him.

The Doctor was a particular kind of preacher, one with 'logic on fire.' Some of his contemporaries had little biblical logic, but much heat; they left you instantly challenged but not permanently helped. Others had much logic, but little fire; they gave sound expositions and taught you. The Doctor had much logic and much fire. That was why he was exciting to listen to—and a touch unpredictable. I do not mean that he was inconsistent, only that he had the same element of surprise, the same ability to unsettle and provoke, that Scripture itself does.

His place in British evangelicalism owed much to his leadership of the Westminster Fellowship of ministers. There he made us think; woe betide the man who spoke before he thought. That was why many of us thought— hard and deeply—and even then did not speak. He only ever cut down those whom he knew could take it, and only in order to make everyone think.

He constantly emphasised the priority of the mind. A clear example of this was at the IVF annual conference at Swanwick in 1956. He was billed to lead an open discussion for over 500 students on 'Guidance.' He entered and sat down on the platform, reluctantly taking off his overcoat. 'Our subject is "Guidance",' he said, 'so where do we begin?' It somehow seemed that he, not we, should speak. After a long silent moment, one student said: 'Oh, it's quite simple. It's just a matter of prayer.'

The Doctor slowly rose, began to don his coat and made as if to leave, saying: 'Very well, there's no more to be said. That's it. We can all go.' Cries of 'No, no' rang out from the hall. 'Well then, what's wrong with that answer? What more must be said?' By then everyone was thinking hard. He proceeded to lead us into a most illuminating and practical

discussion, all the while gently pushing us to thinking out
what Scripture actually said and how to apply it.

He influenced his generation of Evangelicals because he
had a mind that was unafraid. He knew that a biblical mind
could face all the facts—on every subject, from brainwashing through biblical criticism to evolution. If for
example, the Lord were genuinely blessing a group with
whom we did not agree doctrinally, we were not to take the
easy course and dismiss the uncomfortable fact as the mere
appearance of blessing; we were to face the reality and see
what we should learn from it. If some people (to take a quite
different example) thought acupuncture was a quasi-
medical adjunct of eastern mysticism, we were not therefore
to dismiss it but to look at the facts and find the proper
explanation. He was once asked a question about this at the
Westminster Fellowship. It was from a young pastor who
was afraid that a lady in his congregation would be led even
into the occult if she took advice to have acupuncture. The
Doctor gave an impromptu hour-long dissertation on that
subject, in which he encouraged us not to go by myth or
rumour, but gave us facts and helped us to evaluate them.

The Doctor always wanted to make people think. This
was one of his major roles within evangelicalism. He was
not first concerned to make Christians do something; he
knew that it is much easier to produce activity of the body
than of the mind. He wanted people to think biblically for
themselves, knowing that they would then act not out of
emotion or coercion, but conviction. The mind came first
for him, as the only proper route to the heart and will.

That emphasis was needed when he first came into wider
evangelical circles before and after the 1939–45 war. Many
student conferences and Bible conventions were more
remarkable for chorus-singing and 'the challenge of the
higher life' than for genuine Bible teaching. They moved
many, but grounded few. The Doctor had a profound role in
challenging that. Of all people, he argued, students should

think—not repeat choruses like a Sunday school class. Conventions should not offer a dubiously based 'higher life', but think through the whole New Testament teaching on sanctification.

Many such occasions, little by little, have altered their emphasis over the years, not least because of the Doctor's general stimulus to the evangelical world. He would be the first to say that such a role needs to be performed in each generation. Now that he has passed, it needs to be done again, not least in circles that have seen much growth through the Holy Spirit but are in the same danger of superficiality and lack of biblical thought.

Certainly he enabled countless Christians to see and feel that they could be fully committed to the Bible without committing intellectual suicide. That was no mean achievement when biblical thinkers (sadly not always the same as biblical scholars) were few and when the tide of liberal and humanist ideas was surging so strongly against the Bible.

If he was passionate about the mind and about truth, he was even more so about life and vitality. As he concluded the Puritan Conference of 1960, attended by lovers of Reformed theology, adamant for doctrinal precision, he spoke from 1 Corinthians 8:1–3: 'Knowledge puffs up...' Knowledge, he said, is all-important and doctrine is absolutely vital. It must always come first. The conference was purring. But he added, it is possible for us to develop a false view of knowledge. The intellect has priority, but that does not permit a purely intellectual interest. The will and the heart must be involved. If we cannot say we love God, can we say that we know Him? We are dealing with the living God, not with a mere knowledge of Him. Life was paramount.

He challenged the low level of spiritual life in the churches. He was saddened that orthodoxy was often dead, activist but not alive; saddened, for example, that many saw big crusades as the answer to this lack of spiritual life. He simply stood off from the Billy Graham crusades from 1954 onwards and was roundly criticised as being against evangelism. That charge was hard to sustain, when people saw the steady numbers converted under his Sunday evening sermons. His influence in this matter began to grow again, as some at least saw that the claims at the start of a typical crusade ('I believe God is preparing to send a mighty revival...') were not borne out by the results. He could not bear triumphalism from any quarter. At each successive large event he rejoiced as individuals were genuinely converted, but he saw that the church as a whole was unimproved. He wanted and pleaded not for occasional bursts of activity, but revival. He never let us forget that or settle for less.

And he never let us forget history—history in general or our evangelical history in particular. He gave us a sense of the flow of history, so that we could see where we had come from. He gave us back our roots, and with them a strong security. He made us aware of our heritage. He set our day in the context of God's ongoing purposes. He made history live and speak. Few others even attempted that, but history was in his bones as much as the Bible and both kept coming out, the one subservient to the other and constantly illustrating it. This was a crucial contribution.

From that, in part, came his searching of the times through which he lived. He dissented at times from another highly perceptive contemporary, Francis Schaeffer, and is on record as disparaging apologetics. 'Nothing has so caused us to forget God....as our concern for apologetics' he told the 1971 conference of ministers in Wales. I am sure he would deny this, but I always felt that such comments reflected his penchant for hyperbole. 'There is nothing more vital for us than...' he would say, whatever text he was handling. Every text was the most crucial. Despite his strictures, he certainly showed a highly informed awareness of many areas of human life and thought—intellectual, moral, social, aesthetic, psychological, philosophical, medical, economic, historical, spiritual. He knew his age and he made use, discreet but definite (and sometimes devastating), of that awareness. He preached as a mid-20th century preacher, not as one from his beloved 18th century. This knowledge, so thorough in so many disciplines, gave him a unique place in directing the thought and energies of his contemporaries.

All this gave him a leader's ability to speak to and challenge particular situations or trends. He never rested on generalities. He was a big enough man to speak appropriately to different groups. The doctrinaire he kept on challenging about life and power, the more activist about doctrine and truth. Inclusive churchmen he kept reminding about doctrinal clarity, the more separatist about love and acceptance. The tradition-bound had to hear him about liberty, the 'liberated' about order. He would constantly encourage, but he would never let us settle. He was always urging us on, showing by his own life that there was more to be gained.

It was because of all these concerns, especially for truth and life, that he was sometimes involved in controversy. He hated controversy, but was for that reason most suited for it. He always focussed on issues, principles, causes and effects—never on individuals. This was true of the controversy that can be dated precisely as 18 October, 1966. On that Tuesday evening he provoked, surprised and unsettled his hearers from Scripture. He was addressing the crowded opening rally of the Evangelical Alliance's National Assembly of Evangelicals in Westminster Central Hall, under the chairmanship of the Rev John Stott. I recall that, by the end of the meeting, the atmosphere was electric. None of us had been at an occasion like it—the two leading Evangelicals of the day differing in public over a matter of such practical importance.

The Doctor had been invited to speak. It was a measure

of his standing in British evangelicalism that he was the obvious person to address such a gathering of the clans on such as hot subject. Moreover, he had never hidden his approach to it. Over previous years, for example, he had set out his basic principles in two publications from the Inter-Varsity Press: *Maintaining the Evangelical Faith Today* (an IVF presidential address in 1952) and *The Basis of Christian Unity: a study of John 17 and Ephesians 4* (in 1962). In the months prior to October 1966 he had been asked to 'give evidence' to the Evangelical Alliance's 'Commission on Church Unity;' and that Commission had asked him to say in public to the National Assembly of Evangelicals what he had laid before them in private. He was not taking advantage of the meeting, but simply answering that invitation.

On that Tuesday evening he pointed out that the ecumenical movement had put denominations in the melting pot as never before. He noted also that Evangelicals were the least concerned of any about unity and were sadly divided among the various comprehensive denominations. Those who were at one on the basics of the faith were the only ones who could be guilty of schism: separation from liberals was not schism, separation from fellow Evangelicals was. He then said: 'I make an appeal to you evangelical people this evening. What reasons have we for not coming together? Why is it that we are so anxious to hold to our inherited positions?'

The wording of his appeal was for 'fellowship or association,' but it was misunderstood by some—a quite vociferous some—as urging the formation of a evangelical super-denomination. He had never said or wanted that; in any case he was realist enough to know that it was never on. He wanted a cutting of ties with liberal/ecumenical councils and denominations, so that all the evangelical churches could, unfettered, pull together.

Earlier in the meeting John Stott had urged that spiritual unity be expressed visibly. After the Doctor had sat down,

John Stott said: 'I hope no-one will make a precipitate decision after this moving address...I believe Scripture is against him...'

That meeting was a watershed. The Doctor had known that the issue of Evangelicals' practical loyalties could not be avoided: would they stick to their mixed denominations or commit themselves to visible Gospel unity (unity, not organisational union)? In the event, denominational loyalties proved stronger for most. The evangelical scene has not been the same since. The Doctor's appeal had to be made, but (and this is a subjective view) was never likely to be widely heeded. Inherited allegiances (whether to Anglicanism, Methodism, the Baptist Union or other groups) ran very deep. Nevertheless a great and unrepeatable opportunity for united evangelical life and witness was missed.

Before 1966, Evangelicals had been more conscious of their ties to each other than their links to denominations. To be sure, there was a certain individualism about evangelicalism's conferences, conventions, movements and events; no one thought much about the church and we were in general militantly defensive—battling for the truth against the ecumenical monoliths, with a simple clarity and robust cohesion.

After 1966 evangelicalism drifted into various camps. Anglicans, for example, became more self-consciously Anglican. The National Evangelical Anglican Congress at Keele in 1967 affirmed: 'We are deeply committed to the present and future of the Church of England. We believe that God has led us to this commitment...we do not believe secession to be a live issue...' (*Keele '67: The Congress Statement*, p.38). That, it seemed to many, was novel. Evangelical Anglicans had previously spoken as being committed to the Articles and to the Reformation heritage of the Church of England. An almost carte blanche commitment to the Church of England, comprehensive warts and all, was another matter.

In the decade following, Evangelicals in other denominations, at different tempos and in different degrees, also began to see themselves growing in numbers and to believe themselves growing in influence. Either way, denominational affairs took up time and energy that could have (and previously had) gone to inter-evangelical relationships. Evangelicals, denominational and independent, drifted apart.

This was later illustrated, even accentuated, by various events. Nineteen-seventy-one saw the publication, unexpectedly, of a book on *Growing into Union*, by two leading evangelical Anglicans and two Anglo-Catholics. Unintentionally, but effectively, that thwarted some proposed inter-evangelical initiatives on 'the church' and showed that previous evangelical consensus on priorities no longer held. Then Nottingham '77, the successor to the National Evangelical Anglican Congress at Keele, illustrated the Doctor's general thrust about what happens when Evangelicals hold to their inherited, comprehensive structures. Anglican and non-Anglican Evangelicals seemed more distant, despite Nottingham's declared good intentions towards the latter. I declare an interest in a small example of this polarisation. A large evangelical parish, on the personal initiative of its book agent, began taking the *Evangelical Times* in this period. Sales went up to 50 a month, until it came to the notice of the incumbent. Instantly—thinking it too unanglican?—the order was cancelled.

Two contrasting views of the church had surfaced: the mixed or 'comprehensive,' which Evangelicals would try to influence, even capture; and, not the pure or perfect, but the genuinely 'Gospel distinctive,' which would be as inclusive and exclusive as the Gospel itself. The two were not compatible.

Where did this leave the Doctor's influence? Undoubtedly it was diminished in mixed denominational circles. He had

trodden on too many toes (or pricked too many con-
sciences?) to be readily heard there on church issues any
more. I came across this when asked to speak at the Anglican Evangelical Study Conference (the Eclectics) in
October 1968 and 1969, on two related issues, both affected
by and perhaps indirectly arising from October 1966: (1) A
non-Anglican Evangelical's view of Keele's statement on
the church; and (2) Comprehensiveness in the church.
Many individual parish ministers were deeply uneasy about
the Keele direction, but hesitated to say so, feeling unable to
handle debate with those (mainly bright theological college
staff or academics) who were, it seemed to me, writing the
agenda for Anglican evangelicalism.

Nevertheless, many individuals in mixed denominations
still held the Doctor in high respect. They valued his teaching and continued to read his books, which carried his
teaching far and wide, overriding denominational and
national boundaries. (One outstanding example of this was,
and still is, in Operation Mobilisation. Through George
Verwer's initiative it distributed thousands of copies—
300,000 of *Spiritual Depression* alone.)

In the churches that fell the other side of the 1966
watershed the Doctor's influence grew even stronger, as it
needed to. He had to warn against the dangers of self-
righteousness in those who claim to stand for truth. Many
ministers, for example, left the Baptist Union after the
tragic presidential address at its 1971 Assembly which
doubted, indeed denied, the deity of Christ. The Doctor
knew that there were dangers in the seceding mentality.
Those who take a stand can harden and become resentful.
Splits can lead to more splits. In October 1966 he had
appealed to Evangelicals in liberal and mixed denominations to separate from them in order to manifest evangelical unity. Now, on the same basis and for the same goal,
he was urging those who accepted his appeal not to split
from each other. He stressed more than once that such

division is schism, and he continued to set his face against it.

He therefore insisted, with vigour and full biblical back-up, that Evangelicals should not separate over three matters in particular: Calvinism or Arminianism (i.e. the question of the sovereignty of God and the human will); charismatic issues (whether spiritual gifts have ceased); and church issues (i.e. baptism, church government and order). He insisted on the distinction between primary and secondary in matters in belief; and he encouraged the Evangelicals to hold together. He was often the crucial factor, humanly speaking, in their cohesion. His stature shamed some groups into keeping relatively quiet about their distinctives, though some have come more into the open since his passing.

The state of independent evangelicalism since 1966 has not been all that he encouraged and urged it to be. It became clear that not all the blame for evangelical divisions lay the other side of the watershed. Independents were prone to subdivide and did not always keep a sense of proportion when they differed from each other. Little empires tended to form. Those who urged secession seldom tried to make their own grass greener than it was on the denominational side. Some subconsciously expected great blessing to crown their secession or separatist stance, and were a little aggrieved when others seemed to see more growth and spiritual prosperity. The separatist camp often looked uninviting to any would-be seceder.

This situation did not remain static. Some went on, as entrenched as ever in their denominations; others became ever more committed to no-compromise separation. Some in the inclusive denominations, however, came to see that triumphalism is one thing, the triumph of truth quite another. A more biblical realism emerged. They became more aware of who and where their true friends were. At the same time some outside such bodies came to see that a church which is uncompromised doctrinally can be com-

promised just as seriously in other ways; and that cold or
dead orthodoxy is of little use to God or man. They came to
see that blessing cannot be channelled according to paper
lists of ecclesiastical association, but runs much more along
the lines of a people's working relationship with God, His
truth and other Gospel churches.

How would the Doctor have spoken to this situation? We
would all love to know. We can only believe that he would
have done what he always did: set out the same biblical
principles on unity and truth and then applied them
realistically to the actual (not the imagined or theoretical)
situation. He had a way of surprising people...

The Doctor's thinking was consistent, but never static. In
his latter years as he reflected on his ministry and as he gave
more thought to the Holy Spirit and the church, he urged
what had not been immediately apparent in his Westminster ministry. He now saw beyond that, as his summing
up at the Westminster Fellowship on 2 October 1978
showed. I took notes at the time from which these are
extracts:

'Can you see one man preaching twice on a Sunday... the
same man delivering his Bible lecture at the mid-week
meeting...and an address at the prayer meeting? I cannot
see that in the New Testament, I cannot...There is a
dissatisfaction in the churches. I think the people are right;
they feel there is something wrong. So, when anything that
approximates to the New Testament appears, they are
interested. That is not wrong...We say that we are Biblical
men, governed by Scripture. When confronted with Scriptural teaching we say: "That applies only to that time." But
this is a new dispensationalism and very dangerous. It is
wrong to think that much Scripture does not apply now.
This is a basic and fundamental thing...We are Free
Churchmen, but people are feeling that there is a deadness
about us (that is a general statement.) So we should be
profoundly dissatisfied. In revivals you get the people taking

part; so we should reexamine all our activities. We should ask: why is the church now so different from the New Testament and from revival? It is no longer necessary that Paul write I Corinthians 14 to us, but it should be...Much trouble today is because people are ignorant of history; the idea that people should take part is entirely biblical. The one-man ministry has been carried much too far. It is entirely remote from the liveliness of the New Testament. We are all living stones, not dead. We need to recapture this. This is desirable. Our business is to get people to pray, to relate experiences. So the next step is: how do they, when do they take part?

'The New Testament teaches that everyone has some contribution to make, for God does differentiate between person and person. The one who teaches is to be given double honour, but this has hardened now so that one man does everything and others do nothing. One man should expound, because he is the most competent to do so. But in more private meetings all the church should take part—the ideal church is where all wish to take part in prayer...It is as in a family. A parent must never crush a child; a child is not to be cowed and fearful. That is very bad. That is wrong. There should be freedom—controlled and disciplined freedom. Don't prohibit it, control it...Rather I am to do everything that I can to make the church to which I belong conform to the New Testament. There is something right in the ferment today. Our object is edification and the business of the ministry is to exercise this control—to say "This will be profitable/that won't edify." People are right in what they say about the freedom, but it is to be controlled. There is clearly something wrong with things as they are among us. If it is possible for people to go out feeling dull, tired and bored, then that is a travesty of the Christian church. We've got to work this out. We've got to act in a period of transition. We must reject the idea that anything new is wrong...We are still to advocate participation because we believe that life always exposes itself. There are people in our churches who are traditionalists but they are wrong.'

The Doctor found himself dealing, in independent circles, with these two views of the church—the one-man view and the body view. He had at Westminster, for obvious reasons, generally conducted his ministry on the former view—though the earlier Friday discussions and his practice at Sandfields were more open. There seems little doubt, however, that he was leaning away from one man doing everything towards controlled freedom and participation.

His spiritual and intellectual stature made him a difficult, almost impossible, man to emulate. All great men, despite their best efforts, attract imitations. Many great men are poorly served by such disciples. This was sometimes so for the Doctor. Some who copied his method of exposition (verse by verse, sometimes word by word) generally lacked his deep knowledge of Scripture. In his hands that method was informed and controlled by his grasp of the whole counsel of God; in other hands it could degenerate into a weekly airing of the bees in the preacher's bonnet. Their texts varied, but not their message. For them to preach 'But God . . .' could be very dull and repetitive, whereas for him it was so different.

So great was his gifting and stature that many, scarcely aware of so doing, imitated his approach, as I tried to do. In my first weeks in the ministry I quickly learnt that I needed a method that would deliver me as much as possible from my own bees, that would ensure that I was expounding, not imposing. Like some others, I concluded that I needed a different expository approach if I were not to wear Saul's armour.

The Doctor suffered from disciples in other ways. His name and authority were invoked for conflicting causes, especially after his death. (A cynic new on the scene now might wonder how many Doctors there were.) According to the claims, the Doctor was pro or anti charismatic; pro one-man ministry or participation; strong on Reformed doctrine or soft on Arminians; pro unity or pro secession. Quotations 'proved' anything.

On the other hand, some erstwhile disciples became a shade condescending: 'Of course, he was a great preacher, but he was rather quiet on Reformed distinctives...had strange views on the Spirit...was obsessed with revival... made the basic mistake of thinking some truth primary...' Those are the comments of little men. Many claimed him, none owned him. The Gospel lion was no-one's pet. He had a far bigger mind and heart than any who play him up or put him down.

This did not mean that he was infallible. His friends could disagree with him without risking the friendship. Some obviously dissented from him on churchmanship, others on Bible versions, others still were not persuaded that all his comments on the Spirit were biblically sound.

He was not the captive of any group or 'ism' or school or movement. He was bigger than them all. That was his greatness. That secured him his unique place in British evangelicalism. He was Christ-centred and saw all else from that perspective. He had a sense of proportion, a sense of timing, a sense of history, a sense of God.

And he had no sense of self-importance. He hated effusive introductions before he spoke. He got on with the work and forgot himself. He was only concerned with others' praise or criticism insofar as it affected the cause, the Gospel, the name of his Lord. Throughout his 'short, uncertain earthly life and pilgrimage' he counted himself nothing. He was simply our servant for Jesus's sake—but what a servant!

He served to the end, even as his final illness approached, giving himself unstintingly to the churches. I received another illustration of this not long after his death. He had preached annually until 1979 for a friend near Carlisle, but felt he was not strong enough to do so in the spring of 1980.

However, in mid-April he 'felt a lot better' and asked to be allowed to go to preach. A meeting was hastily arranged for 4 May and over 700 people came. His friend, Eddie Stobart, wrote: ' It was a night to be remembered. Showing obvious weakness of body, he was strong in spirit, leaving his congregation in no doubt as to what it meant to be a Christian. Though perspiring heavily and very tired, he was willing to give counsel and help to those who wished to see him after the meeting.' I was present at his last sermon, at the opening in Sussex of Barcombe Baptist Chapel's new building on 8 June 1980. He was to the last leading us further on and higher up.

He always kept calling us back and up to the big things. I recall a powerful address on Romans 14:17 to the Baptist Revival Fellowship in November 1970: 'The kingdom of God is not meat and drink, but righteousness, peace and joy in the Holy Spirit.' He had only to begin on such a verse to demonstrate that there were big issues and little issues—and they were not to be confused. His big themes were the living God, Christ and His cross, the Spirit and His power, the Word and its truth. He kept these before his generation as few others could.

Chapter Two

A KIND OF PURITAN

by

James Packer

Dr Packer is the Professor of Systematic and Historical Theology at Regent College, Vancouver, Canada. The author of many books, he is best known for his international bestseller, *Knowing God*. A contemporary at Oxford of the Doctor's eldest daughter Elizabeth, he and Dr Lloyd-Jones ran the Puritan Conference together for many years.

'Sometimes he's a kind of a Puritan.' So, for quite wrong reasons, said Shakespeare's Maria of the bad-humoured buffoon Malvolio. So, for better reasons, did many say of David Martyn Lloyd-Jones. The verdict was a true one, but it lies open to misunderstanding.

What does it mean to call a person a Puritan? Maria's view has been common from Shakespeare's day to our own: namely, that Puritanism is a matter essentially of temperament and personal disposition, a habit of taking oneself too seriously and playing the role of a natural-born sourpuss and killjoy. Such was Macaulay's notion when he told the world that the Puritans hated bear-baiting not because it gave pain to the bear but because it gave pleasure to the spectators, and such was Mencken's idea when he defined a Puritan as a person who fears that somewhere, somehow, someone may be happy. A variant of this view, often found among Roman Catholics, see Manichean convictions as shaping this sourpuss spirit, as witness the following lines:

> The Puritan through life's sweet garden goes
> And plucks the thorn, and throws away the rose;
> He thinks to please, by this peculiar whim,
> The God who framed and fashioned it for him.

The stereotypes are familiar, but the belief that they catch the essence of Puritanism is nonsense.

Would individuals who felt and behaved according to the stereotypes have been found among the Puritans of history—that is, among the Calvinistic Protestants who sought to reshape or replace the Church of England between the 1560's, when the label 'Puritan' was coined, and the 1660's, when the would-be reformers had finally to admit defeat? No doubt there were some such persons among them, just as there have been in similar movements since. Any group of Christians with high moral standards is likely to attract hangers-on of this kind, from whom the unfriendly world is likely then to form its image of the group in question. But it must be said with emphasis that no Puritan teacher ever approved the ethos of censorious gloom or supposed that pleasure excludes piety and vice versa. Rather, with Calvin, the teachers condemned these attitudes, as showing ingratitude to a kind and generous Creator. And here Dr Lloyd-Jones was right with them. Posturing asceticism was to him childish immaturity, if not indeed superstitious folly. In this he was as purely Puritan, in the historically valid sense of that word, as a man could be. The Puritan pastors of history always insisted that healthy piety would ordinarily be cheerful and full of joy. 'There is no mirth like the mirth of believers,' wrote Richard Baxter. Though grimmish-looking in public and never in his prime smiling for the camera, 'The Doctor' was himself a supremely cheerful, affable, humorous man, and the reality of God's gift of joy, both joy in created things and the joy of salvation, was one of the constant emphases of his ministry.

Authentically Puritan traits do not, then, always coincide with what Puritanism is popularly thought to be; sometimes, as in the present case, they contradict the stereotype directly. Of other elements in the stereotype—pharisaism, philistinism, fanaticism, for instance—the same is true. So I had better lay it down at once in black and white that what this essay will explore is not how far Dr Lloyd-Jones fitted the popular stereotype of a Puritan, but how far he matched up to the historical reality. As I shall show, he knew what real historic Puritanism had been and heartily identified with most of it. Granted, he often said that he was more an 18th-than a 17th-century man; by this he meant that evangelism and revival ministry in the style and with the theology of George Whitefield and Jonathan Edwards was his supreme ideal for the church and his supreme goal for himself. But his references to Puritan writers when preaching, his constant advice to budding and burned-out pastors to read them, his own reading of them (Owen's and Baxter's works were among his wedding presents!) his chairing the annual Puritan and Reformed Studies Conference (later, with changed personnel, the Westminster Conference) from 1950 to 1979, his backing of the Puritan reprint programme of the Banner of Truth Trust, and his support for the ministry of the Evangelical Library, which majors in books by and about the Puritans, all show how he valued the 17th-century material. In an address on 'Puritanism and its Origins' in 1971 he declared that since 1925 'a true and living interest in the Puritans and their works has gripped me, and I am free to confess that my whole ministry has been governed by this.[1] The dependence was always in fact clear and obvious.

My own first meeting with the Doctor took place when Raymond Johnston and I, both still students, went to his vestry to float before his eyes our vision of an annual Puritan Studies Conference and to seek his help in making it a reality. I was struck at the time by the air of suppressed excitement with which he welcomed the idea, as well as by his extreme forthcomingness: not only would he host us at Westminster Chapel, but he would be permanent chairman, and get the ladies of the church to produce free lunches and teas! Thereafter he treated the two days of the conference as an unbreakable engagement, and when one year I could only be present for one day he was very cross and accused me of getting my priorities wrong! Years down the line, when the conference had grown from the 20 who met in 1950 to 200 and more, he told me that he had seen the interest that Raymond and I showed in publicizing Puritan standards of faith and devotion as one of a series of signs that God was starting to revive His work in Britain, and therefore he had given it all the backing he could. Certainly, when he and I met in his vestry over tea at each conference to plan the next one he had always given the matter advance thought and was full of suggestions about both themes and speakers. Every one of the many anniversaries that the conference celebrated was his proposal. At no stage did his interest flag, and the historical acumen which his opinions and conference contributions reflected was always of very high order.

Like the Anglican, J. C. Ryle (whom he much admired) and the Catholic, Hilaire Belloc (about whom he would have felt differently), he had a flair for bringing history to life at a popular level, and he was in himself living proof that, as Belloc once said, 'history adds to a man, giving him, as it were, a great memory of things—like a human memory, but stretched over a longer space than one human life.' The truth is that, though a formidably independent thinker, the Doctor was emotionally a traditionalist, very conscious of his heritage (Welsh, Free Church, and Reformed), very fascinated by it and very respectful towards it. Within that heritage the Puritans of history held a place of honour, as we now see.

At the conference itself, year by year, his contribution was far more significant than that of anyone else. As chairman of each of the first five two-hour sessions, he would elicit, control, and sum up a discussion lasting up to an hour after the paper had been read. Watching him with his head down as the paper-reader spoke you might have thought him near to sleep, but the discussion showed that he had been very much awake! His remarkable memory enabled him, though he took no notes, to remember with exactness all that the speaker had said, and with the lightning mental energy that always marked him he had weighed its implications and decided what he thought about it before ever the general debate began. The overall agenda was to explore the wealth of the Puritan heritage, plus other elements of Reformed history and historical theology, so as to see what guidance this legacy affords for Christian faith, life, and ministry today. As he himself put it, in his last Westminster Conference address, 'one of the chief reasons for our interest in these 17th century men...is that our world is strangely similar to theirs. I, for one, am interested in them mainly for that reason, that we may learn from them, as they battled with the same problems and difficulties which confront us. That is the main purpose of this conference.'[2]

Most of the conferees were ministers (minus wives: Dr Lloyd-Jones disliked the presence of women at what were to him professional meetings, and made no secret of the fact), and accordingly most of the discussion questions which he posed or, more often, drew from the floor were double-barrelled and ministry-related, thus: was there truth and wisdom in what had been presented? and if so, how should we act on it today? The Doctor's mastery of discussion as a teaching tool has often been remarked on, and his skill in handling these particular discussions, keeping them on the point, bringing out the logic of speakers' suggestions, demanding biblical assessment of and backing for all views expressed, feeding in relevant facts that seemed not to be generally known, and finally pulling out of the air, as it seemed (actually, out of the depths of a well-stocked mind) clarifying and encouraging comments to conclude, was to me at least a source of constant admiration.

Also, from 1959 to 1978 he gave the closing conference address. A partial list of his titles shows the wide range and practical thrust of his historical interests. 'Revival: an historical and theological survey' (1959). 'Puritan Perplexities: some lessons from 1640–1662' (1962). 'John Owen on Schism' (1963). 'John Calvin and George Whitefield' (1964). "'Ecclesiola in Ecclesia'" (1965: in a series entitled *Approaches to Reformation of the Church*). 'Henry Jacob and the first Congregational church' (1966). 'Sandemanianism' (1967). 'William Williams and Welsh Calvinistic Methodism' (1968). 'Can we learn from [Reformation and Puritan] history?' (1969). 'Puritanism and its origins' (1971). 'John Knox—the founder of Puritanism' (1972). 'Living the Christian life: new developments in the 18th and 19th century teaching' (1974). 'The French Revolution and after' (1975: in a series entitled *The Christian and the State in Revolutionary Times*). 'Preaching' (1977: in a series entitled *Anglican and Puritan Thinking*). 'John Bunyan: Church Union' (1978). These transcribed addresses, which if reprinted together would make a fascinating book, reveal easy mastery of relevant facts; vivid empathy with historical figures; shrewd discernment of people's motives, purposes, achievements, failures, blind spots, and follies; and great insight in judging how particular events furthered or frustrated the cause of God and truth. Sometimes, to be sure, the deliberately popular, non-technical, simple-man style of presentation borders on the slapdash; sometimes the generalisations are broader and more categorical than the evidence cited can bear; sometimes complex issues are over-simplified. Overall, however, Dr Lloyd-Jones' evident purpose of providing passionate wisdom and vision for spiritual edifying through mental stimulus and challenge was masterfully fulfilled each time, so that the closing address was regularly the high spot of the conference. When folk who were there think back to these gatherings they will remember the Doctor's contribution before that of anyone else.

I undertook to consider how far Dr Lloyd-Jones was

himself in line with the Puritanism that he celebrated so vigorously I must now say some general things to pave the way to that.

He was, to start with, Welsh: which meant that he had a Welshman's view of Englishmen. He saw them—perhaps I had better say, us—as having a genius for compromise and for maintaining inert institutions, but as chronically hazy on matters of principle and hardly ever able to see anything in black and white. He perceived the Church of England as an expression of this spirit, and the Puritans as an exception— from his standpoint, a glorious exception—to it. Regarding me as a latter-day Puritan (which I took as I was meant to do, as a compliment), he once told me that I was not a real Anglican, and predicted with some distress that my fellow-Anglicans would not accept me. Though not a typical Welshman, since he was unsentimental, nor a typical Welsh preacher, since he spoke and thought like a barrister and put no imaginative flights into his sermons, his Welshness—geniality, courtesy, sensitivity, warmth, magnetic vitality—remained pure and potent, and it was as a Welshman contemplating Englishmen that he viewed the Puritans and the battles they fought.

Then, he was a physician by natural inclination and training, and as a physician he brought both to Christians and their problems in the present, and also to his study of Christians and their problems in the past, a rigorously diagnostic habit of mind. Starting from a clear view of what constituted theological and spiritual wholeness, he analysed everything and everyone systematically, as a matter of habit, to detect first of all what was disordered and then also what was lacking; for he recognized that what is not seen, or not said, can be as significant a sign of spiritual or theological ill-health as any actual sin or error. He was, in fact, a brilliant diagnostician both spiritually and theologically, just as he had been medically in his Bart's Hospital and Harley Street days. (Yet he was not always a good judge of

men, being too confident that right belief and zeal would
make up for deficiencies in intelligence and character. Sheer
kindness, too, could blind him to a supporter's limitations.)
One thing that delighted him about the Puritan writers was
that they, too, in their character as physicians of the soul
(their own phrase to describe themselves), were thorough in
diagnostic analysis within the frame of their profound
understanding of what, according to Scripture, constitutes
theological and spiritual well-being, and of the damage that
one-sidedness, imbalance, and tunnel vision can do to one's
Christian life. His appreciation of the Puritans was a case of
deep calling to deep in this regard.

Furthermore, he was a biblical, rational, practical,
pastoral theologian of outstanding gifts and acumen. He
once spoke of a person we knew as having 'a naturally theological mind:' well, we are told that it takes one to know one,
and if I am any judge that is exactly what must be said about
him. Though he never attended a theological college and
was to all intents and purposes self-taught, he read constantly, thought deeply, and during the years that I knew
him could keep his conservative Reformed end up in any
company—indeed, could dominate any theological discussion in which he was involved. I saw him do that as a
member of the portentously-named Group on Differing
Biblical Presuppositions which met periodically at the
British Council of Churches; I also saw him tie a Cambridge
don in knots because of the looseness of the latter's biblicism.
His formidable power in this regard was the fruit of habitu-
ally thinking issues out thoroughly. I am told he was a slow
reader, but nonetheless he regularly went for the big books
on each topic, whether he expected to agree with them or
not. I remember him singing to me the praises of *The Vision
of God*, a highly technical treatise on the theology of spiritual
life and discipline by the Anglo-Catholic Kenneth E. Kirk;
and one lunchtime in the late '60's, when separatism was
much in his thoughts, I found him carrying back to Sion

College library W. H. C. Frend's heavy tome, *The Donatist Church*. No 'smatterbooks' for him! From this standpoint, too, deep called to deep when he turned to the Puritans. The thorough theological discipline that marked all their thinking gave him much pleasure and their great length and painstaking exhaustiveness, which lesser mortals nowadays find so exhausting, put them right up his alley.

Again, there was a prophetic quality about his ministry which during the years when I knew him isolated him from the religious establishments and the mainstream religious cultures of both England and Wales. He had his admirers, of course, clerical as well as lay, but while woolly sentimentalism in Welsh chapels and anti-intellectualism among English Evangelicals and unbelief of the Bible and its gospel both sides of the border were coming under his lash, his peers in official Christianity treated him as scarcely more than an extremely able freak. Being themselves consciously and complacently 'progressive' they saw him as a throwback to a type of ministry that as a general pattern had long since ceased to be viable. They could not deny his ability but they could not approve or take seriously what he was doing. Swimming against the stream, standing for unpopular truth, criticizing conventional complacency, exposing folly in both the world and the church, prodding people to think about things they had no wish to think about, displaying the bankruptcy of modernity and recalling its proud exponents to the old paths, has never been a prescription for popularity in the corridors of power, and it was not so in the Doctor's case.

He was, to be sure, strong enough to cope with the isolation, and it was in fact given him in the post-war years to see the quality of evangelical teaching in England and Wales change for the better through his own weaving back into it the binding thread of Reformed theology—a thread which had snapped after Spurgeon was defeated in the Downgrade controversy, and Keswick teaching swamped

Anglican Calvinism, and liberalism and the social gospel captured the pulpits of Wales. Ultimately responsible for his ministry having this happy impact was Douglas Johnson, first General Secretary of the Inter-Varsity Fellowship, who both drew the Doctor into student work, where he could shape the outlook of the rising generation of evangelical leaders, and also persuaded him to found his influential ministers' fraternal, the Westminster Fellowship, which in effect made him bishop to literally hundreds of clergy in all denominations.

Yet deep-level isolation from most of his ecclesiastical peers was a permanent part of the Doctor's experience, and this, I think, gave him a special sense of affinity with the Puritans, who were the odd men out in relation to the Anglican establishment in the century after the Reformation. As we shall see in a moment, he viewed them as classic instances of Christian determination to stop at nothing, and to refuse no form of unpopularity and rejection, in order to get God's church into fully scriptural shape; and his own mind-set, natural as well as spiritual (for I suspect it would have been Lloyd-Jones *contra mundum* as a matter of mental habit, even if he had never become a Christian) was powerfully reinforced by the Puritan example.

The final point needing to be noted at this stage is that he was a dyed-in-the-wool Reformed churchman—not, that is, an institutionalist (which is what the word tends to mean when used of Anglicans), but one who saw that in Scripture the church is central to both the fulfilling of God's purposes and the furthering of His praise, and one for whom therefore the state of the church was always a matter of prime concern. Overall, it is not too much to say that his preaching, first to last, started from, revolved round, and homed upon, just two areas: one, the state of the church, for which his final remedy was Holy Ghost revival through a return to the old paths of faith and practice; the other, the state of the world, for which his final remedy was the biblical gospel of the three R's—ruin, redemption, regeneration—set forth in the Holy Spirit's power. He described himself as primarily an evangelist, but in fact the condition of the church weighed upon him as heavily as did that of the lost. He did not think that any Anglican, not even a Puritan Anglican, was or could be as seriously concerned about the church as he was himself, and during the '60's he occasionally put the boot into me on that point. His ecclesiology had developed over the years: ordained a Presbyterian and officially one to his dying day, he became in polity 'a convinced Independent' (his phrase to me), and ceased to baptize covenant children, though retaining affusion as his mode of baptizing adults. This combination of tenets and procedures was unusual if not unique. But he would never make polity an issue; he urged, rather, that evangelical churches should accept without question each other's varieties of organization and usage provided these did not directly contradict Scripture, and concentrate together on the common quest for doctrinal purity, spiritual profundity, and missionary vitality, under the guidance and authority of God's written Word. It was thus, to his mind, that true Christian unity would be shown and the church's real health promoted.

At first, therefore, he left on one side the question of denominations. But over the years he came to think that since there was little hope of the main Protestant churches in England and Wales accepting biblical reform of faith and life and seeking spiritual revival together, since too their links with the World Council of Churches were compromising their future (for the Doctor never doubted that a single super-church based on doctrinal horse-trading lay at the end of the WCC road), the wisest course was for evangelical ministers and congregations to withdraw from these bodies and form a new 'non-denominational' association of old-fashioned Independent type. He once told me that he had privately believed that something of this kind would have to happen ever since J. Gresham Machen was put out of the ministry of the Presbyterian Church of the USA in 1936, and thus became a living proof of how resistant to biblical authority and reform mainline churches can be. In the '60's, following the commemoration of the 1662 ejectment of 2,000 Puritan clergy, the Doctor began to publicize his view, and to call on his denominationally-involved peers within evangelicalism to separate. His gestures evoked strong feelings both ways. At a large gathering of the non-separatist Evangelical Alliance in London in 1966, believing that he had been briefed to do this and giving his opportunist instincts full rein, he pulled out all the stops in making this plea, and John Stott rose from the chair to argue against him. That night my phone rang in Oxford and a woman's voice greeted me with the words: 'Jim—is John Stott mad?' Next day one who had been at the meeting told me that my friend Martyn Lloyd-Jones had gone off his rocker, and how glad he was that John Stott acted as he did.

How did the Doctor put his case? Essentially, his argument was three-pronged: that separation was prudent in the light of the unattractive ecumenical rapprochements into which mainline denominations were being drawn; that separation was an effective and glorious, even necessary, way of manifesting evangelical unity, which it was really schismatic not to take; and that separation was a present duty, since Evangelicals were guilty by association of all the evils currently found in their own denominations. No matter how vigorously one opposed these evils and sought to change them, one was ruinously compromised by them: only by withdrawal could one's integrity be recovered. Understandably, some of this failed to convince, and while acknowledging their freedom to withdraw if it seemed right most of England's evangelical ministers in doctrinally-mixed church bodies concluded that God was calling them to stay where they were and go on fighting there. The way that in the last 15 years of his life Dr Lloyd-Jones highlighted this issue, and the pressure he put on Anglicans in particular over it, led to individual estrangements, from which the present writer was not exempt; it disrupted evangelical community (for those who backed the Doctor and saw themselves as separated felt that they would not themselves be compromised should they collaborate with unseparated brethren); and it diminished the Doctor's overall influence in England, which was at least a pity and perhaps a tragedy. To his own understanding, however, he was doing no more (and no less) than maintaining in a necessary present-day form something biblical and Puritan—namely, the holy zeal that repudiates half measures, and the holy impatience which , when things are out of joint in the church, insists on 'reformation without tarrying' so that God may be glorified. For this spirit was to him the real heart of Puritanism, as we shall now see.

In the addresses, 'Puritanism and its Origins' and 'John Knox—the founder of Puritanism,' his notion of its essence is made very clear. He rejects what he calls 'the Anglican view' of Puritanism as 'essentially pastoral theology' according to Greenham, Rogers, and Perkins, and of Puritans as clergy who while pursuing this interest stayed in the Church of England even though reforms they sought were not forthcoming. He rightly observes that this view deals only with how the word 'Puritan' was used historically, not with the human reality to which it was applied.[3] With M. M. Knappen he sees Puritanism as a mentality that first appeared as early as William Tyndale, one that starts with independent Bible study and insists on applying the fruits of that study to the reordering of church life; a spirit that demands 'reformation without tarrying,' and that will challenge the magistrate's control of the church and break with the ecclesiastical establishment whenever necessary in order to secure that reformation. Application of biblical truth was and always will be central in Puritanism: 'There is no such thing, it seems to me, as a theoretical or academic Puritan.

There are people who are interested in Puritanism as an idea; but they are traitors to Puritanism unless they apply its teachings; for application is always the characteristic of the true Puritan.'[4] And the church as such was and remains the prime object of this application; the Puritan study of piety and pastoral care was, as a matter of history, 'subsidiary to the desire for true reform of the church. Indeed, the underlying argument is that only a truly Reformed church...guarantees the possibility of that full flowering of the truly religious type of life.'[5] In sum, then: 'The Puritan is primarily concerned about a pure church, a truly Reformed church. Men may like aspects of the Puritan teaching, their great emphasis on the doctrine of grace, and their emphasis on pastoral theology; but however much a man may admire these aspects of Puritanism, if his first concern is not for a pure church, a gathering of saints, he surely has no right to call himself a Puritan...if we fail to put the doctrine of the church in a central position we are departing from the true Puritan attitude, the Puritan outlook, the Puritan spirit, and the Puritan understanding.'[6]

Is this delineation of the Puritan mentality right? Basically, yes, though two qualifying comments are perhaps in order. The first is that the Puritans of history were reformed mediaevals, who inherited the mediaeval sense of the wholeness of life and the involvement of the individual with the group—a perception that we, with our compartmental and individualistic way of thinking about life, can easily overlook and ignore. For the Puritans, as for that marvellously modern man John Calvin who preceded them, the church's confession, order, discipline, and worship; the Christian's personal godliness and uprightness; and the justice and moderation (balance) that should mark every aspect of socio-politico-economic life in the human community; all formed parts of a single great whole that required comprehensive attention from those who would please God, however much present circumstances might require them to concentrate on one or another of these matters in a way that would make it seem for the moment to be their one exclusive interest. It is therefore really a false question to ask which of these concerns is regularly and characteristically subordinated to which—in other words, which under ordinary circumstances has priority in their thinking. Everything in individual, institutional, church and community life was linked in the Puritan mind with everything else, and it all had to be 'holiness to the Lord.' Each item in their range of concerns was thus coordinate with all the rest. That, I think, is the truest way to focus what historic Puritanism was about.

The second comment is that we must not minimize the variety of views within Puritanism on specific questions of policy. The Puritans did not differ much in their ultimate goals, nor in their theological principles, nor in their sense of the urgency of action against scandalous things, nor in their judgment that the honour of God and the welfare of Christians were always directly bound up with the current state of the church; but they frequently differed among themselves as to when and in what form action to remedy abuses and reinforce righteousness could best be taken. It would thus be misleading to generalize about them as if at each stage one group and one line of action have more right to be called Puritan than another—Presbyterian national-churchmen opposing toleration, for instance, rather than Independent gathered-churchmen supporting it, or vice versa.

There were many matters on which men with an equal right to be called Puritans—good, active, devoted, consistent Puritans, who prayed and longed incessantly for a church that was in all respects biblically pure—took different lines, and we must avoid generalisations that suggest that those who took the one were more authentically Puritan than those who took the other. As Dr Lloyd-Jones himself once noted, 'until about 1640 you had that kind of original

Puritan who was essentially Anglican, and who was non-Separatist of course; then you had the Presbyterian type of Puritan, also non-Separatist; then right at the other extreme you had the Separatists quite plain and clear and open'—to which groupings were then added the Independents, who practised 'occasional conformity' with the Church of England and 'have been rightly called semi-Separatists.'[7] Yet he, with historians generally, was surely right to think of these as divisions within a body of people whose common outlook on basics made it right to call them all Puritans, whether they were so called in their own day or not. That illustrates my point exactly. No doubt on occasion it was tempting to Dr Lloyd-Jones and his admirers to think of their own preferred options within the Puritan spectrum as 'really' Puritan in a way that other options were not. But such temptations have to be resisted, at least by those for whom history is more than a resource for propaganda.

Concerning the separation campaign, in which the Doctor's commitment to Puritan ideals of church purity found its final expression, a question may be asked about his apparent lack of realism. It was observed that, while speaking forcefully in public about the issue of principle, he never gave substance to his vision by producing, or getting others to produce, a blueprint for the new para-denomi-nation (the 'non-denominational' denomination) that he had in view. He seemed at one time to look to a small anti-ecumenical body, the British Evangelical Council, to provide the necessary structural network, but no serious planning seems ever to have been done. Why was this? I once asked him whether he was not really saying that we should all join the Fellowship of Independent Evangelical Churches; he replied that that would not do, but did not say why not, nor what the alternative was, save that something new was called for.

Though he disliked organizing and always had in mind that the more highly organized a venture was the less

spiritual was it likely to be, he was a competent enough
manager and must have seen that some organizing would
be needed to effect any new grouping. I have wondered, I
confess, whether he was not more interested in making the
gesture of calling for separation, with the accompanying
criticism of evangelical Anglicans, Baptists in the Baptist
Union ('in it to win it'), and the world ecumenical movement, than he was in seeing the gesture succeed; whether,
anticipating rejection as Isaiah and Jeremiah were told to
anticipate rejection, his main purpose was not, rather, to
leave a testimony the significance of which, though ignored
in his own day, might be seen afterwards. He once observed
to me with reference, as I recall, to the fall of David Lloyd-
George, whose political acumen he had once admired, that
you cannot be a leader if you do not have followers, and he
was certainly shrewd enough to foresee that, humanly
speaking, he could not expect many followers on this particular issue. Probably the truest thing to say about his
campaign of words without plans is that he was testing the
waters, looking to see if the Holy Spirit would use what he
said to evoke major support and a widespread desire for
action, and he would not risk prejudicing his own prophetic
role in the process by any appearance of wanting to be a
denominational boss. And who will blame him for that?

Though Dr Lloyd-Jones and I did not wholly agree about
church polity and policy, we were together in thinking that
the Puritan spirit is in essence New Testament Christianity,
and as such something with which we ought to identify
today. What, now, was most notably Puritan about his own
ministry? Over and above matters already mentioned, I
single out the following items.

First, his concept of theology as a rational, practical
study corresponded perfectly to William Perkins' definition
of it as 'the science of living blessedly for ever' and his view
of the Bible as the source of theology (i.e., as God's revealed
truth), and of the system of thought that the Bible yields,

was in entire accord with that classic of Puritan theology, the Westminster Confession.

Second, his practice of preaching was altogether Puritan in its philosophy, method, and substance, even though it was entirely 20th century in its style and verbal form. Doctrine, reason, and 'use'—taking truths from texts, confirming them by other Scripture passages plus rational reflection, and then applying them—was the regular pattern. As declaration to us of God's work, preaching was praise; as instruction in God's ways with us, preaching was food; in both respects, it was the climax of public worship, and was to be honoured as such. Christ and gospel grace, set forth with relevance to present human need and perplexity, must be central always, albeit in the large frame of the whole counsel of God. In the application (of which, for the Doctor, the introduction was really part) one must speak to the times and seek to get inside one's hearers, speaking directly to their anxieties and their guilt before God. A simple, serious, plain-talking idiom, without frivolous illustrations, purple passages, or flights of fancy, suits this purpose best. (The phrase 'noble negligence,' first used of Richard Baxter's writings, fits Dr Lloyd-Jones' transcribed sermons and lectures admirably; persuasive man-to-man clarity, speech that was 'familiar' in the Puritan sense of that word, was what he was always after, and no attempt at verbal elegance was ever made.) Unction from God, giving liberty and forthrightness, empathy and energy, passion and compassion, and enabling one to get inside people, was to be sought on each occasion for the act of preaching so that, in Baxter's words, the preacher might always be said to have

> ...preached as one that ne'er should preach again,
> And as a dying man to dying men.

Continuous systematic wide-swinging exposition of chapters and whole books of Scripture, with as many sermons on each text as it was felt to warrant as part of the larger design, was a fruitful way to preach. Sermons might reasonably be up to an hour long at any time. All this was as Puritan as could be.

Third, the Doctor conceived Christian experience in Puritan terms. His understanding hinged on two principles: first, the primacy of the mind in man, as guide to his will and judge of his feelings; second, the indirectness of the work of the Holy Spirit, who teaches and moves us by first making us actively learn and then rousing us to move ourselves. When the Spirit is at work, illuminating and imparting, he stirs mind and feelings together to an affective awareness of divine realities; God, Christ, grace, pardon, adoption, new creation, and the rest; Christianity is therefore, to use the Puritan word, 'experimental' (we would say, experiential) in its very essence, and the idea that the best Christianity is that into which least emotion enters is a shallow and absurd middle-class English reaction against strong feelings of any sort. Such an idea merits both ridicule, since it is silly, and tears, since it quenches the Spirit.

Conversion was individual response to the crucified, risen, and enthroned Christ who ever and to all says 'Come to me.' Coming to Christ involves repentance (leaving sin, and making Christ one's Master) as well as faith (admitting sin and inability, and taking Christ as one's Saviour). Preachers should constantly point their hearers to Christ and celebrate the peace, joy, change of heart and new resources for living that those who come to Him will find. Conventional 20th-century evangelism, to the Doctor's mind, had three great weaknesses: its manipulative emotionalism, displacing intellectual persuasion, was a kind of brainwashing that encouraged false conversions; the standard form of appeal ('now I give you an opportunity to respond . . . I want you to get up out of your seat and come forward . . .'), in which the preacher acts as if he were the

Holy Spirit, has the same unhappy tendency; and the constant failure to insist on radical and thorough repentance in conversion sentences true converts to shallow and stunted growth thereafter. Perceiving these weaknesses led him to say on occasion that certain evangelists were not preaching the Gospel at all, and to stand apart from modern institutionalized evangelism on principle, so that the difference between its standards and his would not be obscured.

In teaching holiness, the life of obedience to Christ whereby one abides in Him, Dr Lloyd-Jones saw quietist passivity as a kind of modern demon possessing evangelical minds and needing explicit exorcism. Slogans like 'let go and let God,' 'stop trying and start trusting,' seemed to him from this standpoint so misleading as to be scandalous. The formulae of holiness are 'do this,' 'don't do that again,' 'pray first, then act,' and wisdom is to guide always in the application of biblical principles. Determination and effort are needed for the practice of holy living, since opposition from indwelling sin is multiform and constant, as Galations 5:16–17 shows. The Doctor parted from the Puritans in declining to read Romans 7:14–25 as testimony to this conflict between the spirit (the regenerate self) and the flesh (indwelling sin); he argued, unconvincingly in my view, that this passage delineates the final stage of pre-regenerate life. But he was entirely with the Puritans in stressing the lifelong reality of the spirit-flesh conflict and the folly of any perfectionist claims to have got beyond it.

Spiritual depression, a condition distinct from though often linked with the clinical depression that physicians and psychiatrists treat, was a problem to which the Doctor devoted attention. The condition has at its heart unbelief of God's gracious promises. The remedy for it is to learn to fight the feelings that unbelief begets by keeping one's spiritual eyes on God's faithfulness to His promises as He disciplines his children, and by talking to oneself in the style of Psalm 42 about the certainty that some day one will be praising God for turning one's sorrow into joy.

Assurance of God's everlasting love and of heaven to come was to him the supreme blessing in his life, and the supreme form of assurance, which all Christians should seek, was the direct witness of God's Spirit with our spirit that we are children and heirs of God. Equating this witness, of which Romans 8:15–17 speaks, with the seal of the Spirit (Ephesians 1:13, 4:30; cf. II Corinthians 1:22), with baptism with the Spirit (John 1:33), and with receiving the Spirit in some passages of Acts, the Doctor always spoke of it as a particular occasional experience, and illustrated it from a wide range of testimonies to intense and transforming moments of assurance that saints from Pascal to Edwards to Moody, with Puritans like John Flavel among them, had put on record. He had himself enjoyed one such experience while reading a book on heaven, as he told me in a private conversation 30 years ago in which he tried out on me the line of exposition summarized above. He lectured at the first Puritan Conference on this theme, commending the Puritan doctrine of direct assurance as a neglected truth that we needed to recover and in elaborate treatments (all now in print) of the Romans, Ephesians, and John texts he gave it high exposure during the second half of his London ministry. While some Puritans understood Romans 8:16 and Ephesians 1:13 as he did, others took the Spirit's witness to refer to a constant quality of experience rather than to one single moment of experience, and understood the seal of Ephesians 1:13 to be the gift of the Spirit upon believing rather than a work of the Spirit some time after believing; and the case for the latter view against the former seems conclusive. But it was characteristic of all Puritans to seek, and urge others to seek, the clearest experiential assurance of our adoption that God will give, in whatever form it comes, and in reviving and highlighting this emphasis the Doctor once again endorsed the Puritan perspective and revealed his Puritan roots.

Finally, the Puritans, with Christians of every age till this century, viewed dying well as the crown upon a godly life. Dr Lloyd-Jones often stressed in his preaching the need to be ready for death, and he told a colleague towards the close of his life that he saw it as the final work of his ministry to make a good end. Thus he maintained the Puritan view of things to the last.

Only at one point did he go beyond 17th-century Puritan teaching on Christian experience: namely, in his embrace of Jonathan Edwards' belief that cyclical revival is God's main and regular way of extending His kingdom. Revival, on this view, is an outpouring of the Holy Spirit on the church which deepens Christian experience enormously. God however is sovereign in determining when the outpouring shall occur; Christians may and should pray and prepare for it, but they cannot precipitate it. God works to His own timetable. Now, there is nothing of this in the Puritans. Though they all recognized that the Reformation was, among other things, a revival of true religion, and though men like John Howe had vivid expectations of quickening for Christians when the Spirit was poured out to herald the latter-day glory, the Puritans did not at any stage interpret their own ministry and the history of their own times in terms of the cyclical vision, whereby a day of small things leads on to days of great things for individual congregations and the wider community around. Dr Lloyd-Jones did, however, think in these terms, and it was a source of sadness to him that he never saw revival in England, at Westminster Chapel, as in real measure he had seen it in his South Wales pastorate in 1929–31. How his belief about the sovereignty of God in revival related to the certainty he seemed to show that an alliance of separated churches would have unique spiritual vitality and power, much beyond anything that had preceded its formation, was something that to my knowledge he never explained, and I think that real inconsistency was present here; for certainly the Edwardsean doctrine of revival was in his heart all along. But the greatest men can fall into wishful thinking.

Sometimes 'a kind of Puritan'? Yes, most of the time in fact. Spurgeon in his own day was called the last of the Puritans, but the title surely passed to the Doctor while he was alive, and maybe still belongs to him. Yet, please God, it will not be his for ever. For part of his legacy to the world was men—pastors, young and middle-aged, for whom his Puritanism was an inspiration and he himself, as Americans would say, a role-model. No doubt there have been among his admirers immaturities, imprudences, unspiritual apings, and downright failures, and the 15 years of separatist drumbeating does appear in retrospect as something of a scorched-earth era in English evangelical life, when much that was of value was destroyed. But the Puritan type of godliness is still New Testament Christianity at its noblest and most thorough-going, and the God of the Puritans is not dead, and it will be right for us to look to God to raise up, perhaps from the ranks of those whom the Doctor inspired in his lifetime, perhaps from a younger age group, persons who will be clear-sighted enough to discern what Puritan principles of preaching, praying and living require as the 21st century approaches, and who with that will be big enough, intellectually and spiritually, to carry the mighty torch of Puritan ministry that the Doctor has passed to us.

In one sense, of course, it has to be said of the greatest Puritans, Owen, Baxter, Goodwin, Sibbes, Perkins, and Howe, and of their greatest followers over three centuries, Edwards, Spurgeon, Ryle, and now Dr Lloyd-Jones, that we shall not see their like again; each great man is unique. In another sense, however, we may hope and should pray that tomorrow's church will be blessed with many like them in stature, principles, wisdom, gifts, and godliness, and so in every generation until the Lord comes. Men who faithfully maintain the essence of the Christianity that the Doctor stood for are the memorial that he himself would have

desired. May such a memorial be forthcoming; for there is
nothing today that the church needs more.

NOTES

PC = Puritan and Reformed Studies Conference Report
WC = Westminster Conference Report
All reports were privately printed

1. 'Puritanism and its Origins' in *The Good Fight of Faith* (WC, 1971),
   p.72.
2. 'John Bunyan: Church Union' in *Light from John Bunyan* (WC, 1978),
   p.86).
3. *The Good Fight...*, p.73.
4. 'John Knox—the founder of Puritanism' in *Becoming a Christian* (WC,
   1972), p.102.
5. *The Good Fight...*, p.86.
6. ibid., pp.89 f.
7. 'Henry Jacob and the First Congregational Church' in *One Steadfast
   High Intent* (PC, 1966), pp.59f.

Chapter Three

THE DOCTOR AS A DOCTOR

by

Gaius Davies

Dr Gaius Davies is a consultant psychiatrist at King's College Hospital, London. Like 'The Doctor,' he trained at St Bartholomew's Hospital (Barts). He was involved with Dr Martyn Lloyd-Jones in both medical and Welsh life, and spoke at the Doctor's memorial service in Westminster Chapel in 1981.

When I was a medical student at Barts, and a regular attender at Westminster Chapel on Sundays and Fridays, my English friends would sometimes say to me on Fridays: 'Are you going to hear the prophet this weekend?' It was, of course, a compliment that they should recognise Dr Lloyd-Jones' ministry as a prophetic one: yet I was put out, since for us he was in 1948 simply 'The Doctor'. That large group of us who were medical students of many denominations went to Westminster for the regular, systematic teaching. We did not know then that the title of doctor in the history of the Christian church carried the meaning of being an honoured teacher.

Yet, first and foremost, he was a doctor of medicine. The great contribution he made to the church was because he was trained as a medical man, and because he remained to the end of his long life passionately interested in every aspect of medicine, reading the medical journals that came out week by week and month by month. He was not only interested in conventional or establishment medicine, but he was also insatiably curious about other forms of treatment: what is now so well-known as alternative medicine. It was his training in medicine that formed his mind, so that he received his degree of Doctor of Medicine from London

University at a very early age. I shall argue that he owed to this training and interest—under God's providential guidance—some important features of his remarkable ministry.

Not everyone agrees with the obvious fact that he remained at heart a doctor of medicine. When I spoke of Dr Lloyd-Jones' contribution to medicine at his memorial service, I was rebuked by the Rev Omri Jenkins for stressing that he was a doctor first. In his kind way Mr Jenkins then proved my point with an amusing reference to a meeting of ministers at which the topic of acupuncture was raised; Dr Lloyd-Jones had spoken on the subject (without preparation) for over an hour after the subject was broached. This sufficiently established what I am now still convinced of, that he enjoyed applying his mind to medical topics to the end of his days. As he once put it, after he had prepared the two sermons for Sunday, he would enjoy that week's issue of the *Lancet* and the *British Medical Journal* as relaxation and light relief.

Martyn Lloyd-Jones was one of a large number of young Welshmen who made the journey to London in order to find a place in one of its many famous medical schools. Among the many Welsh names in medical rolls of honour, I think his deserves a unique distinction. His ability led him to qualify exceptionally early and he also passed the Membership examination of the Royal College of Physicians at a young age.

The outward and visible sign of his intellectual distinction was the recognition given him early in his career by Sir Thomas Horder, then one of the leading teachers in London and well known as an honoured physician to the most famous in the land—those who visited his busy Harley Street practice or called him out to their homes. Horder was one of the earliest to bring research to the bedside. He gave Dr Lloyd-Jones his opportunity to work on a disease of the heart, subacute bacterial endocarditis. It was his thesis, giving an account of this work, which earned Martyn Lloyd-Jones the degree of Doctor of Medicine, of London University.

Later in life his intellectual achievements and his long ministry might quite honourably have been recognised by a number of universities with their doctorates. It is, after all, a good custom to honour those who are worthy in this way: yet Dr Lloyd-Jones chose not to accept any such honour and distinction. I know that this was a statement, on his part, of his firm convictions about the limited value of academic training in the Christian ministry. It was also a clear demonstration of a modest and humble turning away from such academic honours in following what he thought his plain duty. These academic titles had, after all, ensnared many: they were part of the knowledge which puffs up, not of the love which builds up.

Yet his refusal to accept other doctorates would be dismissed by him as saying that he preferred to be content with what Barts and London University had given him. They had brought him the distinction of being chief assistant to Sir Thomas Horder. The prospects of fame and wealth were certainly before him: as we all know, he chose to leave them to become a minister of the Gospel. When he left Barts, what did he take with him of lasting value?

St Bartholomew's Hospital is proud of its ancient traditions and there are always those who were trained at other medical schools who would say: 'You can always tell a Barts man, but you can't tell him much!' Doubtless this implies some conceit or pride in Barts men, and some envy and jealousy on the part of those who went to other hospitals. I think all of us who went to Barts basked in the reflected glory of its great names: those who had fiercely fought in the battle to advance knowledge and improve medical care. Among young Barts men Dr Lloyd-Jones had already achieved a considerable pre-eminence. In his case you could not tell him much because he had worked so hard and seemed so effortlessly to be able to encompass the field of medical knowledge. In the early 1920's so much more depended on the clinical acumen, the sharpness of observation, and the ability to deduce the correct diagnosis and treatment—qualities of the doctor himself. Today it seems routine to rely on tests of various kinds which were not then available. When Dr Lloyd-Jones was teaching at Barts he was helping to train the minds of the juniors and the medical students: he was teaching them a method.

I remember Dr Douglas Johnson describing how he heard of this remarkable young medical teacher, and how he went from King's College Hospital one day to try and sneak in to a ward round or demonstration and hear Dr Lloyd-Jones in action. Later on, when I arrived in London in 1947 for the first time, Dr Johnson in his typical fashion advised me to hasten to the Friday evening meetings conducted by Dr Lloyd-Jones at Westminster Chapel. He told me I would see the Socratic method in action, and the methods of teaching and reasoning which the Doctor had learned in his early training with Horder and other famous teachers, being applied to problems of the Christian life.

I had seen nothing like those Friday evening discussions, and I doubt if I knew precisely what the Socratic method was! Like so many hundreds who attended, what we seemed to join in was, apparently, a free-for-all discussion of any selected topic of Christian belief or practice. After the opening of the meeting with a customary reading, prayer or hymn, the rest of the procedure was quite new to me. Looking back, I see it as a process of being taught to think: just that, at first. Then, if we stuck with it (and many found it too hard and gave up) there was the possibility of being taught to think in a Christian way, and to strengthen the sinews of our minds.

The views of members of the audience were sought by Dr Lloyd-Jones as chairman and then discussed as fully as possible, showing with wit and humour where such views logically led. I remember being full of admiration for those who spoke up: one voice I recall above others was that of Fred Catherwood, later to be well-known! I feel ashamed as I look back, at my silence; I was as mixed up in my thinking as any and should have been one of those publicly helped to be sorted out. When Mrs Lloyd-Jones once asked me why I did not speak up on Friday nights, my reply was that I considered it unwise to stand in the path of a steam-roller. But the Doctor was a very gentle steam-roller, and he was particularly kind to the young and weak in the faith.

The method that Dr Lloyd-Jones took from his medical training was once described by him as follows: Horder would put up a number of diagnostic solutions to a patient's puzzling condition as if they were skittles. Then, in turn, he would try in discussion to knock down each skittle: the one that remained was the correct one. This process involved observation and logical deduction. It involved thinking, and a real live intellectual debate without fear or favour. It should not rely on quoting authority but on demonstrating the truth.

In a word, I believe that, in taking this method into his Christian work, Dr Lloyd-Jones brought back the importance of thinking and rehabilitated the intellectual functions that had been so much neglected by Christians of his day. 'Don't pray, think!' Such a remark can have a proper application: he taught many of us that to think through and apply what we believed was as important as any stress we had been taught to lay on experience and devotional aspects of our lives; indeed, it was to love God with all our minds. It was to give an intellectual and doctrinal backbone to what might otherwise make us rather like supine jelly-fish in some aspects of our lives.

Many conferences throughout the country and in many parts of the world saw the full force of this method of discussion and debate. Of course Dr Lloyd-Jones was working as a Mr Valiant-for-Truth. I do not think it takes away

rom that to point out that this thinker and debater had
earned some special skills at the bedside and in the ward
rounds and conferences of St Bartholomew's Hospital.

His links with the developing Inter-Varsity Fellowship
are well known, and his close and long association with Dr
Douglas Johnson led to many fruitful conferences and pub-
ications. Though there have been accounts of the development of the IVF (now the UCCF) and of the Christian
Medical Fellowship, I do not think that we have ever been
given the 'secret history' of the evangelical movement
between the '30's and the '80's of this century. So much has
happened, so many different developments have grown up
and become accepted. It is my belief that the close association between two medical men who had left the prospects of
glittering prizes for the work of God's kingdom will feature
argely in a true and proper account of Christian work in the
middle of the 20th century.

Both Dr Douglas Johnson and Dr Lloyd-Jones shared a
training which left its mark on mind and character. Without
disparaging other kinds of intellectual preparation for life,
one reflects on the example that London medical students
had to work in special ways. For instance, to learn midwifery
it was an important discipline to accompany the local district nurses in their tasks as midwives. It meant seeing life in
the raw with babies being born in conditions that occasionally reminded one of Dr Barnardo's days. To be 'on the
district' was an important month in a medical student's life.
I once heard Dr Lloyd-Jones remark that every candidate
for the ministry might benefit greatly from a month on the
district! By now, of course, much practical experience *is*
included in theological students' training: they work in
hospitals and hospices in order to learn the kind of skills
which Dr Lloyd-Jones was referring to in his slightly joking
remark.

If the IVF and the CMF had its own bishops and apostles,
Dr Lloyd-Jones would surely be one of the leading figures.

His work with the study group that the CMF formed extended over 25 years. He enjoyed it because, in a sense, he was back with his fellow medical men. But he brought to the study group his enormous theological learning and wide reading of so many subjects. He brought a discipline that was applied with wit and humour. The study group led to many subjects being treated in what are now standard works of evangelical scholarship.

In addition to his own brilliant addresses on many themes, he did even more working behind the scenes. He was a superb catalyst and loved to encourage and help others. It was not only reprints of old classical works which he helped to publish, but original books too.

If a man of Dr Lloyd-Jones' gifts undergoes a proper medical training, then he emerges as someone who has experienced at first hand the rigours of scientific method. I believe that, in a remarkable way, his thinking as a scientist was also put to the service of the faith. Consider three areas where his service was of great value: in assessing the developing ministry of healing; in his attitude to psychology generally; and in his opposition to Freudian psychoanalysis in particular.

Dr Lloyd-Jones believed strongly in the miraculous, and therefore in the possibility of divine healing. Yet there were many claims being made of spiritual healing which he was very critical of: he sought to define miracle in practical and New Testament ways. He thought such healing was immediate, complete and lasting and owed nothing to natural processes, but to direct divine action as in our Lord's signs and wonders. His great exponent of this view was Dr B. B. Warfield, though he did not limit himself to such an exposition as Warfield's. He was critical of some healers and their methods, since they tended to undervalue or even devalue some of the basic New Testament teaching. One obvious example is that God is sovereign in His decision to grant healing or not. Anything that tended to the magical or superstitious was bound to be rejected since ultimately it did not tend to glorify God or to adorn the doctrine of the Bible.

I remember one surgeon who was totally taken up with the Churches' Council of Healing telling me, in the late '40's, that the healing movement would sweep through the evangelical churches were it not for the qualified opposition of one man—Dr Lloyd-Jones. We know that, in spite of his cautions, there has been a tremendous growth of healing ministries. When I see some of the casualties of a wrong emphasis on healing, I wish that the Christian and scientific rigour of Dr Lloyd-Jones' mind had prevailed in keeping the claims and the practices of the healing ministry within a more thoroughly Christian framework.

I was always impressed with the way Dr Lloyd-Jones stated the negatives before he moved on to the positive statements he could make in exposition. There were two great enemies of the Gospel that frequently came under fire: philosophy and psychology. In his opposition to philosophy, Dr Lloyd-Jones would have often echoed the words of Blaise Pascal in the famous document of 1654 found after Pascal's death: especially the statements he jotted down beginning 'God of Abraham, God of Isaac, God of Jacob, not of the philosophers and scholars.... He is to be found only by the ways taught in the Gospel.' Others are more competent to deal with Dr Lloyd-Jones' endless fight with those who were trying to evacuate the faith of its true meaning and substitute some new version of human philosophy. All I know is that he brought all his power to bear in the attack on philosophy, and that his use of wit and sarcasm to laugh at some of those who were the enemies of the faith was often most effective.

He was profoundly interested in psychology, and showed great skill in applying his understanding of it to both persons and movements. But popular psychology he abhorred, and he was merciless in his criticism.

We must remember that in the years 1930–50 there was a vast amount of preaching which was actually little more than restating what looked like Christian truths in what turned out to be another brand of popular psychology. I often think of some of the leading writers of the day as weathercocks in the pulpit: listen to them, and you could tell which way the wind of popular psychology was blowing at the time. It was Dr Lloyd-Jones' scientific approach, as much as his loyalty to the Bible, that made him mock the easy and cheap psychologies which were masquerading as Christian teaching.

His fascination with biography and learning the lineaments of the man he was studying led him to eschew the interpretation of men's developments in terms of psychological theory. He wanted facts, not interpretations, and his mind was stored with what seemed an illimitable supply of biographical and historical knowledge. Against such a background of erudition (which he hardly ever displayed simply for effect) he judged many modern attempts at understanding as glib and superficial. He believed in depth psychology, but not in the sense the Freudians used the phrase. Rather, he wanted to understand the individual's special characteristics and the depth of the work of grace in the soul. For this, writers like Jonathan Edwards and the Puritans seemed to him to have a better grasp of biblical psychology. In modern psychology he looked for a balanced view and supported such things as learning theory, which need not of necessity contradict Christian faith.

I have never heard Dr Lloyd-Jones criticise by name the writings of such popular psychologisers of religion as Dr Leslie D. Weatherhead. He was only interested in contrasting ideas he found wanting with the truth of the Gospel. He made the remark on one occasion, when asked why he did not engage in more public controversy, that of course people loved to see two dogs fighting in the street. By the same token he could have increased his popularity, or the circulation of the *Westminster Record*, by attacking opponents by name: he chose not to do so.

There was one notable exception: Dr William Sargant, a physician famous as a psychiatrist in charge of his department at St Thomas's Hospital, London. Dr Sargant wrote a best-seller called *Battle for the Mind*: it is not often that a working psychiatrist sells a quarter of a million copies of a book. His work was in many ways an attack on John Wesley for preaching hell-fire and using a conversion technique based on it. On the whole, Dr Sargant's book was an attack on all aspects of conversion.

Dr Lloyd-Jones gave an address reprinted as a booklet called *Conversions: psychological and spiritual*. It is a model, to my mind, of how the Christian response should be made: accepting some criticisms of modern evangelistic developments but showing the profound difference between a response based on pressures of a psychological kind, and a true conversion wrought by grace, mediated by the Word and the work of the Spirit.

Again, it is typical of the way it was done that Dr Sargant afterwards sent Dr Lloyd-Jones every reprint of his publications. And as he told me, he signed his letters: Affectionately, Will. Thus can be shown how it is possible to be a terrible judge in regard to ideas, but full of charity towards persons (to quote Dr Andre Schlemmer in another connection).

Dr Lloyd-Jones, although a great polemicist, aimed in this attack to achieve what always concerned him: a balanced view based on the truth. He saw science as part of God's common grace, and found that this was in its way as amazing as God's saving grace. He was interested in what doctors were doing in psychiatry and psychological medicine as part of his encyclopaedic interest in advancing knowledge. In his last years as a doctor with Sir Thomas Horder he had found how often it was not a physical problem, but a spiritual and psychological one, which led to a patient's illness. Before holistic medicine became popular, he did his best to practise whole-person doctoring.

Perhaps the vast majority of ministers in the churches believe with W. H. Auden that Freud is now part of the air we breathe:

> To us he is no more a person
> Now but a whole climate of opinion.

Many notable leaders in the churches have sought to create a synthesis of Freudian and Christian teaching. Some have made a cornerstone of such things as Otto Rank's birth trauma theories so that ecclesiastics (I am credibly informed) were to be seen undergoing the 'birthing' treatment and similar procedures based on neo-Freudian depth psychology.

Dr Lloyd-Jones was totally opposed to such syncretistic amalgams of any psychology with the Christian faith. Today there are paperbacks on many bookshelves showing from the writings of such distinguished scientists as Karl Popper and Peter Medawar that much of Freud's writings belongs to the realm of pseudo-science and pseudo-religion. But Dr Lloyd-Jones was saying this long ago when he wrote a preface to a little book called *The Menace of the New Psychology*. He warned against accepting Freud or Jung uncritically, and urged that their teaching should be tested critically and much of it rejected.

In the decades since he thus showed his opposition, the juggernaut of Freudian movements, particularly in the USA, has been slowed down, and largely corrected in its bad influences, by the growth of biological psychiatry and behaviour theory and other methods of treatment based on a more scientific application of learning theories.

Although he was not trained in psychological medicine, I always felt that Dr Lloyd-Jones had a special interest and aptitude for it. It was my privilege to invite him back to his old hospital to give a lecture on treating the whole man. It was a masterly review of what might be called psychosomatic medicine from a Christian viewpoint. He showed how doctors should always consider factors in illness and development which were physical, psychological and spiritual. Not only in that lecture but in many of his reprinted lectures he showed his down-to-earth way of applying his understanding of these three aspects.

Even in many of his sermons the same psychological insights are shown: it is not at all surprising that his book of sermons entitled *Spiritual Depression* is still a bestseller after many years.

I wish there had been time for Dr Lloyd-Jones to give himself to more detailed criticism of the wilder shores of speculation, offering themselves as an attractive mixture of clinical psychology and theology: mixtures which sometimes seem to contain a bit of everything, with little or no critical appraisal. Perhaps he decided such was not his main task, and therefore avoided controversy which might have proved fruitless.

But in assessing the *popular* presentation of Freud and his followers (as opposed to strictly medical papers or books) it was surely right of Dr Lloyd-Jones to regard 'the climate of opinion' created by Freud's followers as an atmosphere polluted by many half-truths and lies, mixed with much that may have been good in its original intent. Today we are all interested in preserving a better environment, and in the ecology of grace it may be that a fresh understanding of what Dr Lloyd-Jones saw as the essence of Christian teaching may make for a healthier climate, a purer atmosphere for the mind and spirit.

When he left the practice of medicine Dr Lloyd-Jones seemed to turn his back on fame and wealth: but I think he found a much larger practice, especially as a counsellor.

Others will recall the fact that his specific medical talents and knowledge led him to be of great help to many cases when he first worked as a minister in Aberavon. The local doctors who may have felt he was an interloper came to know him as a valued colleague. But inevitably as the work became greater in its pressures and time was pressing, he was unable to be a kind of unofficial medical specialist to many doctors and patients. Yet his function as a counsellor became more and more important.

In his study, at Westminster Chapel, by telephone and by letter many sought his good counsel. On his many preaching engagements away from London he would be consulted by those in need of help. His was a vast practice, rewarded far more richly than he would have been had he stayed in Harley Street or worked in a London teaching hospital. It was not only his wisdom and spiritual knowledge but the application of his medical skills which made him such a reliable counsellor.

There is no mistake so dreadful to a doctor as attributing symptoms to some psychological pressures which really require proper physical care and diagnosis and treatment. Dr Lloyd-Jones did not hesitate to advise a physician or a psychiatrist when he thought it was the right course: we will never know how many he helped in this way by his medical skill and up-to-date knowledge.

But as a counsellor one of the most remarkable things to be noticed was that he seemed incapable of being shocked: this was remarked to me by one of his neighbours, a member of his church. I wonder if his early medical training contributed to this unexpected capacity of being able to listen without expressing condemnation and judgment such as most of us do when we are shocked?

It is said that three qualities are important in the counsellor: a personal warmth which is careful to be non-possessive, an ability to tune in with empathy to the needs of the person who is seeking counsel, and a genuineness in the whole approach. These were qualities amply shown in Dr Lloyd-Jones' type of counselling: added to them were of course spiritual qualities unique to him as a man of God.

It will be obvious to anyone who has read thus far that I feel the affection and hero-worship towards Dr Lloyd-Jones which so many of us as his students felt when he had us under his spell. It was a byword that we imitated him, and that you could tell from our speech, construction of sentences, and many other idiosyncrasies that we imitated without being wholly aware of how great the influence was upon us. I expect many young painters similarly would have been proud to belong to the school of Raphael or Titian: in due course they would develop their own style though still showing where they were trained, and by whom. Yet the Doctor himself deplored the cult of personality and all the modern notions of it created by the media.

It was evident from his early days at Barts that he had enough intellectual power to drive several turbines. I venture to think that his medical discipline helped him to use his powers well, just as it must have been a constant struggle to deny himself the pride which would vitiate everything. He was a very humble man, ever aware of the dangers that our sinful hearts lead us into. He may have done battle with many other intellectuals, but like his Lord it was true that the common people heard him gladly. In Wales he told me how he preached over the heads of the distinguished ministers in the first seats, in order to reach the ordinary folk in the pews beyond.

It is difficult to be a doctor without some love and compassion for people: the Doctor had a boundless charity mixed with his curiosity to know more about people—again part of the medical inheritance he carried with him everywhere.

It is worth quoting in full Dr Schlemmer's remarks about the French Reformed teacher Auguste Lecerf, for they apply to the Doctor too:

> Although there was something of the grand seigneur about his bearing, no one could have been more simple, more friendly or

more finely comprehensive in his personal dealings. A terrible
judge in regard to ideas, he was full of charity in regard to
persons; but, holding in horror all display of sentiment and all
mere emotionalism, his good nature was often veiled by a
malicious sense of humour.

I was immensely struck by the first occasions I visited his
home and saw the essential homeliness of that side of his
life: I had seen many Christian leaders at close quarters
since childhood, and I was frequently more impressed by
their personal vanity or self-importance than by their
graciousness. but with Dr Martyn Lloyd-Jones there was a
splendid continuity between the father and husband at
home—offering you the food with some disarming remark
that he hoped tomorrow's sermon would not be stodgy after
all the good food—and the remarkable figure that would
seem to soar in the pulpit the next day.

There were wittily unkind medical students who told me
I would see him in his Geneva gown soaring like a black bat
from the pulpit. There may have been some truth in the
observation, but it did not penetrate to the heart of the man.
For in his heart and mind he more resembled the skylark,
described in lines of Wordsworth which I first heard the
Doctor quote from the pulpit. He was indeed able to be full
of down-to-earth commonsense, and also to take spiritual
wings and be a pilgrim of the sky in proclaiming the truth.
He was, thus

> Type of the wise who soar, but never roam
> True to the kindred points of heaven and home.

I am thankful that Providence prepared him for his
remarkable career in the way it did. And when serious
illness affected him twice, all who were privileged to see or
know of his fortitude in suffering, and his balanced views on
looking to God for healing while still using the best that
science could give, saw grace in action. *Soli Deo gloria.*

Chapter Four

THE DOCTOR AS A PREACHER

by

Peter Lewis

The Rev Peter Lewis is the minister of Cornerstone Evangelical Church, Nottingham. He has a wide speaking ministry and serves on the Council of the Evangelical Alliance. He preached the sermon at the memorial service to Dr Martyn Lloyd-Jones in Westminster Chapel in 1981.

What is preaching?' Dr Lloyd-Jones once asked a gathering of preachers and theologians. He answered his own question. It is, he said, 'logic on fire, eloquent reason.' And if any preacher exhibited the soul of that definition it was Martyn Lloyd-Jones himself. Was there a preacher of his generation who so uniquely combined intellect and passion, argument and persuasion, formidable apologetic abilities laid out in defence of the historic Christian faith and irresistible personal magnetism, as he wooed and won his hearers? A former Archbishop of Canterbury used to say that all preachers may be divided into three classes—preachers you cannot listen to, preachers you can listen to and preachers you cannot help listening to. The subject of this book was emphatically a preacher of the last type.

Yet it was not by artifice that the Doctor gripped the attention. The combination of clear reasoning and urgent passion was no mere formula: it was the expression and outflow of the man himself, the man of God. Someone once asked C. H. Spurgeon how they could communicate with the people and reach them as he did. 'It's very simple', he said. 'Get on fire for God and the people will come to see you burn!' When you heard Dr Lloyd-Jones preach you saw a man burn for God.

It started quietly enough: a straightforward introduction

to the passage and theme before the preacher and his congregation if he were speaking to Christians, or an easy, familiar sharing of the present situation around them with its perplexities and disappointments if it were a message to non-Christians. Within a few minutes, however, quite swiftly though without dramatic suddenness there would come a deepening intensity into the voice, the words quickening their pace, the body becoming the rigid, almost quivering, instrument of the speaker's fierce passion, and before one knew it one was swept into the sustained motion and progress of the whole sermon. It was, to modify a favourite story of his, the advocate taking the witness box, adding personal testimony to irrefutable argument: a man who had seen 'infinities and immensities' in this Gospel concerning Jesus Christ, the Son of God, and who knew it had power to lift men and women to God for ever.

However, if we are to understand the full significance of Dr Martyn Lloyd-Jones' life as a preacher, we must not begin with the phenomenon of his own preaching but with the biblical principles which lay behind it: out of which it grew and by which it was conditioned. He himself sets out these principles, as he understood them, in his book *Preaching and Preachers*, the opening three chapters of which form a direct and pressing challenge to evangelical priorities in our own day.

The first chapter is entitled '*The Primacy of Preaching*' and at the beginning he declares himself unequivocally: 'To use the work of preaching is the highest and the greatest and the most glorious calling to which anyone can ever be called.' This is not simply a piece of personal testimony, much less the admission of a personal indulgence. He continues: 'If you want something in addition to that I would say without any hesitation that the most urgent need in the Christian church today is true preaching; and as it is the greatest and the most urgent need in the church, it is obviously the greatest need of the world also.'

Characteristically he begins by surveying the present scene and then applies biblical principles to it. He sees the widespread decline in preaching as due to a number of factors ranging from the suspicion of oratory in society at large to a failure of faith, a crisis of confidence, in the church in particular. This last point is much the more important. The church has lost her faith in the reason for preaching and in the act of preaching. In the one case, what he describes as 'the loss of belief in the authority of the Scriptures, and a diminution in the belief of the truth' has led away from proclamation and ultimatum to suggestion and speculation, from the pulpit having a unique message of its own to its commenting, favourably or otherwise, on trends in society and fashionable political thought, from doctrinal and ethical absolutes to religious and moral relativism. In regard to the act of preaching itself, calm 'addresses' have replaced passionate testimony, the essayist has supplanted the prophet, liturgy has been enlarged as real 'worship' while the sermon has been reduced as something that follows 'the worship,' and personal counselling has claimed precedence over the public exposition and application of Scripture.

Over against these trends and their defenders he sets the clear priorities of Scripture as God's unchanging pronouncement on the matter. The primary work of Christ in His earthly ministry he points out was not physical healing or social relief or political reform. The physical healings were 'signs' that pointed to profounder needs and possibilities. The great thing was: 'Seek ye first the Kingdom of God and His righteousness.' In comparison with that, all material, physical and social needs took second place. On the most famous occasion of Jesus dealing with a 'practical' problem, hunger, in the feeding of the five thousand, Jesus turned His back on the popular response 'and went up to a mountain Himself alone.' Comments Dr Lloyd-Jones: 'He regarded that as a temptation, as something that would side-track Him.' Similarly He refused to involve Himself in dispute involving an inheritance and replied to the request for arbitration, 'Man, who made me a judge or a divider over you?' Again the Doctor comments: 'It is not that these things do not need to be done; justice and fair play and righteousness have their place; but He had not come to do these things.'

In perfect consistency with His own priorities, Jesus, in commissioning His apostles, commissioned them to be *preachers* (Lk 24:47), witnesses to Him (Acts 1:8). When the promised Holy Spirit came at Pentecost, it was with this immediate result: they *preached* with boldness the death and resurrection of Jesus, the Son of God, and God's call to the world to repent that it might receive the forgiveness of sins and the eternal life of Christ (Acts 2:36–38; 3:17–21; 4:10–12). Nothing therefore was allowed to qualify or reduce the priority of this work in the New Testament church, not even the social needs within the fellowship of God's people, which were indeed to be met (Acts 2:44, 45) but met by other means: 'It is not right that we should give up preaching the word of God to serve tables. Therefore, brethren, pick out from among you seven men of good repute, full of the Spirit and of wisdom, whom we may appoint to this duty' (Acts 6:2–4).

'Now there' concludes the Doctor, 'the priorities are laid down once and for ever. This is the primary task of the church . . . and we must not allow anything to deflect us from this, however good the cause, however great the need.' This was clearly the priority of the apostle Paul to the end of his preaching career. In his letters to Timothy he reminds the young evangelist that the church is 'the pillar and ground of the truth', on which Dr Lloyd-Jones comments: 'She is not a social organisation or institution, not a political society, not a cultural society, but "the pillar and the ground of the truth."' Hence Paul's great emphasis in the last of his letters is on the need for preaching: 'The things that thou hast heard of me among many witnesses, the same commit thou to faithful men, who shall be able to teach others also ... Preach the word; be instant in season, out of season; reprove, rebuke, exhort with all long-suffering and doctrine' (1 Tim 3:15; 2 Tim 4:2).

Dr Lloyd-Jones ends, again typically, with the supportive argument of church history which, he says, 'fully confirms' the apostolic priorities:

> Is it not clear, as you take a bird's eye view of church history, that the decadent periods and eras in the history of the church have always been those periods when preaching had declined? What is it that always heralds the dawn of a reformation or of a revival? It is renewed preaching. Not only a new interest in preaching but a new kind of preaching. A revival of true preaching has always heralded these great movements in the history of the church. And, of course, when the reformation and revival come they have always led to great and notable periods of the greatest preaching that the church has ever known. As that was true in the beginning as described in the book of Acts, it was, also, after the Protestant Reformation. Luther, Calvin, Knox, Latimer, Ridley—all these men were great preachers. In the 17th century you had exactly the same thing—the great Puritan preachers and others. And in the 18th century, Jonathan Edwards, Whitefield, the Wesleys, Rowlands and Harris were all great preachers. It was an era of great preaching. Whenever you get reformation and revival this is always and inevitably the result.

I want to turn now from the Scriptural and theological rationale of preaching which is further developed in the second and third chapters of *Preaching and Preachers* (published by Hodder and Stoughton) to demonstrate from Dr Lloyd-Jones' own preaching how he both proved and illustrated these things. He himself expressed the belief that 'every preacher should be, as it were, at least three types or kinds of preacher. There is the preaching which is primarily evangelistic. This should take place at least once each week.

There is the preaching which is instructional teaching but mainly experimental. That I generally did on a Sunday morning. There is more purely instructional type of preaching which I personally did on a week-night.' It will be helpful if we see the Doctor 'in action' as a preacher on each of these occasions, but I venture to say that it is the first type of preaching, evangelistic preaching, which shows us most memorably and most effectively his greatness as a preacher.

Speaking personally, of all the qualities that characterised the Doctor's ministry I find it is the power of *his evangelistic preaching* which still thrills, impels and challenges me most as a preacher and pastor. The prominence he gave to evangelism confirms my growing feeling that however sound and effective our teaching ministries may be, and however solid and well taught the churches we build up, under God, yet when we come to die our chief concern and greatest comfort, as we survey our ministries, will be the lives we have changed and the souls we have led to the Saviour. If our eyes are upon a system we shall cultivate devotees of a system, theological clubs where what distinguishes us from other Christian believers becomes our abiding and engrossing concern. But if our eyes are upon a present and personal God, holy and loving, who seeks out sinners and offers salvation to them by the death of His own Son, and if we absorb and share His immeasurable love for men and women, then whatever our other—and legitimate—concerns we shall be characterised in our ministries by the passion of the soul-seeker and the power of the soul-winner.

I recall on one occasion in my study the Doctor telling me of a company of leading ministers (by no means all evangelical) with whom he used to meet on a regular basis to discuss theological matters. He challenged the views and quite basic positions of many of them repeatedly and the battle often waxed hot and strong. However on one occasion when the talk got round to their various views of their ministries, he told them that he saw himself primarily as an evangelist. 'And they all laughed!' he added in meaningful tones. They saw him as a theologian or a teacher or a church leader and evidently thought 'the work of an evangelist' (2 Tim 4:5) a good many notches beneath these other accomplishments. Dr Lloyd-Jones did not. He knew what was the greatest glory of the greatest calling—and it was not the dignity of leadership or the excellence of intellectual attainments or even the fulness of theological learning but the glory of God in the salvation of souls.

In singling out the elements which made the Doctor a mighty evangelist from the beginning of his ministry in Wales, I think I must start with his interest in people. He was not a preacher interested only in sermons—any more than he had been a doctor interested only in bodies. Stories of his involvement in the lives and troubles of working men and women in Aberavon, South Wales, in his first ministry, can be read in the biography of Iain Murray, *D. Martyn Lloyd-Jones, The First Forty Years*, as well as the little book, *Memories of Sandfields*, by his wife, Bethan. Such was his (almost uncanny) ability to get behind a person's appearance and even their own sincere estimate of their trouble, to the real trouble and its cure, that it was commonly said that he had the old apostolic gift of wisdom spoken of in Paul's first letter to the Corinthians (1 Cor 12:8). Exegetical matters apart, this interest in people, this remarkable (almost x-ray!) insight into the characters of those who came for pastoral counsel, was throughout his life and ministry one of the most God-given and effective gifts he possessed. This profound interest in people affected his whole pulpit manner, his approach to preaching and his method in preaching. As to his approach, there appears a very revealing passage, in the Doctor's own words, in Iain Murray's biography:

I am not and have never been, a typical Welsh preacher. I felt that in preaching the first thing that you had to do was to demonstrate to the people that what you were going to do was very relevant and urgently important. The Welsh style of preaching started with a verse and the preacher then told you the connection and analysed the words, but the man of the world did not know what he was talking about and was not interested. I started with the man whom I wanted to listen, the patient. It was a medical approach really—here is a patient, a person in trouble, an ignorant man who has been to the quacks, and so I deal with all that in the introduction. I wanted to get the listener and *then* come to my exposition. They started with their exposition and ended with a bit of application.

No less orientated to the position, capacities and needs of his hearers was his method as he proceeded, from the introduction to the heart of his message. He was, utterly and every moment, determined to take his hearers with him step by step to the heart of his message and, if possible, into the heart of God Himself. He did not start half way up the ladder but at its lowest rung. He seemed to take in hand the weakest, to wait for the slowest, to turn back in repetition or recapitulation as he progressed through his sermon and its argumentation step by step, yet all the time advancing to his goal. He never forgot his hearers even in his zeal for the truth he was expounding, addressing himself to their difficulties and 'blocks' repeatedly lest they be left behind and robbed of the grand opportunity before them. It was at this point that his hearers, sometimes with reluctance, often astonishment, found themselves led forward by, as it were, logic holding one hand and passion holding the other, a total experience that shook sceptics to their roots and dramatically changed attitudes and lives.

The following example illustrates this perfectly. The Rev Leigh Powell of Canada, in a tribute to the Doctor shortly after his death, recalls taking to Westminster Chapel a friend, an 'unemotional mathematician', who sat stirred to the depths as the Doctor 'ascended the ladder of Paul's logic in Romans.' Leigh Powell writes: ' "As he was preaching", he told me, "I said, Ah, yes, *but*—and then he answered the *but*, until I had no *buts* left." ' That was it! Again and again he showed people the untenableness of their position, the arbitrariness of their prejudices and the reality in God which they must one day confront. The presentation of truth was to their minds, but the effect on their emotions was tremendous, and the transformation of their wills and lives inevitably followed. It was a method and a progression in the tradition of Jonathan Edwards, Dr Lloyd-Jones' great mentor, but it was apostolic before it was Edwardsean! Quoting Paul's words 'God be thanked that ye were the servants of sin, but ye have obeyed from the heart that form of doctrine which was delivered you' (Rom 6:17), Dr Lloyd-Jones traces the method of God in all effective preaching:

> What had been delivered or preached to them was the truth, and truth is addressed primarily to the mind. As the mind grasps it, and understands it, the affections are kindled and moved, and so in turn the will is persuaded and obedience is the outcome. In other words the obedience is not the result of direct pressure on the will, it is the result of an enlightened mind and a softened heart. To me this is a crucial point.

Behind all his evangelistic preaching was the conviction that in spite of the enormous advances in techniques in science, medicine and engineering, in spite of truly revolutionary changes in society and in the daily lives of men and women, families and communities, still, the essential things, the paramount things, remained the same. Man in sin was the same as ever, failing to make it without God, failing to build his world or even to maintain his own domestic or personal peace: a failure for all his progress as the history of the 20th century has shown in its unfolding and terrible drama of war, corruption and marriage breakdown. And God's way of salvation too remained the same: unequalled and unexcelled, His only Son Jesus a persistent challenge to every generation, His Atonement man's only redemption from sin, His righteousness man's only means of justification before a holy God. The Doctor regarded as 'monstrously shallow' the idea that television, education, politics, or world events had fundamentally altered either the character and needs of man or the church's task in meeting that need and confronting that character:

> Never has there been a greater opportunity for preaching than there is today, because we are living in an age of disillusionment. The Victorian age, last century, was an age of optimism. People were carried away by the theory of evolution and development, and the poets sang about the coming of the 'parliament of man and the federation of the world.' We would banish war and all would be well, and the world would be one great nation. They really believed that sort of thing. Nobody believes it now apart from an odd representative here and there of the old 'social gospel' of the pre-1914 era. We have lived to see the fallacy of that old optimistic liberalism, and we are living in an age of disillusionment when men are desperate. That is why we are witnessing this student protest and every other kind of protest; that is why people are taking drugs…Is not this then the very time when the door is wide open for the preaching of the Gospel? The age in which we are living is so similar to the first century in many respects. The old world was exhausted then. The flowering period of Greek philosophy had come and gone, Rome in a sense had passed her zenith and there was the same kind of tiredness and weariness, with consequent turning to pleasure and amusement. The same is so true today; and so far from saying that we must have less preaching and turn more and more to other devices and expedients, I say that we have a heaven-sent opportunity for preaching.

His evangelistic preaching may be summarised under what has long been known in Reformed circles as 'the three R's', namely, ruin, redemption and regeneration: the fall of man and his consequent helplessness, the cross of Christ and its way of atonement, and the necessity of the new birth, the birth 'from above', if men were to live new lives. One very important addition to be made, which he discovered for himself and made in the early years of his ministry, was the mighty gospel truth of justification in which God the Judge declares the believing sinner to be guiltless, righteous and forever acceptable in Christ His Son, our Redeemer.

Yet all that I have said about his approach, his method, his content and his convictions about both his Gospel and his hearers fall short of explaining him—as much as paper and print can ever 'explain' great preaching. The final, crucial exceptional element of truly great Gospel preaching is not, in the final analysis, in the man at all. Dr Lloyd-Jones was a great logician and clear thinker, but as he himself said 'No one has ever been "reasoned" into the Kingdom of God.' He preached with zeal and passion, but still many are proof against emotion, however sincere. The Doctor himself comes to the heart of the matter when he writes, 'True preaching after all is God acting. It is not just a man uttering words; it is God using him. He is being used of God.' This is the unique factor in effective preaching. It takes up a simple sermon by a man of very average abilities and attainments and makes it mightier than the greatest philosophical effusion or oratorial display, mighty to the pulling down of strongholds. God is using it! The Holy Spirit is accompanying it. It is reaching the hearts of the hearers with power. Dr Lloyd-Jones, for all his gifts, never relied on his gifts. He scorned to preach 'great' sermons, that the excellency of the power might be of God. He perfectly embodied Paul's attitude at Corinth: 'And I was with you in weakness, and in fear, and in much trembling.

And my speech and my preaching was not with enticing words of man's wisdom, but in demonstration of the Spirit and the power: That your faith should not stand in the wisdom of men, but in the power of God' (1 Cor 2:3–5).

Consequently the one thing he prayed for, the one thing he relied on, the one thing he waited for and the one thing above all else and beyond most other preachers of his generation which thousands felt under his preaching was the unction, or anointing, of the Holy Spirit: that scarcely definable accompaniment of solemn, sacred, searching truth as proceeding from the eternal presence of God, that breath of the still small voice which somehow goes beyond words, even God-words, so that the form of truth yields up its divine power. There was nothing formal about this, nothing automatic, nothing inevitable. It might come early or late in the sermon—it might not come at all; usually it came well on into the discourse, after the ground had been cleared of many prejudices, fears and errors and a foundation in great truth laid. But the preacher was never content to build the sermon and leave it an imposing but empty structure: he wanted it to be filled with the Holy Spirit even as it was raised in the minds and hearts of his hearers. So, often toward the end, it came; with the preacher's rising passion but not identical with it, from it but not of it: more than argument, more than conviction: the affirmation of God reaching the heart of the hearers, bringing them to final surrender—and worship. Leigh Powell, in the memorial tribute to Dr Lloyd-Jones earlier cited, perceptively recalls exactly this feature of preaching at 'the Chapel': 'At times—often toward the end of the sermon, he seemed to be hovering, waiting for something,' adding 'Sometimes the wind of the Spirit would come and sweep us and him aloft and we would mount with wings like eagles into the awesome and felt presence of God.' Neither the Doctor's own preaching, nor his view of preaching itself, can be understood without this supreme element which he called 'unction.'

The second type of preaching in which every preacher must regularly engage was, he believed, directed to believers, being instructional and experimental, inculcating Scripture and applying it to the lives of its Christian hearers. His own Sunday morning ministry at Westminster Chapel was of this kind and was an outstanding feature of his pulpit ministry. Here he used his teaching gifts to great effect, building up not only the same congregation (estimated at 1,200 in the morning and up to 2,000 in the evening) but also thousands of students over the years, whose Christian understanding and commitment was permanently deepened and matured, enabling them in turn to teach others where Providence led them and to build others up in the Christian faith.

In ministering to his congregation at this level week by week, he followed the way of the old Reformers and Puritans in the systematic exposition and application of Scripture. Connected series of sermons, long and short, characterised his long London ministry. As well as the great 13-year series of Friday night Bible studies on Paul's letter to the Romans, there was, on Sunday mornings, the eight-year series on Ephesians (256 sermons) now published in eight volumes by the Banner of Truth Trust; a series of 197 sermons stretching over six years on the early chapters of John's Gospel, some of which have been published as *Joy Unspeakable* and *Prove All Things*; a series of 122 sermons on the early chapters of the Acts of the Apostles, over three years; and an earlier series of 60 sermons on the Sermon on the Mount, over two years. Besides these and other series there were many shorter, immensely valuable, series over a period of months on such subjects as Spiritual Depression (1954), Revival (1959), Baptism in the Spirit (1964, '65), and on shorter passages of Scripture, often in the evening sermons, such as Psalm 107, Isaiah 5 and 40, Ezekiel 36, John 3 and 5 and 1 Peter 1 and 2. (Most of these and many

others are becoming available on tape to a new generation
through the Martyn Lloyd Jones Recordings Trust, who
have already published a catalogue of 500 tapes of exceptionally high sound quality and are in the process of com-
pleting the commercial availability of about 1,800 of Dr
Lloyd-Jones' sermons.)

This unceasing reference to Scripture is a crucial factor in
any evaluation of the Doctor as a preacher. To him the
Bible was not a starting point from which we 'advanced,'
leaving behind apostolic teaching for our own opinions or
philosphy. He believed that the Bible was what it claimed to
be—the unique, perfect, sufficient and authoritative revelation of God, humbling us and exalting us, demanding our
closest attention and touching our lives at every point with
the sanctifying power of its truth. He believed that churches
and congregations of God's people were built up or 'edified'
under a preaching ministry precisely as the preacher sur-
rendered himself to the revelation which God had given,
faithfully expounding apostolic truth, guarding and sharing
the deposit of faith which was given for all time and could
never be set aside (2 Tim 1:13–14).

The preacher's task was to understand, and to help his
people to understand, this revelation. The preacher was not
to leave his intellect behind when he entered the pulpit—
the doctor had little time for shallow and superficial ministries of the 'blessed thought' type—but he was to use his
intelligence, every ounce of it, to 'think God's thoughts after
him,' in Pascal's famous phrase. Dr Lloyd-Jones' own
remarkable intellectual gifts were obvious, yet he kept the
intellectual element very firmly in its place, humble in the
very area where he might have been most self-reliant—the
area of his profound and agile intellect.

For him, consequently, a truly expository ministry was
bound to be a *doctrinal* one. This meant that he based his
preaching on the great doctrines of Scripture rather than
tracing the stories of Bible characters or summarising the

content of Bible books as had been common with older
evangelical contemporaries. He saw the need for doctrine in
the evangelical churches if they were to survive, let alone
develop. At a time when many were crying down doctrine
as divisive or even irrelevant he perceived it to be of the very
essence of Christian life: the motivation of all witness, the
ground of all rejoicing and the source of real power for
Christian living (John 17:17). People needed to know who
they were and why they were the people they had become.
They needed to know what God had done for them in Christ
the Redeemer and the height to which He had lifted them in
making them sons and daughters of God. 'Understand who
you are and you will live as you ought' was, in various ways,
a dictum continually repeated, explained and enforced.

This constant application of Scripture truth to the lives of
his hearers was a major and crucial element even of his most
profound doctrinal teaching. Like the Puritan preachers in
their own systematic pulpit teaching and preaching he
never finished a sermon without applying the doctrine to
the hearts and lives of his hearers—indeed in his case, as we
saw earlier, the 'application' was sustained throughout the
sermon from the start. The end of all his teaching was 'that
according to the riches of his glory he may grant you to be
strengthened with might through his Spirit in the inner
man, and that Christ may dwell in your hearts through
faith; that you being rooted and grounded in love, may have
power to comprehend with all the saints what is the breadth
and length and height and depth, and to know the love of
Christ which surpasses knowledge, that you may be filled
with all the fulness of God' (Eph 3:16–19).

Finally, there was his Friday night ministry and his
practice of the third type of preaching: preaching which was
more purely instructional, sustaining a higher and more
demanding level of thought in the study of Scripture. Early
on in his Westminster ministry, in the late 40's and early
50's, Dr Lloyd-Jones gave a prolonged series on Christian

doctrine. He had discovered how 'patchy' the knowledge of Christians, even those of long standing in evangelical churches, was and how unaware they were of their roots in Reformed, Protestant thinking. By the mid 50's, however, he felt he could proceed with a close and prolonged study of one of the greatest books in the Bible—Paul's epistle to the Romans. For no less than 13 years he wrestled with and absorbed and expounded the great mind of the inspired apostle.

It was a high adventure, not only for himself and his own church members, but also for the hundreds of 'Friday-nighters', including ministers and church leaders of other denominations, who flocked to the Chapel from all over London and beyond to sit at the feet of Paul's great admirer. Here his outstanding teaching gifts were stretched and exercised to their utmost as he expounded the epistle chapter by chapter, section by section, with studied and expert clarity, reading much but quoting little, unravelling the tangled thought of conflicting opinions and setting his own understanding of the revelation clearly before the people, making the reasoning accessible to every intent listener. This remarkable ability to distil long hours of reading, to penetrate to the heart of the controverted matters, to isolate and expound the main elements of a doctrine or a closely argued piece of inspired reasoning, was among the greatest and most useful of all Dr Lloyd-Jones' pulpit gifts.

How profoundly this preacher understood his favourite apostle can in my opinion be best judged from the two volumes (out of those so far published) on Romans 5 and 6, entitled 'Assurance' and 'The New Man' respectively. The volume on Romans 6 alone will show how personally and originally and effectively Dr Lloyd-Jones entered the mind of Paul. If I may venture to express a personal opinion at this point I believe it contains the greatest contribution which the Doctor made to the Christian church in the matter of theological thinking. His message is the most radically life-transforming one that this writer, at any rate, knows.

Among the many notable features of these six volumes is the fact that, throughout, the Doctor is still preaching— even in the profoundest, most demanding reaches of Paul's thought. This will be no surprise to those who knew his ministry for themselves, but it deserves to be noted. Just read the two volumes on Romans 8—'The Sons of God' and 'The Final Perseverance of the Saints'—to see the preacher take over from the theologian! The Doctor once said to me, 'I am coming to the conclusion that the only satisfactory way of teaching theology is in sermonic form.' Certainly to hear on tape or to read these theological expositions 'in sermonic form' is to rise up deeply satisfied in God and His ways with men. Those who poured out of 'the Chapel' into Buckingham Gate from those Bible studies *felt* the truth of Proverbs 3:13–18: 'Happy is the man who finds wisdom, and the man who gets understanding ... for the gain from it is better than gain from silver and its profit better than gold ... Her ways are ways of pleasantness and all her paths are peace. She is a tree of life to those who lay hold of her; those who hold her fast are called happy.'

In conclusion, it is evident from any study of his ministry and its widespread effect, that in the history of the pulpit in Britain the preaching of Martyn Lloyd-Jones is outstanding. He takes his place in a long line of great preachers since the Protestant Reformation who have stood for the reformation and renewal of the church, the evangelization and awakening of the world around it, and the pastoral counsel and good of souls precious to God and His ministers. Some of these men lived and laboured during the church's hard times, others reaped a glorious harvest in times of revival. Dr Lloyd-Jones always regarded himself as 'an 18th-century man' in his deepest sympathies, notwithstanding his Puritan theology and methods: he longed above all to see revival. His call, however, was to minister outside it, to remind the church of its necessity and perhaps to prepare a new generation for God's best and greatest work in the world. In this respect also his ministry goes on.

Chapter Five

AN INTERVIEW

by

Carl Henry

Dr Carl Henry is the founding editor of *Christianity Today*, in whose pages this interview first appeared in 1980. He is now a lecturer-at-large for World Vision, and holds several Visiting Professorships. Dr Henry has written many books, including *God, Revelation and Authority*, which appeared in six volumes.

Question: Your early credentials as a gifted young physician presaged a brilliant medical career. What prodded you toward the pulpit, and was there a deep struggle?

Answer: Yes, there was a very great struggle. It went on throughout my last 18 months in medicine. I literally lost over 20 pounds in weight. Friends said, why not continue with medicine and preach occasionally? I tried that, but it didn't satisfy. I was more interested ultimately in people than in their physical diseases. I became increasingly impressed that most of my patients were suffering from functional and not organic troubles.

Q: What influences shaped your decision?

A: I belonged to a Welsh Presbyterian church in London. But I was greatly attracted by Dr John A. Hutton, later to become editor of *The British Weekly*, who was then minister of Westminster Chapel where I attended occasionally. While he was not an expository preacher he was very dramatic and impressed me with the power of God to change men's lives. The time came when I no longer wanted to be a physician who acts as a preacher only occasionally; I wanted to be a preacher who at times might act as a physician. To my surprise, my decision got tremendous publicity in the press because of my staff position with Lord

Horder, physician to the royal family.

Q: By the early 1930's, I'm told, word had spread of your 'gift of wisdom' in diagnosing spiritual malady and of your scientific exposition of Scripture.

A: I deliberately went to South Wales, to a small mission centre of 93 members, to do pioneer work. The mission, under the Welsh Presbyterian Church, was in both a mining district and a centre of steel and tinplate works. Many of the people were dock labourers. Partly because of the extensive press coverage—some of it annoyed me greatly—the church was filled from the very first. There were amazing conversions. In my 11½ years the church grew to 530 members and the attendance ran at about 850.

Q: When did you first meet G. Campbell Morgan whom you succeeded at Westminster Chapel?

A: I went to hear him during meetings he was conducting in Swansea. A friend of his in the congregation introduced me to him. I didn't see him again until early December 1935, when on a miserably foggy night I spoke at a Bible Witness rally in the Albert Hall, the biggest hall in London. Campbell Morgan was present and almost the next day I got a letter from him inviting me to preach in Westminster Chapel on the last Sunday in 1935. In 1937, when I was in the States to address preassembly evangelism meetings of the then United Presbyterian Church (North), my itinerary took me to Philadelphia. There the presiding minister told me that in the congregation would be a Dr G. Campbell Morgan who had arrived the previous night from England. My heart sank. From the pulpit I noticed him sitting in the front. Just as I began to preach I saw him pulling out his watch; he was going to time me. For some reason that stimulated me, and we had a good service. The first one to greet me at the close was Campbell Morgan; then, as people gathered, he slipped away. I knew intuitively that he was weighing an invitation to me to join him. That June night in 1937 he decided to invite me to Westminster Chapel. When he later learned that I was scheduled for a teaching post in a Welsh theological college the following year, he asked me to come for the interim to alternate preaching services with him. In September 1938, I came; six weeks later I received a unanimous call to serve as associate pastor.

Q: What was it like to labour in the shadow of such a giant?

A: He was a great pulpit master, in many ways the greatest I have ever heard. He was also a very kind and very generous man. But I always wanted to be myself; I never wanted to duplicate him or any other preacher. My main concern was to convey the message to the best of my ability. I believed the message and that God would honour my efforts. Between us we alternated morning and evening services monthly. Our congregations were almost identical in number during the entire year we ministered together before the war.

Q: What impact did World War II have?

A: It was shattering. I well remember Sunday morning, September 3, 1939. A radio bulletin was to be given at 11 o'clock, so we delayed the service until the unsettling announcement came: *war*! Immediately everyone expected air raids over London. Since our Chapel had no facilities for sheltering people, we dismissed the congregation. That very day, in fact, an air raid warning sounded, though it was a false alarm. People who could move out of London did so and our congregation dwindled to about 300. We blacked out the church windows and moved the evening service to mid-afternoon. In a flying bomb attack a bomb dropped just across the road in June 1944 and blew off half the Chapel roof, so that for 14 weeks we met in a borrowed hall with about 150 people. Only 100 to 200 were left of Campbell Morgan's great congregation. Campbell Morgan retired in 1943 and died in 1945.

Q: Were you ever discouraged to the point of wanting to forego a pulpit ministry?

A: No, never. During the war I travelled extensively throughout Britain, at least two days a week, for combined meetings or special services. In 1947 many people urged me to take the superintendency of the Forward Movement of the Welsh Presbyterian Church, but I stayed in war-scarred London. The congregation had slowly begun to build, and at the end of the war roughly 500 people attended quite regularly.

Q: Once the Nazis were repelled, what happened?

A: People began to return to London. But we lost the vast majority of our membership; the pre-war remnant that remained was middle-aged and elderly. We developed a virtually new congregation. In 1948 attendance reached 1,300–1,400 people and we opened the first gallery. The National Centenary Exposition in 1951 brought throngs to London, and for the first time since Campbell Morgan's day the Chapel was again completely filled as 2,500 persons at times crowded the auditorium, first gallery, and balcony.

Q: If not in numbers, how does one then measure the effectiveness of such a large pulpit ministry?

A: By an atmosphere of expectancy in the services, for one thing. We placed notices in the pews that the minister was available for private conference after each service. I spent well over an hour service after service with individuals seeking conversion or counsel.

Q: Word reached America that because you were not only steeped in Scripture but also abreast of medicine, science, and history, non-evangelical intellectuals were attracted to your preaching.

A: I was invited to speak at the Inter-Varsity Fellowship conference in 1936. During the war years I served as their president. Students came in large numbers, especially after the war. The New Testament scholar, Professor R. V. G. Tasker, attended on Sunday nights; he forsook liberalism and told me that under my ministry he became convinced of original sin and the wrath of God, and that led to a complete change. There were others in whom an evangelical faith was revived. ˙

Q: You and I met in 1966, I believe, to discuss the projected Berlin World Congress on Evangelism. You declined to be either a participant or observer. You were also, I think, the only minister of a major church in London that did not cooperate in the Graham Crusades? What kept you on the sidelines?

A: This is a very vital and difficult matter. I have always believed that nothing but a revival—a visitation of the Holy Spirit, in distinction from an evangelistic campaign— can deal with the situation of the church and of the world. The Welsh Presbyterian church had roots in the great 18th-century evangelical revival, when the power of the Spirit of God came upon preachers and churches, and large numbers were converted. I have never been happy about organized campaigns. In the 1820s a very subtle and unfortunate change took place, especially in the United States, from Azahel Nettleton's emphasis on revival to Charles G. Finney's on evangelism. There are two positions. When things were not going well, the old approach was for ministers and deacons to call a day of fasting and prayer and to plead with God to visit them with power. Today's alternative is an evangelistic campaign: ministers ask, 'whom shall we get as evangelist?' Then they organize and ask God's blessing on this. I belong to the old school.

Q: What specific reservations do you have about modern evangelism as such?

A: I am unhappy about organized campaigns and even more about the invitation system of calling people forward. Mark you, I consider Billy Graham an utterly honest, sincere, and genuine man. He, in fact, asked me in 1963 to be chairman of the first Congress on Evangelism, then projected for Rome, not Berlin. I said I'd make a bargain: if he would stop the general sponsorship of his campaigns— stop having liberals and Roman Catholics on the plat-

form—and drop the invitation system, I would wholeheartedly support him and chair the congress. We talked for
about three hours, but he didn't accept these conditions.

I just can't subscribe to the idea that either congresses or
campaigns really deal with the situation. The facts, I feel,
substantiate my point of view: in spite of all that has been
done in the last 20 or 25 years, the spiritual situation has
deteriorated rather than improved. I am convinced that
nothing can avail but churches and ministers on their knees
in total dependence on God. As long as you go on organizing, people will not fall on their knees and implore God to
come and heal them. It seems to me that the campaign
approach trusts ultimately in techniques rather than in the
power of the Spirit. Graham certainly preaches the Gospel.
I would never criticize him on that score. What I have
criticized, for example, is that in the Glasgow campaign he
had John Sutherland Bonnell address the ministers' meetings. I challenged that. Graham replied, 'You know, I have
more fellowship with John Sutherland Bonnell than with
many evangelical ministers.' I replied, 'Now it may be that
Bonnell is a nicer chap than Lloyd-Jones—I'll not argue
that. But real fellowship is something else: I can genuinely
fellowship only with someone who holds the same basic
truths that I do.'

Q: You haven't been a Keswick enthusiast either?

A: I refused to speak there. I was unhappy about the
so-called Keswick message concerning sanctification. I
considered it unscriptural and have tried to show why in my
volumes on Romans 6 and 8. To me, sanctification is a
process, and the Keswick formula 'Let go and let God' is
quite unscriptural. Today Keswick no longer requires
speakers to adhere to the doctrine of a modified perfectionism.

Q: What great emphases do Evangelicals too much
neglect?

A: To me, the missing note in modern evangelicalism is

the matter of godliness, or what was once called spirituality. We Evangelicals are too smug, too self-satisfied, too healthy. The notion of being humbled under the mighty hand of God has gone. We live too much in the realm of a pseudo-intellectualism and an emphasis upon the will. The heart is being ignored. I see no hope until we return to the great emphasis of Jonathan Edwards who, though a brilliant intellect and outstanding philosopher, put ultimate emphasis upon the heart. By the heart I mean the whole man, with special emphasis on the emotional element. Today a vague sentimentality has replaced deep emotion. People are no longer humble; there is little fear of the Lord. Modern evangelicalism is very unlike the evangelicalism of the 18th century and of the Puritans. I'm unhappy about this. The genuine evangelicalism is that older evangelicalism.

Q: Was it not also intellectually and theologically powerful?

A: Tremendously so. But today we have a pseudo-intellectualism that is theologically shallow. We need both brilliant theological comprehension and the warm heart. When I first came to England evangelicalism was non-theological, pietistic, and sentimental, and I stressed engaging the intellect to its maximum. But now many Evangelicals are far too conscious of their intellects; some are preoccupied with secondary things like the Christian view of art or of drama or of politics.

Q: You would surely want the Christian intellectual dimension to be strong enough to expose the shallowness of all speculative alternatives to the great truths of revelation?

A: Of course. But that alone is not enough. The most important chapter in the Bible today from the standpoint of modern preaching is 1 Corinthians 2. Without the demonstration of the Spirit's power, all theology leads to nothing. My key verse, in a sense, is Romans 6:17, 'Ye have obeyed from the heart the form of sound words delivered unto you.' While truth comes primarily to the intellect it must move the heart, which then, in turn moves the will. Today many people go no farther than having the form of sound words; others place their emphasis upon decision. Both approaches ignore the heart.

Q: What evangelical gains and losses are noteworthy in Anglican circles and in the Free Churches of Britain?

A: The main trouble at the moment is confusion.

Q: In the Free Churches as well as the Anglican church?

A: Yes; particularly among the Anglicans, but among the others as well.

Q: Why so?

A: Because the technical linguistic and ecclesiastical 'experts' have wrested control from the theologians. Concessions have been made to so-called scholarship, and there has been a slide toward a liberal view of the Scriptures and of particular doctrines. James Barr's *Fundamentalism* correctly represents some of this country's prominent Evangelicals as having quietly and subtly crossed the line by concessions to higher criticism. At stake is the loss of a doctrine of the full inspiration and inerrancy of Scripture.

Q: In view of the loss to England, what do you think of the evangelical exodus, that is, of James Packer's move to Canada, of Colin Brown's to the United States, and of John Stott's heavy overseas ministry?

A: I have great regard for these men. It's very sad when a country loses evangelical scholars and leaders. They should stay here in Britain and fight. But it's hard to fight things out in a mixed denominational situation. Anglican evangelicalism today has an identity crisis; the same holds for other compromised churches, many of whose leaders and teachers of students disown basic Christian doctrines. For dedicated Evangelicals to labour in such circles ultimately suggests that these truths do not matter. Today priority must be given anew to the doctrine of the church. Too many people regard institutional organizations as the church. I believe in *evangelical ecumenism*. I believe Evangelicals should combine forces—not to form a new denomination, but for fellowship and cooperation. Such mutual strengthening is the hopeful way into the future.

Q: You have a great sense of humour, your friends say, but seldom use it in the pulpit.

A: I find it very difficult to be humorous in the pulpit. I always feel in the pulpit that I am in the terrible position of standing between God and souls that may go to hell. That position is too appalling for humour.

Q: You've cancelled four months of preaching engagements, I'm told, because of your hospitalization and recovery last year. Friends are eager for some word of your physical condition.

A: I'm such a sinner that God has always had to compel me to do things. I struggled a year and half before entering the ministry. Then, in the beginning of 1968—I was 68—I naturally thought of retiring. But I carried on until, when facing major surgery in March that year, God clearly signalled me to leave Westminster Chapel in order to put my sermons into print and to prepare spiritual reminiscences. That was God's assurance that the surgery, though serious and radical, would be successful. I shall curtail itinerant preaching and concentrate on writing. The last six of my 12 volumes on the Epistle to the Romans and the last two of the eight volumes on Ephesians are soon going to press, and I am ready now to commence spiritual autobiography.

Q: What do you think Christianity ought to say to the economic situation today?

A: I think the great message we must preach is God's judgment on men and on the world. Because man is a sinner, any human contrivance is doomed to fail; the only hope for the world is the return of Christ—nothing else. It amazes me that Evangelicals have suddenly taken such an interest in politics: to do so would have made sense 50 or 100 years ago, but such efforts now seem to me sheer folly, for we are in a dissolving world. All my life I've opposed setting 'times and seasons,' but I feel increasingly that we may be in the last times.

Q: What undergirds that conviction?

A: To me 1967, the year that the Jews occupied all of Jerusalem, was very crucial. Luke 21:43 is one of the most significant prophetic verses: 'Jerusalem' it reads 'shall be trodden down of the Gentiles *until* the time of the Gentiles be fulfilled.' It seems to me that that took place in 1967—something crucially important that had not occurred in 2,000 years. Luke 21:43 is one fixed point. But I am equally impressed by Romans 11 which speaks of a great spiritual return among the Jews before the end of time. While this seems to be developing, something even more spectacular may be indicated. We sometimes tend to foreshorten events, yet I have a feeling that we are in the period of the end.

Q: Would you agree that even if we might have only 24 or 48 hours, to withhold a witness in the political or any other arena is to withdraw prematurely from the social responsibility of the Christian and to distrust the providence of God? Might He not do something even in the last few hours that He had not done before? The closer we get to the end time, isn't it that much more important to address public conscience? Must we not press the claims of Christ in all the arenas of society and remind people, whether they receive Christ or not, of the criteria by which the returning King will judge men and nations?

A: No; I'm afraid I don't agree. It seems to me that our Lord's own emphasis is quite different, even opposed to this. Take Luke 17 where we read, 'As it was in the days of Noah, so shall it be also in the days of the Son of man. They did eat, they drank, they married wives . . . until the day that Noah entered into the ark, and the flood came . . .' You can't reform the world. That's why I disagree entirely with the 'social and cultural mandate' teaching and its appeal to Genesis 1:28. It seems to me to forget completely the Fall. You can't Christianize the world. The end time is going to be like the time of the Flood. The condition of the modern world proves that what we must preach more than ever is 'Escape from the wrath to come!' The situation is critical. I believe that Christian people—but not the church—should get involved in politics and in social affairs. The kingdom task of the church is to save men from the wrath to come by bringing them to Christ. This is what I believe and emphasize. The main function of politics, culture, and all these things is to restrain evil. They can never do an ultimately positive work. Surely the history of the world demonstrates that. You can never Christianize the world.

Q: Let's grant that the regenerate church is the new society and the only enduring society, that the world as such can never be Christianized and turned into the new society, and that apart from regeneration there is no participation in the kingdom of God. Having said that, does not the church nonetheless have a mission of light and salt in the world? Even if the institutional church is not to be politically engaged, does not Christ wish to expand His victory over evil and sin and all the forces that would destroy Him, by penetrating the social order with Christians to exemplify godliness and justice? Are they not to work for good laws and a just society, even though they cannot hope to Christianize society?

A: Certainly. Such effort prevents the world from putrefying. But I regard it as entirely negative. I do not regard it as anything positive.

Q: Is it not possible that here or there at some point Christian effort might bring about what in quotation marks might be called 'Christian culture'?

A: No. It will never come. All Scripture is against that. It's impossible. In the present world situation—surely it has never been more critical—all civilization is rocking, and we are facing collapse, morally, politically, and in every other way. I would have thought that surely at this time our urgent message should be, 'Flee from the wrath to come!'

Q: Would you therefore encourage young people to consider the pulpit ministry or a missionary call above every other vocational call?

A: No. That's something I have never done and never would do. Such a decision must be a personal call from God. But seeing the critical danger of the world we must surely urge people to escape. It's amazing that any Christian could be concerned about anything else at this present time.

Q: Would you be happier if Sir Fred Catherwood, your son-in-law, were in the Christian ministry rather than in his present political work in the European Parliament?

A: No. I wouldn't. In fact, I was glad he resisted when pressure was brought upon him to go into the ministry. I've always tried to keep men out of the ministry. In my opinion a man should enter the ministry only if he cannot stay out of it.

Q: Did you indicate to him the remarkable contribution that he could make in the political arena?

A: Yes. But I also said that he should never—speaking as a Christian—claim that '*this* is the Christian political view.' That approach was the mistake of Abraham Kuyper. Kuyper placed himself in a compromise position: a Christian minister becoming Prime Minister and then needing to form a coalition with Roman Catholics and claiming Christian sanction for specific political positions.

Q: Was there some ambiguity about evangelical doctrine in your own earliest preaching?

A: In the early part of my ministry I preached regeneration as the great message, but not justification (George Whitefield did the same for a time, you know). I preached what I was sure of. I neglected the Atonement, but within about two years I came to see that was an incomplete message.

Q: Do you think that present-day evangelical preaching too much neglects the doctrines of Atonement and justification while emphasizing the need for the new birth, and thus unwittingly gives the impression that God tolerates sin?

A: Precisely.

Q: Do you see any prospect for evangelical renewal in England?

A: I really don't. Nothing but a great outpouring of the Spirit—which is what I meant by revival—can possibly retrieve the situation.

Q: How would you chart the next 20 years of world history, if we have them? What will give way, and what will endure?

A: I'm afraid I see nothing but collapse. I think that democracy is the ultimate position politically; we've passed through all other forms of government. But beyond democracy there now looms either dictatorship or complete chaos. The end is more likely: 666 is the number of man, and this is democracy—man worshipping himself, his own likeness. I'm not sure at all that we have 20 years. Several factors are present that have never been present before. In the past, great civilizations in various parts of the world would collapse but would not devastate the rest of the world. Today the world is one vast whole. What happens in one place happens everywhere. I think we are witnessing the breakdown of politics. I think even the world is seeing that. Civilization is collapsing.

Q: What parting word have you for the secular man or woman who does not take Jesus Christ seriously?

A: I can only say: 'Flee from the wrath to come' and 'Believe on the Lord Jesus Christ'.

Chapter Six

WITH EVANGELICAL STUDENTS

by

Chua Wee-hian

Chua Wee-hian is the general secretary of the International Fellowship of Evangelical Students, whose first chairman and subsequent president was Martyn Lloyd-Jones. Chua Wee-hian, who comes from Singapore, first met the Doctor while studying in London during the 1950's.

Many people are unaware of the major part played by Dr Martyn Lloyd-Jones in one of the most remarkable movements of God's Spirit in the world of students.

Today, in well over a hundred nations, there are committed groups of Christian students witnessing to the power and grace of Jesus Christ. Some of these are phenomenally huge, both in numbers and in spiritual impact. Consider the Varsity Christian Fellowship, Singapore. Some 1,500 students are involved with this Christian Union. (The National University of Singapore has an enrolment of 12,000.) A sizable proportion of the teaching staff are committed Christians. In its relatively brief history the Fellowship of Evangelical Students of Singapore, to which the VCF is affiliated, has had the joy of witnessing many of its graduates playing key roles in government, the different professions and the church.

In Anglophone Africa there has been astounding growth. Nigeria alone has around 200 Christian Unions involving over 30,000 college and university students. Its annual conference attracts 5,000. The mind boggles when planning for such events is in the hands of students operating with a minimum of funds and technological equipment. In neighbouring Ghana, evangelistic missions are often times of spiritual harvest, when literally hundreds of students profess faith in Jesus Christ.

The older and more established student movements, like those in Britain (Universities and Colleges Christian Fellowship), the United States and Canada (both known as Inter Varsity Christian Fellowship) and Norway (Norges Kristelige Student—og Skoleungdomslag), have maintained a strong evangelical witness. They have not lost their vitality in evangelism. Each year hundreds of students are nurtured in their faith and equipped to live and serve God in their academic communities.

These national evangelical student movements, and those in 70 other nations, are all members of the International Fellowship of Evangelical Students (IFES.) They pool their manpower and resources to pioneer and establish ongoing Christian Fellowships in another 30 countries. A conservative estimate indicates that more than 270,000 high school and university students are linked together in the IFES family.

Dr Martyn Lloyd-Jones was one of the founding fathers of IFES. He played a vital part in its inception and its formative years of growth. He was acquainted with the predecessor of IFES, the International Conference of Evangelical Students. He had the distinction of addressing 900 or more students who gathered at Cambridge University for the 1939 conference. Since 1934, European evangelical students had profited enormously from these fraternal gatherings. Many had to maintain their evangelical position amidst ridicule from theologically liberal church leaders. They were greatly refreshed by the excellent Bible expositions and their faith was confirmed through fellowship with like-minded student believers.

It was in April 1946 that the leaders of various European evangelical movements met again. They had been through the holocaust and devastation of World War II. Some who had attended the 1939 Cambridge conference had lost their lives; Europe in general was licking the wounds of war. But in addition to the European leaders, delegates from the USA, Canada and Australia were present. In the dismal political climate and in the face of human helplessness, a new vision was kindled. Students must be reached for Christ! The Swiss were challenged to minister to German students. The North Americans enthusiastically agreed to plant Christian Fellowships in the Caribbean and parts of Latin America. At the same time American soldiers on duty in war-devastated Japan, who had been involved with IVCF, were praying for the start of a Japanese witness in the universities there. Amazingly, this prayer of faith was answered within a matter of months. In 1947 two Japanese Christian students met for prayer and Bible study in a bombed classroom of Waseda University. That was the beginning of the KGK, the Japanese Evangelical Students Union.

For such a missionary vision to become reality, an international body had to be organised with clear objectives, an evangelical basis of faith and a workable constitution. There were going to be problems: of ecclesiastical differences, of language and of methods of operation.

The Doctor was one of three British delegates at this historic conference. All were united and unanimous in bringing about the birth of this worldwide body—the IFES. In the debates and discussions that took place, it was the good Doctor who presented proposals, clause by clause, and ably argued for various amendments to be included in the new constitution. The minutes of the 1946 IFES general committee bore tribute to his skills: 'The committee was greatly indebted to the able, patient and very clear manner in which Dr Lloyd-Jones presented the amendments.' No easy task at such an international meeting!

It was therefore no surprise that the Doctor was elected vice-chairman of the newly-formed Fellowship. It was agreed that the new body would be formally ratified at the

ollowing general committee. In August 1947 delegates from
en nations convened at Phillips Brooks House, Harvard
University. The chairman was in fact unable to be present
and so Dr Lloyd-Jones presided over the assembly. At
Harvard the participants affirmed the importance of being
both a biblical and a genuinely international movement. All
member movements of the IFES had to be unreservedly
committed to the supreme authority of the holy Scriptures.
Sound doctrine, combined with Spirit-generated warmth,
must characterise each national affiliate. But in addition,
conscious as he was of the possible domination of powerful
countries over the weaker ones, the Doctor guided the
general committee to accept the need for an 'open' Fellowship. Each movement must be encouraged to develop its
own style of leadership, suited to its cultural ethos; no group
should impose on another its pattern of work. So the basic
quality of indigeneity was affirmed at the very outset of this
organization. The fact that Dr Lloyd-Jones was Welsh
helped considerably. Some delegates were amused when he
insisted that he would not allow the English or the Church
of England to formulate his Christian perception of truth!

One of the delightful tasks of the Doctor, as presiding
officer of the 1947 committee, was that of welcoming the
China Inter Varsity Christian Fellowship as a full member
of the IFES. It was significant for him, as he had been
closely involved with the China Inland Mission (now known
as the Overseas Missionary Fellowship.) But more impor-
ant, it heralded a new era when Christian students from
countries with little or no evangelical heritage could be
welcomed as members of this new worldwide Fellowship.

The spiritual leadership that the Doctor exhibited at that
assembly stirred Archbishop Howard Mowll of Sydney to
propose that Dr Lloyd-Jones should visit university centres
worldwide. He could then address Christian students and
encourage the emerging movements; he would admirably
serve the role of the IFES ambassador-at-large. As it turned

out, although he felt greatly honoured by the confidence
that the IFES delegates had in him, the Doctor's duties a
Westminster Chapel prevented him from making extensive
tours of the Fellowship. But he did accept invitations in the
summer months to speak at various national conferences in
continental Europe.

From 1947 to 1958 the IFES benefited immensely from
the leadership of the Doctor. He presided as chairman of the
executive committee and also at the triennial general com
mittees. He was no figurehead chairman. He was always
available for consultation, and whenever he chaired a meet
ing everyone knew that he had gone through the agenda
with thoroughness. C. Stacey Woods, the first general
secretary of IFES, constantly spoke of his friendship with
the Doctor. Each session, whether private or public, resul
ted in a renewed zeal to serve the Lord and to remain
steadfast to His Word.

As chairman, Dr Lloyd-Jones guided his committee
with wisdom. He refused to allow his members to sidetrack
on to trivia or petty issues. He worked at biblical, rather
than pragmatic, solutions to the major issues. Yet in spite of
his spiritual stature the Doctor was never a dictator. He
listened to debates with sensitivity and great patience. He
encouraged all members to participate actively in the dis
cussion. He would sometimes remind those who were arti
culate in English to consider their brothers whose mother
tongues were different: they had their distinctive contribu
tions to make.

When I speak to those who served on the executive
committee under the Doctor's leadership, they invariably
refer to the evening discussions. These were always intro
duced by the Doctor himself. No business items were per
mitted. The members were to tackle contemporary issues
Sometimes these might include a critique on the unification
of the church as advocated by ecumenicals. Inevitably
there would be a stimulating discussion of the presupposi

tions adopted by different ecclesiastical camps. 'What then is the biblical view?', he would pertinently challenge his fellow committee members. On other evenings they might explore current trends in theology, ethics and society. The Doctor never allowed these topics to remain in the realm of the academic. The principles deduced and agreed in their debates were applied to student work or to the church at large. Many executive committee members valued those times when the Doctor stimulated them to think biblically and to act with integrity.

One morning, following an entire evening's discussion on the authority of Scripture and the dangers of theological compromise, there was a crucial item on the business agenda. It was only a matter of months since the IFES had been legally constituted; yet the leaders had already to work through the implications of their evangelical basis and constitution. A Lutheran professor made a dramatic appeal to the IFES delegates to admit his country's movement as a full member. The particular group was affiliated to the World Student Christian Federation. In the IFES constitution, affiliation to a theologically liberal student organization precludes membership in IFES. But the professor recommended that the IFES should modify this position, so that his movement could be admitted. He eloquently pleaded that this would be a great encouragement to the evangelical students who formed an influential wing in this theologically mixed Lutheran student organization.

The delegates were caught on the horns of a dilemma. The arguments were persuasive; the professor was a godly evangelical theologian. Besides, like all new international bodies, IFES could do with new members! But the discussions of the previous night sharpened the perceptions of several members. After a long and heated discussion, the movement from Finland was not granted membership in IFES. And yet the Doctor did not close the door to the Finnish Evangelicals. He urged them to rethink their position, and indeed suggested publicly that they should continue to have personal and informal links with IFES. In the event, it was not until 1964 that a truly evangelical Finnish Lutheran Student Mission was welcomed into the world-wide IFES. The original Finnish movement had by then weakened considerably, both in numbers and spiritual impact. The 'new' evangelical movement continues to grow.

In the summer of 1959, at the IFES general committee in Paris, Dr Lloyd Jones relinquished his post as chairman. There were spontaneous tributes to his leadership from the delegates. They also elected him as president, looking forward, doubtless, to the presidential addresses that he would deliver. Their hopes were not unfounded; the Doctor's presidential addresses were of noteworthy calibre. In Paris he chose the theme of 'Authority', relating it to the Bible, the authority of Jesus Christ, and the church. These talks were later expanded and published by Inter Varsity Press for the blessing and benefit of many readers.

Four years later, at Nyack, New York, he grappled with the thorny issue of Christian unity. The Doctor was aware that IFES groups had been criticized by liberal churchmen and others for being divisive and unwilling to maintain the unity of the Spirit in the bond of peace. He selected the same passages and texts that ecumenical leaders would employ to champion their dream for unity. In his robust and characteristic style he expounded Ephesians 4 and John 17. He examined the contexts of the 'unity texts' with thoroughness. There was, he affirmed, no room for schism and party feuding in the Christian church. But believers had to 'speak the truth in love.' Unity was not a general uniformity which rejects biblical doctrine. We had no right to pit love against truth—both go together. Unity must always be a unity in the truth, in the revealed Word of God. These expositions were repeated in other Christian gatherings and finally published under the title *The*

Basis of Christian Unity.

The last occasion on which the Doctor addressed an IFES conference was in August 1971. Just before the general committee there was a special staff consultation. Each morning Dr Lloyd-Jones spoke on what it meant to be an evangelical Christian. He warned us against the pitfall of evangelical respectability. Evangelical scholarship had already made its mark in the theological world. Evangelical leadership was evidently penetrating ecclesiastical structures in several countries. Like the children of Israel, it was possible for us to forget God in the midst of our apparent successes. He exhorted us to be valiant for truth; we must never allow our doctrines to be diluted by persuasive philosophies. We were to study God's Word with diligence and to proclaim it with boldness, clarity and urgency (2 Tim 4:2).

The delegates who were at the general committee heard him expound 1 Samuel 4. His message was on the absence of God. It was possible for Christians to be so preoccupied with themselves and their activities—even Christian ones—that they left God out of their reckoning. That message was used by God's Spirit to convict many of us of sin and insensitivity to His glory. It resulted in confession and repentance, and a new sense of joy.

One evening at the same committee the Doctor paid tribute to the retiring general secretary, C. Stacey Woods. The entire assembly rolled with uncontrollable laughter as Dr Lloyd-Jones proceeded to relate anecdotes about the founding fathers of the Fellowship. One British leader had been so self-effacing that he would lock himself in a toilet when a group photograph was being taken. On another occasion a well-known Hungarian professor was reeling like a drunken sailor when he accidentally bumped into the Doctor. The latter was at first perplexed with the behaviour of his colleague, whom he knew to be a teetotaller! His analytical mind then recalled that a few delegates had complained about upset stomachs caused by the conference food. The abilities of the Doctor as a master story-teller endeared him to all.

When I was a theological student in London during the late '60's and early '70's I used to worship regularly at Westminster Chapel. Large crowds of students—both British and those from overseas—flocked to hear the Doctor. We would furiously scribble notes. Sometimes, indeed, we were admonished not to concentrate on note-taking lest we fail to meet the Lord Himself. Dr Lloyd-Jones' preaching always brought us face to face with the triune God. It also taught us to think biblically. Those of us from overseas found this discipline invaluable when we returned to our home countries. Faced with ethical compromise and with the current fads and fashions of materialistic societies, how thankful we were to test everything from Scripture. It was the Doctor who set us an example in thinking and acting biblically. I know a friend from Hong Kong who spent Sunday mornings reading through the copious notes that he had made when he sat under the Doctor's ministry. He used to attend a church that was rather deficient in expository preaching. These notes supplemented his spiritual diet. When the Doctor's sermons were published by the Banner of Truth Trust, this friend would read and meditate on them. He is an enthusiast in recommending the Doctor's books to other Christians!

In my travels I've met Christian leaders who were deeply influenced by the Doctor's preaching; some are well-known pastors and lay preachers. I know of at least three medical doctors in Singapore who often occupy the pulpits of their churches. They enjoy the reputation of providing solid meat for their hearers. When others ask them their 'secret' of sermon preparation they will most probably hear about Dr Lloyd-Jones and the way he proclaimed the Word of God.

Two Ghanaian Christians used to attend Westminster Chapel in the '50's and '60's. One was the Rev Gottfried

Osei-Mensah. After his training as an engineer he returned to Accra, where he spent three years serving God as a travelling secretary for the Pan African Fellowship of Evangelical Students. He developed his preaching and teaching skills in his ministry among students throughout English-speaking Africa. In 1972 he became the pastor of Nairobi Baptist Church, with a large and flourishing congregation. From 1976 to 1984 Gottfried was well-known in the evangelical world because of his leadership as executive secretary of the Lausanne Committee for World Evangelization. He has preached in every continent, challenging Christians to fresh thrusts in evangelism and world mission. Not only was the Doctor a mentor and example to Gottfried's preaching, but Gottfried used to invite friends and neighbours in Accra to his home to listen to Dr Lloyd-Jones' messages recorded on large reel tapes.

These tapes (all 200 of them) were given to Gottfried's fellow-countryman Dr Felix Konotey Ahulu. As a medical student he had experienced tremendous blessings at Westminster Chapel. In fact, on my first day in England, it was Felix who invited me to that church. Before Felix returned with his wife to Ghana, he had specially asked the Doctor to let him have as many tapes as possible. His own father—who was a village chief as well as a pastor—listened to the tapes with rapt attention, exclaiming, 'This is Holy Ghost inspired preaching!'

Felix kept a journal, and a few extracts from his personal diary show the marked influence that the Doctor has had on his life:

The Doctor was quick to recognise spiritual gems in other nationalities. One Sunday morning during his six-month series of sermons on revival he broke with his usual tradition of not easily mentioning people by name from the pulpit, to tell us how the previous Sunday, after the morning service, Uganda's William Nagenda and Festo Kivengere went to see him in the vestry. 'Did you know, my friend,' the Doctor asked us, 'that in East Africa, when you gave a testimony, you did not stop at why and how you became a Christian? You carried on right up to today—this is *true* Christianity, my friend.'

My indebtedness and that of many others to Dr Martyn Lloyd-Jones springs from his concern that believers should know that they have only just begun—and that there is a journey to be journeyed to heaven, a fight to be fought on earth, and wonderful things in store for the saint. A more personal indebtedness to the Doctor was when he married me to Rosemary, a member of Rev John Stott's church, as we both journey together in this 'our short uncertain earthly life and pilgrimage.'

But without a doubt, the greatest thing the Doctor has ever said, as far as I am concerned, was not found in a sermon. It was in his long prayer one Sunday morning, and I have never forgotten it. Whenever I am in a corner, spiritually, and I remember that one sentence, God's sovereignty just floods my heart, and I am released. Many, many people the world over who have heard the Doctor *pray* can say the same.

It was the Doctor's custom to concentrate on systematic and solid teaching on Sunday mornings and also on Friday evenings. From 1958 to 1962 his expositions were on Paul's Epistle to the Ephesians. From the autumn of 1959 to the summer of the following year he preached a series on 'Revival', and our eyes were opened to the sovereign visitation of God's Spirit. The theme was reinforced with passages from Scripture, and profusely illustrated by accounts of spiritual awakening in Britain and North America. This longing for revival has lodged in my own mind and heart for some years. Some time ago I was conversing with a pastor friend who used to attend the Chapel with me, and we rejoiced to learn that we have both been preaching this urgent necessity. Our inspiration had stemmed from those formative years of our lives when we heard the Doctor expound this great theme.

On Sunday evenings the Doctor's sermons had a strong evangelistic slant. Many of us brought our non-Christian friends to hear him. An Iranian student turned to me after one of these meetings and solemnly reflected, 'Although I have been to a Christian mission school, tonight this man deeply disturbed me. He showed me my heart, and also what God is really like.' The cost of discipleship was too high for him, and as far as I know, he did not profess faith in Christ. But he had heard the gospel proclaimed clearly and succinctly.

I also recall a night in May 1958, after a moving evangelistic sermon. I noticed an English student from Imperial College looking rather troubled. A few minutes later we were both walking away from the Chapel towards Buckingham Palace. I plucked up courage, introduced myself, and began to talk to him. I realized immediately that he was under deep conviction of sin. That night he had heard the Doctor preaching on God as the supreme Judge, and the finality of His judgment. Colin W. knew that he would be condemned; his formal religion could not put him right with God. I shared with him from my New Testament, passages relating to Christ the Saviour and His free offer of salvation. We saw that he could become a child of God if he were to receive Christ into his life (Jn 1:12). After pausing for a minute or two, Colin in simple faith invited the Lord Jesus into his life. We were standing by the railings of Buckingham Palace. There and then he had become a child of God. What a setting! God had used the preaching of the Doctor to convict Colin of sin and righteousness and his need of a Saviour. Or, more correctly, the Holy Spirit had applied God's Word—His law and His demands on this student's life. I simply had the privilege of being a witness, pointing Colin to an all-sufficient Saviour.

Some who 'know' the Doctor only through his sermons and books might find it difficult to imagine that he could also be a very warm friend and counsellor. But the first two general secretaries of the UCCF Britain (formerly known as IVF), Dr Douglas Johnson and Dr Oliver Barclay, often sought his advice. He offered them unstinting support and counsel. My own predecessor as IFES general secretary, Stacey Woods, valued his friendship. As for me, whenever I asked to see him he was always available. Until the very end of his life he maintained a keen interest in IFES, and his daughter Elizabeth and her husband, Sir Fred Catherwood, kept him informed because of their close links with the Fellowship.

I benefited from my sessions with the Doctor. We would discuss the charismatic renewal in the church, for example, and how IFES should respond to it. Before answering my queries, he would ask searching questions so that the big and crucial issues could be identified. Then he would wisely offer counsel on how best to handle the problems that arose. Then there was the critical matter relating to Roman Catholic students assuming leadership positions in our Christian Fellowships. The Doctor rejoiced to hear of large numbers of these students turning to Christ and experiencing new birth and new life. Many of these students would have no qualms in signing an evangelical basis of faith. This meant that they could become active members and even leaders in our local groups. But what of their links with a church that still subscribes to certain tenets that are contrary to Scripture? If they did not know the difference between these and the fundamentals of the evangelical faith, should they not be disqualified from holding office?

He asked how the IFES executive dealt with this problem. I explained that we approached it by summoning our member movements to a greater evangelical awareness, which meant the constant need to re-affirm our basis of faith. In positively teaching the central truths of revealed faith, we had to expose erroneous doctrines. He was supportive of this approach. But even before I could amplify the pastoral dimension of the problem, his sharp mind had anticipated this. 'You do know that if Catholic students were to repudiate the doctrines of their church, that could also be interpreted as a rejection of their families.' My mind flashed to several instances and case-histories reported by our Latin American and French staff workers. The Doctor further advised us to make sure that these Catholic students felt accepted as persons. They must be encouraged to search the Scriptures. As they grow, then they must discern truth from error. After each visit, I was thankful to be encouraged by the Lord's servant.

Another of our leaders, Dr Robin Wells, was a postgraduate student when he attended Westminster Chapel. When he returned to work as a chemist in Pretoria, South Africa, he continued to maintain links with the Doctor as well as with the Chapel. He vigorously promoted Reformed literature, and he saw to it that all his friends studying in London would go to hear the Doctor. In 1979 he returned to Britain and served as the associates secretary of the UCCF. Two years later he was made general secretary. Robin also had access to the Doctor. He found him most gracious and generous with his time. At the Doctor's memorial service, Robin was one of the evangelical leaders who spoke appreciatively of Dr Lloyd-Jones' influence and contribution to the evangelical world of students, particularly in the UCCF.

From this brief account of the Doctor's involvement in the evangelical world of students, we can learn a few vital lessons on spiritual leadership.

First, the Doctor was in no way the sole master-mind or the brains behind the growth of IFES. Right from the outset he knew that it was a corporate effort. God was raising an international task force of students, graduates and staff to accomplish His purpose in the academic world. Dr Lloyd-Jones' responsibilities as chairman and president were to encourage those who were on the front line of the battlefield. He taught them to recognise the enemy and the sins that could easily affect and divide the evangelical 'soldiers'.

Secondly, his breadth of vision was always international. When certain national movements tried to impose their patterns of government on others, he resisted. He was a man with great foresight. He was aware of the dangers of Western domination, and, all along, he encouraged leadership from countries that could be termed in his time 'receiving countries,' that is, those who were receiving missionaries from the West. He firmly believed that if national Christian students and leaders had God's Word and Spirit, they would be more than equals in an international fellowship.

Thirdly, he set an example for thorough Bible study and exposition. He made the executive committee members think biblically and act decisively. His submission to Holy Scripture and his constant reliance on its Author—a triune God—have helped many to remain steadfast to the biblical revelation and to depend upon God's power. His expository preaching has raised up hundreds of preachers in the mission field, as well as in the local churches, to proclaim 'the whole counsel of God.'

Fourthly, the way in which he presided over committee meetings enabled future generations of IFES leaders to major on the issues that really matter. The fundamentals of the faith have always been in the forefront of the IFES. Secondary matters have obviously their importance and place. But these were never overstressed by leaders in a way that would lead to unnecessary schism and division. The Doctor taught us the crucial need to be united in the Lord and in His Word.

And finally, his availability as a counsellor and friend meant a lot to younger leaders. Those of us who are in this position require encouragement from time to time—and sometimes rebuke—from an older saint who cares for us. The Doctor's availability to leaders of student movements, and his godly counsel, sustained many of us; and we thank God for his life and ministry.

Chapter Seven

A FAMILY PORTRAIT (1)

by

Frederick Catherwood

Sir Frederick Catherwood is Dr Lloyd-Jones' son-in-law, and a member of the European Parliament in Strasbourg. Like the Doctor, he is a former chairman of the IVF (now UCCF), and currently serves as treasurer of the International Fellowship of Evangelical Students. An ex-president of the Fellowship of Independent Evangelical Churches, he led the young people's discussion class at Westminster Chapel during the Doctor's ministry there. This chapter, originally given as a talk for the Evangelical Library, was later published by the Evangelical Movement of Wales.

Shortly after I started coming to Westminster Chapel with my parents and sisters in 1948, my father took it into his head to ask Dr and Mrs Lloyd-Jones for a holiday in the west of Ireland. I remember lecturing him, as sons do, and saying, 'Two thousand people come to this church and thousands more come to hear him preach elsewhere—why do you think they would want to accept *your* invitation?' Thus do 23-year-old sons know better than their parents! And I could not imagine the great Doctor on the golf links, playing tennis or fishing, or doing any of the things we did. But I was wrong. They came. And they played golf—not admittedly with skill, but with enormous enthusiasm. And for the first time I saw the other side of the most powerful Christian preacher and teacher.

It was his teaching which had drawn us first. In 1947 we began to come, first of all, to the Friday night discussions which filled the Institute Hall, to hear him make the audience work out the Christian attitude to the questions *they* had raised. He knew how to teach not only so that you did not forget, but so that in future you knew how to begin on any problems which came up. It was always scripturally based. 'You think that Paul may have said something about it? Paul wrote a number of letters, which one was it in?'

Ephesians? Very well, there are six chapters in Ephesians, which chapter?' And so on, until the exact quotation was found, and then put in its context, and then compared with other parts of the Bible on the same subject, until finally we were all quite clear what the Bible was saying, not because *he* had told us, but because he had made us work it through for ourselves.

Then we had to apply it—and here he would try to make us separate our well-worn prejudices from the balance of biblical teaching. 'Yes indeed, I understand that point of view, Mr Catherwood—and holding that, as you do, you would also logically hold the following, would you not?' You would cautiously assent. 'And that being so...' And as he took you another step down your road of error you would begin to see where you were going and would hesitate. 'Come, come, Mr Catherwood, you do agree that that is the logic of your position, do you not?' And having seen at last where your logic took you, you would be forced back to the beginning and, having recanted in full public view, would never make that mistake again! He once apologized for pressing me so hard. He said, 'You can take it, but there are others who hold the views you are putting who could not take it, and I'm really teaching them through you.'

As I learnt myself later on, discussions are not easy to lead. In a talk or sermon, *you* map out your own logical route and you don't have to prepare for all the objections and diversions. But in leading a discussion anything may arise, and if you've not got the whole framework within which your doctrinal theme sits, then you're lost. If the line of thought is irrelevant, you have to persuade the contributor, very gently, that it really *is* another subject. If it *is* relevant, you have to know where and how it fits, so that the contributor can be led to the connection, and that facet of the truth can be properly illuminated. But that requires a wide knowledge of the subject and of all the arguments; and that needs not only a well-stocked mind, but the ability to assess arguments against the framework of doctrine, and the spiritual sensitivity to detect in those arguments a tendency to truth or to error.

The Doctor's vast reading not only gave him a knowledge of the arguments, but his supreme medical skill as a diagnostician gave him a superbly analytical and logical mind. You could see him separating out the strands in the argument, dividing the false from the true, showing why certain strands were dangerous and would not hold, which strands were true and could be relied on, and where they needed strengthening with others before they could be put to the test.

He showed our generation clearly that the strand of pietistic evangelicalism, the muscular Christianity of the varsity and public school camps, the devotional piety of the Brethren, the emotional dedication of the great conventions, the revivalism of the big interdenominational missions, was not enough. He, almost alone, stopped the retreat in face of the liberal humanism which the church had not dared to meet head on. He led the evangelical wing of the church back into the centre of theological argument, not by conceding a thing, but by going back to its foundation in the Reformation. He, almost alone to begin with, wove in again the strong central strand of Reformed theology to evangelical teaching—a strand which had almost snapped off in the late 19th century, when Spurgeon seemed to lose to the rising tide of liberalism in the 'downgrade' controversy. That Reformed theology which illuminated the immense logical sweep of the Christian Gospel, like the great mutually-supporting arches of a majestic cathedral, came as a revelation to those of us brought up on a diet of blessed thoughts and texts for the day.

And having read through Calvin and the Westminster Confession, through Hodge and Berkhof, having seen that the Reformed doctrine of the sovereignty of God the Creator transformed the natural sciences and indeed the whole of society, having seen evolution as no more than speculative metaphysics, and liberalism and higher criticism for old-fashioned heresies, we tended to forget that the majestic vaulted roof of Christian doctrine was to cover and protect the human relationships of a *living church*. But Dr Lloyd-Jones did not. All the doctrine was dead without the strand of love, a passionate love for God—a love which God would return, flooding us with an overwhelming sense of His presence and a love for each other, by which all men would know that we were God's children.

As he set out these two strands, both Calvinists and charismatics claimed him for themselves alone. But that was totally to misunderstand his teaching—that both strands were absolutely essential parts of Christian belief, that the one called for the other, and that in each Christian life they had to be woven strongly together. Strength and warmth, warmth and strength.

In pulpit appearance he looked the Calvinist rather than the charismatic. In his austere Geneva gown, in his lack of any personal references, in his feeling that the awe of the Gospel forbade jokes and that the power of the message itself produced emotion enough, in his hatred of any artificial bonhomie or breeziness, and in the sheer weight of the authority with which he preached, he was about as far from ecstasy or dance-drama as you can get. Yet he was the most human of men.

I remember, one late autumn Sunday evening in the early '50's, sitting through an hour's thundering sermon, quaking at the thought that at the end I was to go to see him to ask for his elder daughter's hand in marriage. I had rehearsed my lines most carefully, but when at last I crossed the vestry threshold his welcome was so warm that I never had a chance to say a thing! And for the next 28 years until he died that warmth and affection never diminished.

Not only in the family, where he was deeply devoted to each and every one, but in the wider family of church and

ministers, he was the most warm-hearted of men. I have a
constant picture of him sitting in a red armchair engaged in
long telephone conversations with ministers or others with
problems. We would get a wave and a smile as we came in.
Grandchildren would rush in in pyjamas to get a kiss on their
way to bed; and on the call would go, as he quietly and gently
untangled the mental knots into which someone at the other
end had tied themselves, or sympathized with someone in
distress, or encouraged someone faced with opposition.
And I know how it felt, for he did the same with us.

When he talked to you about your problems, he was
thinking of *you* entirely—never remotely about himself. You
had not only his undivided attention but his total commitment, until the problems had been sorted out to his satisfaction and to yours. There were exceptions. His eldest grand-
son, aged eight, at a quiet tete-à-tete lunch when both were
quietly reading, looked up at him suddenly and said, 'What
do you think about sex?'!

He had, in dealing with personal problems, both a vast
range of knowledge, secular and spiritual, and an inspired
common sense. There was the nurse in bed at her parents'
house, being looked after by a fellow nurse. She had a
soaring temperature which came down to normal every
evening by the time the GP called round. No one could
make sense of the symptoms. Dr Lloyd-Jones got everyone
out of the sick room and asked the nurse, 'Why did the
hospital dismiss you?' She hadn't dared to tell her parents,
and had come home with a feigned illness and with the
other partner in collusion to report the high temperature
and maintain their desperate cover. Dr Lloyd-Jones looked
at the patient, not at the temperature chart, and knew she
wasn't ill. My recollection is that he prescribed a speedy
recovery followed by a dose of moral courage.

He was always, of course, in much demand for problems
on the frontiers of medicine and the Christian faith. A friend
of mine was a depressive and his whole life was transformed

when Doctor was able to show him the sure foundations of faith on which he could build, and from which he could fight the depressive doubts by which he had been continuously attacked.

He was not only generous with his time. He was generous with his money. He was, of course, like all Cardiganshire Welsh, very careful with money, but he hardly ever used it for himself. However small his ministerial salary, he gave regularly and generously. and whenever he found he had more than he needed, from an inheritance or latterly from book royalties, he at once started to ask who in the family needed it. I thought I had married a poor minister's daughter without expectations, but that was where we got a loan for the deposit to buy our first home. The thought that he might spend any money on himself never even seemed to occur to him. And he was just as generous to his grandchildren.

While I always regarded his views with the greatest respect, not so his grandchildren. To them he was only '*Dadcu*' (the Welsh for grand-dad), and whatever views he held were there to be disputed together with the views of the rest of their elders. He was like an old lion with young cubs which darted in and out where no one else would dare to go, while he tolerated from them what he would tolerate from no one else.

And within the family debate, where he did not have to worry about misrepresentation, he would set them off with the most outrageous statements, and as they came spluttering back, 'You can't *possibly* say that,' he would defend them with all his forensic skill.

We used to have tremendous discussions in the family about politics. Although he had, throughout his public life, attacked the idea of a social gospel and , as a kind of overrun from that, tended to the view that there was no Christian attitude to politics, he was nevertheless fascinated by the whole political process. He used to watch political debate on television with enormous zest and report to us on the programmes we had missed.

He always wanted to know about the politicians we had met—and he met quite a number himself. He and Mrs Lloyd-Jones had a wedding present from Lloyd George, whom Doctor used to admire greatly, and who came at least once to hear him in Westminster Chapel. He had spoken on a platform with Stafford Cripps; Ernest Marples once gave him a rather right-wing book, which he passed on to me; and, of course, he knew many of the Welsh politicians particularly well. Cledwyn Hughes and George Thomas, the Speaker of the House of Commons, had a great admiration for him, and it was almost certainly the latter who recommended him for a high public honour which, as a Christian minister, he felt bound to refuse. Not only was he known in Wales—I met Lord Mackay, the Lord Advocate of Scotland, who knew all about the lecture on Martyn Lloyd-Jones and his books.

What interested him in politics was, I think, the clash of personality. For him politics was people. He did not believe that there was a particularly Christian view of politics. It was more a matter of the capacity to make the right judgments. Lloyd George's private life did not override his capacity to make better political judgments than others who did not have his political genius. What Doctor did object to was the hypocrisy of a politician disregarding his marriage vows and then taking a high moral tone about the sanctity of contracts.

It was his capacity to be interested in everything that was going on which gave him such a breadth of mind. He read the newspapers till the end of his long illness. Then one Thursday he asked Pam Harris, a close friend of the family, to cancel *The Times* after Saturday, and he died on Sunday morning. He had kept up his medical reading too and his capacity for diagnosis was just as sharp as ever.

But perhaps his greatest attribute was his visionary

prophetic capacity. He saw very early on the potential of student work, and during the war he was the president and the inspiration of the Inter-Varsity Fellowship, working in a superb partnership with Dr Douglas Johnson. Together they steered the movement away from muscular Christianity, the hearty and shallow evangelicalism of the day, and based it firmly on the rock of Christian truth. Douglas Johnson's successor, Dr Oliver Barclay, attended Westminster Chapel in the '50's and Dr Robin Wells, the present general secretary, was a member when he lived in London in the '60's.

Immediately after the war he was one of the founders of the International Fellowship of Evangelical Students, with Stacey Woods, who was also general secretary of the American movement, as its first general secretary. IFES now has member movements in 75 countries; so his vision of what could be done through student movements in the world's universities has begun to come to pass.

He kept in touch with both the British movement and the IFES. The last quadrennial general committee of IFES he attended was in Austria in 1971, with another co-founder of IFES, John Bolten, a German-born American who had given the movement the old castle at Mittershill for student conferences.

John Bolten was—and is, (like so many of the Doctor's friends)—a tremendous character, who had been a first-world-war Bavarian officer and after the war felt, with other Bavarian officers, that the army had been let down by communists and socialists and that the Versailles Treaty had to be revised. They felt they needed a popular politician and went out and found a good rabble-rouser calling himself Adolf Hitler. It wasn't long before they wanted to drop him, but he was not the sort of person who took to being dropped, and John Bolten, discovering his family was on one of the first of Hitler's hit lists, emigrated to America where he became a Christian and, incidentally, made a fortune.

Martyn Lloyd-Jones, John Bolten, Stacey Woods the Australian, René Pache the Swiss, and others—all tremendous characters—were lifelong friends who respected, trusted and encouraged each other, a group of pioneers who separately and together did great things for God. And though less well-known than his work in Britain, I'm not sure that this international work may not well be more far-reaching in the end.

When he retired, he had 13 busy years in writing, preaching and—after much urging—television. He had been very dismissive of television—arguing that it was in one ear and out the other, and that the real media of communication were still preaching and writing. But eventually he was persuaded, first for BBC Wales and then occasionally for the wider UK network. He did one series on Whitefield, taking a TV camera team around with him, and took to it just like a professional.

He had no fear of famous TV interviewers. Joan Bakewell —known as the intelligent man's pin-up—was impressed by his complete indifference to trendy thinking to which most clerics seemed to want to bow. She said he was the first person to tell her frankly she was not a Christian. She knew perfectly well she was not, but all TV clergymen had insisted to her fury that she was *really*. But she couldn't understand how in this day and age he got anyone to listen to such old-fashioned ideas. 'Tell me', replied the Doctor, 'of any politician today who, in this day and age, can still fill the Free Trade Hall in Manchester.'

If there is any one quality by which I remember him, it is his gentleness. He was a strong character. He had strong views and he could put them most powerfully. He had a formidable personality and the capacity, if he wished to use it, to crush opponents. Yet to all in need, and within the family circle, he was the gentlest of people, always helpful, most anxious not to be in the way or to put anyone out, sitting peacefully in his armchair in our house in

Cambridgeshire correcting manuscripts or reading a book, while the TV was on, while everyone flew in and out or talked their heads off. Nothing disturbed him. Then last thing at night we would have prayers. Someone would fetch his Bible and everyone would stop what they were doing, come in and start chatting. This would go on for maybe a full half-hour, and he would join in while the Bible lay on his lap. And then at last, as the talk subsided, he would read a passage and then pray to the heavenly Father he knew so well, trusted so completely and loved so dearly. That is how I remember him.

Chapter Eight

A FAMILY PORTRAIT (2)

by

Elizabeth Catherwood

(Lady) Elizabeth Catherwood is Martyn Lloyd-Jones' elder daughter. With her sister, Ann, she was deeply involved in her father's many activities. She has prepared the manuscripts of nearly all his books for their publishers, and she now serves with Mrs Lloyd-Jones as the Doctor's literary executrix. A trustee of the Banner of Truth, editor of Prisca Press for Marshall Pickering, and member of the UCCF council, Elizabeth Catherwood is also a speaker at many women's meetings and occasional broadcaster on radio. This article is an abridged version of a talk given for the Evangelical Library in Westminster Chapel, and was first published by the Evangelical Movement of Wales as *Martyn Lloyd-Jones, the Man and His Books.*

Mine is a great subject, and I am very aware as I start on it that many of you, friends, ministers, really his sons in the faith; members of the Westminster Fraternal and the West-minster Conferences—you all know so much about my father and his love of books, and I am perfectly certain that as time goes on you are going to say, 'She hasn't mentioned that', or 'I don't agree with her about that'—quite likely. I can really only deal with this personally, and if I leave anything out or if I don't put the emphasis that you wanted please forgive me. I can only do it, as I say, as I myself saw him.

If I am to be quite honest, I think I must say that on a very human personal level I miss him along the whole line of reading almost more than any other way. A lot of my friends who had lost those dear to them had said to me, 'You know, it is the little things that bring back your loss to you', and I had heard them and had understood the kind of thing they meant. But I must say that really one of the most shattering experiences I had was after the great mixture of sadness and of glory, after the funeral service in Wales and the thanksgiving service in Westminster Chapel, with the sense we had that he had gone to be with the Lord in glory and that his weakness was now over. A few weeks later I was in the public library and I was looking along the biography shelves. I had recently been reading the lives of all that remarkable family of Bensons, Archbishop Benson, and his able sons, the one who wrote for *Punch*, E. F. Benson, and all the rest of them. I had been reading them, and suddenly on the bookshelf I saw a book called *Edward King: Bishop of Lincoln*. Ah, I thought, now he must have been around about the same period as Bishop Benson, who had also at some point been at Lincoln; and I thought, when I get home I must ask my... and I realized I couldn't ask him. It was then I realized the great loss I was suffering: this great reader, this friend of mine in reading, he wasn't there any more to talk about it. And, you see, I knew perfectly well... I mean, how many of us had heard of Bishop King? Not many of us, I am sure. But *he* would have known about Bishop King. He would have known where he came from, where he went to, what his relationship with Benson was, where they disagreed, how evangelical he was, all these things. And he is not there any more to answer these questions.

I still find (and I am sure that in all this I am speaking for my sister Ann as much as myself) that so often when I find a new writer—not new in themselves, but new to me—I really miss this. Recently I was told—and I am very grateful for this—about that remarkable little book *The Force of Truth* by Thomas Scott. But somehow the edge of the enjoyment has gone because I can't go to my father and talk to him about Thomas Scott. 'Wasn't it remarkable the way that he wrote this book?' and so on. So I do miss him in this way, because, as I say, it is a line along which I peculiarly appreciated him and all he had to give.

Fred has given this picture already of his sitting in his armchair. We have a photograph of him in the family—it is my favourite of all the photographs: some of you may have seen it—one of him in profile, reading. And that is exactly how I think of him. This oasis of peace in the middle of all the life that was going on around us, this peaceful man sitting there with a book on his knee, enjoying it and wanting us to enjoy it as well.

Now my early memories right back are connected with him and reading. I remember quite well sitting in his study in Aberavon, a room lined with books from floor to ceiling, often over the floor as well, on the desk, theology everywhere. And here I was, in my pre-school days, sitting on his knee while he very seriously read to me from *The Littlest One: His Book*. I don't know how many of you know it; it's an enchanting book, from the '20's and '30's, of poems for children. And I remember him very earnestly discussing the characters of Jane and Emily Jane with me: why Emily Jane was so much nicer than Jane, or what it was about Jane that wasn't pleasant. He was perfectly prepared on reading to come down, as it were, to this level. It was something that he enjoyed doing.

Then of course he himself, I know, has said—and here again, when I re-read what he had to say in *Preaching and Preachers*, I wondered what I could say that he hadn't already said; perhaps I am really just underlining some of these things—he said how always on holiday he would read a great deal. This takes me back to another early memory. I remember staying in Wales. I was again fairly young, it was the mid 1930's, on that lovely sandy beach in Borth. It was a boiling hot summer day. (I know we always tend to think it was like this when we were children, but this really was a boiling hot day.) I was gambolling about in a bathing costume, and digging and paddling and all the rest of it. Everybody else was on the beach, in the amount of undress that was allowed in the mid 1930's. We were all hot, and there we all were in this glorious sunshine sunbathing, as I said, and playing. In front of a rock, over to one corner of the beach, was my father, fully clothed, in a grey suit with a hat upon his head, his usual hat, shoes, socks, waistcoat, the whole thing, sitting bolt upright, leaning against the rock and reading *The Divine Imperative* by Brunner. And this was on a sunbathing beach! You see, he read like this. He always read in the mornings in the summer holidays. But the great thing about it was that we never resented this. Ann and I took this as part of him. He was a great reader. It was his work, it was his enjoyment. It was part of him and so it became part of us.

As I talk about this reading of his, perhaps I had better fill in a little of the background. He came from a family that was always interested in reading. His father was not a very well-educated man, but he was a man who was interested in the whole world around him. He read the newspapers carefully and methodically. He read one or two religious papers as well. My father's older brother, who died in the flu epidemic in 1918, was also a great reader who not only read but also wrote poetry. We don't know what the poetry itself was like, though we do have one or two little exercise books of rather charming first-world-war type of poems. He apparently knew Robert Graves and Siegfried Sassoon, so he is interesting, this older brother; he was in that kind of literary background. Tragically, as I say, he died. His younger brother also was a literary figure. He went to Oxford and there he knew Ronald Knox and met Evelyn Waugh. And, even more interestingly, my uncle was actually in the same tutorial group as C. S. Lewis. So, you see, they were a reading family, with much talk about books and authors and writers.

Now as we look at my father as a reader, and come on to how he handled his reading, I wouldn't be true to his tradition, would I, if I didn't start with the negative. You remember how he told us that we must always start with the negative; so I shall start in this way.

First of all, then he disliked paperbacks very much indeed. All of us in the family, grandchildren, children, everybody, tried to persuade him that books were very expensive nowadays. The students, of course, as you can imagine, were very ferocious about this—how could they afford to buy books at £10.95? and so on—and he did grudgingly agree that perhaps this was true. But it is interesting *why* he disliked paperbacks. Books to him were friends that you kept for life, and you can't keep these paperbacks, they fall apart. You just bend them open and they are finished, aren't they? He did have a kind of unwilling allowance of those halfway-house books—I can't remember what they're called, but they are in sort of stiff paperback format. Them, perhaps, he could tolerate, but by and large he did not like the paperback world in which he now found himself, and was, I think, never quite happy that one or two of his own books came out like this, though, as I say, he allowed it for the sake of the expense.

The other thing that is interesting about him is that he didn't like digests at all. He says at one point in *Preaching and Preachers*, 'I am not a believer in digests and encyclopaedias, which encourage a "ready-reckoner" mentality rather than thought.' When you think about it, of course, this is very typical of him. He couldn't bear anything potted, as it were. He didn't like shortened versions of things He didn't like biographies which were just a few broad sweeps of facts. He liked biography to start about 200 years before the birth of the subject and then work up to it. He liked his books to be full books. He didn't like this modern habit of thinking that you had a lot of knowledge if you just knew a few headings, and so digests and encyclopaedias were not for him. The *Reader's Digest* did go in and out of the house, but very rarely would you find him looking at it. I will be coming back to this dislike of potted things later on.

Another thing he disliked was an over-concentration—I must underline that—an *over-concentration* on style for its own sake. Now, of course, he liked all books to be well written. He himself enjoyed a good style. What worried him was when the style took over, as it were, from the contents; if they were mannered books, he couldn't bear them. He has a very interesting passage, you may remember, in *Preaching and Preachers*, when he says that he thinks that this was part of the cause of the downfall of the pulpit and preaching. You see, preachers had begun producing beautifully styled essays instead of preaching the Word. It was interesting, too, with regard to the style, how sometimes he really disliked something that was beautifully written, because the content was wrong. I remember having quite a discussion with him about Tennyson's poem 'Crossing the Bar'.

> Sunset and evening star
>   And one clear call for me!
> And may there be no moaning of the bar
>   When I put out to sea.

I thought this was the most beautiful poetry. He said, 'But it's wrong. It's wrong. The truth is:

> Safe into the haven guide;
>   O receive my soul at last!

Christians don't go out to sea when they die, they come into the haven.' I said, 'But it is beautiful, isn't it?' He said, 'The beauty doesn't matter, it's *wrong*.'

Here, of course, I must mention the whole question of his style in his own books—in his Ephesians, Romans and all the rest. My goodness, he did have some problem with his editors! Especially I remember one day right at the beginning, one of the first books he brought out. A very earnest editor—it was a very early book—sent him back his manuscript covered in alterations. You know the kind of thing: 'nevertheless' instead of 'but', 'although' instead of something else, an adjective suggested instead of a noun, or a note in the margin saying, 'Don't you think there are too many adverbs in this line?' My father almost threw the manuscript at me and said, 'Cross it all out. Put it back into the original and leave it alone.' And it was interesting how towards the end he said to me, 'When you come to the editing of the books, don't agonize too much over the words.'

Now he was perfectly prepared for anything that was repetitive to be cut out. He didn't mind the first paragraphs being cut back, but he was exasperated by this desperate fuss about the exact word all the time. 'Don't worry about it,' he said. 'This is the truth of God. Let the truth go out.' And I must say it is very interesting how many people had said to all of us in the family, 'It's great reading his books, we can hear him as we read them.' That is the point. It was the content that mattered. This was the thing on which you concentrated. Of course you made the words as clear as you could for people to understand, but you didn't fuss and fiddle on about the style.

Another thing about him was that he really didn't enjoy novels. He didn't disapprove of novels; he didn't object to other people reading them, in moderation as with everything else (though I think he did sometimes feel that too much novel reading was a waste of time); but he himself didn't enjoy them. He actively disliked Dickens and Hardy. 'Depressing men,' he used to say. Dickens, I think, probably because of his intense assault on the emotions—twanging on your heart strings, with everyone dying by inches and that kind of thing. I don't think he could take this. And Hardy with his cynical pessimism. He disliked them.

As I say, then, novels in general he didn't enjoy, but there was one great exception. And that was Sir Walter Scott. Now Scott he really had enjoyed tremendously. Time was at a premium in his ministerial life, and I don't remember his reading him much. But Scott was a novelist whom he loved, and the funny thing about it was, of course, that the bits which the rest of us always skip, the first hundred pages of every Scott novel, that was the bit he liked best. Here was Scott building up his background. He loved it.

This leads me on to something else at which he was very good. He would often put us in touch with other writers of whom we hadn't heard. I'll be coming on to this again a little later on, but it was he, for instance, who introduced me to John Buchan. During the war he produced a few copies of Buchan and said, 'I think you'll enjoy these.' (Buchan, again of course, is in a Scott mould in a way.)

But there was one lesson, I think, that he always taught us—and here I come on to something else that he felt strongly against in reading—and that was that reading must never become like a drug. Fred has memories of his talking about people who are always wandering about with their noses in books. I always have an uncomfortable feeling that he may have been referring perhaps to me, perhaps to Ann, perhaps to both of us. There was a time, I remember quite well, when I evolved a system whereby I could dress and undress while reading a book at the same time! Now this kind of thing, I think, worried him a little. In other words, reading can very quickly become a drug. I think that is why perhaps he had slight reservations about novels as well. One must never allow reading to take control of one. The Christian reader is to be in control of his reading as well as everything else. So that was a danger.

He also made a very clear point of the fact, that never, never should one read just to impress other people. He said, 'I have emphasized the place and value of reading, but if your chief reason for reading is to parade it and make a display of your knowledge, it is obviously bad in every sense.'

Again he felt very strongly that you should never read just to get ideas which you then regurgitated. He said, 'We are not meant to be gramophone records, or tape-recording machines.' I remember sometimes his expressing some anxiety about various speakers who, because of their love for the writers of the 17th, 18th and 19th centuries, would produce the thoughts of the 17th, 18th and 19th centuries, often in the language of the 17th, 18th and 19th century. He used to worry sometimes about a person. 'Goodness,' we would say, 'isn't he able!' 'Yes,' he would say, 'but I think

that what he really is is just a good student.' This did not
mean that he didn't want people to work or to conentrate on
their work, but that they should not just be people who read
things and could then reproduce them. Reading was much
more than that—much more. Here I go on to perhaps one of
his most significant statements about reading—and now I
am moving on to the positive.

He said, 'In a sense one should not go to books for ideas;
the business of books is to make one think ... The function of
reading is to stimulate us in general, to stimulate us to
think, to think for ourselves. Take all you read', he said,
'and masticate it thoroughly.' It is rather like Bacon, isn't
it? You know how he said that some books are meant to be
tasted, others to be swallowed—and some, he said, are to be
chewed and digested. That was the reading that my father
approved of. You chewed and you digested your books, so
that they became part of you. You were then stimulated.
You thought, and what came out was, as it were, your
quintessence of all the reading, but it was yours. It wasn't
originality for originality's sake. That is not what he meant.
You took all this wisdom of all the ages, and you made it a
part of you. You were stimulated, you thought better, and
as a result you spoke better.

So then, what were the marks of his own reading? Well,
you may be disappointed at this, but he was not a quick
reader. I am sure most people thought that he got through
books at the rate of knots. He didn't. He wished he could.
My mother said that he often said, 'Do you know, there are
so many books to be read, I wish I could read more quickly.'
But he was basically a slow reader. He once apparently sent
away, in answer to some advertisement, for a book that told
you how to read more quickly. It was one of these books that
told you to look at the middle of the page and all the other
words would float into it, and all would be well. But in the
end he came back to his own method of reading, and he read
in his own way. He read a lot, yes, but he didn't read it

quickly. But, of course, the great thing about him was his phenomenal (and I use the word advisedly) memory. He remembered what he read. And I think he remembered what he read because of these things that I have talked about before: because he concentrated on the content, and because of—I cannot think how to put it in a better way—this mastication principle. Because he read in this way, he remembered it all.

Fred has referred to his knowledge of the New Testament, and it is interesting here to note that he was not at all a rote learner. He actually could not learn by heart. If one were to tell him to sit down and learn a four-line verse, he was quite incapable of doing it. But if he was preaching and began a passage from Paul, a verse would come to his mind and he would often go through about 15 verses without stopping, absolutely correctly (in the Authorised Version) because he knew it; the contents had mastered him, so it came into his mind. So the slowness of the reading didn't matter. He contained all that he read.

May I say, incidentally (though she would probably be very annoyed if she knew I was saying this), that my mother, I think, could certainly hold a candle to him in the Old Testament. He would often have to turn to her for some of the stories—if he wanted to know the names of the three daughters of Job, for instance. Mother would know them, the three of them. This kind of thing happened often. She has a good knowledge of the Old Testament stories, and he would often turn to her and say, 'Now where does that story about So-and-so come?' But on the New Testament, the epistles of Paul, he was matchless.

With regard to his general reading, I think the amazing thing was its breadth, the extent of it. As I say, it is so difficult to know how to begin to handle it all. He was a very wide reader indeed. Fred has mentioned some of it, and really I can only underline some of the ways in which he read. I have already mentioned the function of reading as a

stimulus; that was to him most important. But he added to
this when he said, 'What then is the main purpose and
function of reading? It is to provide information.' He read
widely for information It was interesting how important
that was in so many fields. Take, for instance, the Westminster Conferences, how he would round it all off with the
last lecture. He would have his subject and I am sure we all
remember how he had read everything, how he had got the
facts; how too, he chaired all these meetings, and how he
knew all the speakers' facts, often as well as they did, and
sometimes a little better. I remember, once in the early
days, his reminding the speaker of something that he hadn't
actually put into his lecture. He read widely for information
of that kind.

He also read for information in other ways, and this is
where I often think that he had, certainly as far as I was
concerned, a lot to teach us. He read for information on very
basic things, and here we have a very interesting story in
our immediate family. Our elder son, Christopher, had to
have a series of eye operations, and at one point when my
father was away Christopher began producing some very
unpleasant frightening symptoms, which completely baffled
the doctors. It was almost like that bit in that poem about
Christopher Robin:

> All sorts and conditions
> Of famous physicians
> Came hurrying round
> At a run.

They were called in to consider the strange, distressing
symptoms that this boy had, and they began to discuss what
it was—was it something psychiatric, was it this and that,
and nobody knew the answer. In the end they were going to
send him to a series of specialists. At this point my father
came back from his holidays. He came back to find us all

very anxious about Christopher, and he got us to tell him the whole story of what was apparently a medical mystery. 'The next time you take him to the hospital,' said my father, 'I am coming up with you.'

So when Christopher and I went up to the out-patients, my father came with us. Now the 'old boy network' amongst doctors is terrific. Doctors can always go in and say, 'I'm a doctor', and all is fine. They let him in, and he asked the young houseman if he could see Christopher's notes. Imagine what would have happened if one of us had asked to see his notes! You know what it is like in hospitals if you want to see something, a temperature chart or anything. However, there was this old doctor; well, he couldn't do any harm with just the notes. So they handed them to him and while Christopher was being seen he sat going through the notes carefully and accurately.

When the consultation was over and he had made his own notes, he didn't say anything. (That is another thing, by the way. He said that you should never read without having a note pad at your side and a pencil, so that anything you read, anything that struck you, you could write it down.) When he came home, he got out his notes, and then went to the huge book of medicine which is brought out afresh every year and tells you about every medicine that is produced. (Any doctor knows what I mean.) He went to this; he always had one of these. He looked at his notes and found that at certain point Christopher had been given a certain drug. He found out about the drug in his compendium of medicine, and read the side-effects of the drug, and he found the answer to Christopher's problem. You see, instead of just talking about things, airing theories—and may I say his winged words about the current state of young doctors were marvellously clear afterwards!—he *read*. He never put forward theories and great ideas on things that could be a matter of fact. He always made certain that he knew his facts. Of course, once we had discovered about this medicine it was passed back to the doctors, who all had to agree that yes, of course, this was the reason, and everything was perfectly all right and the symptoms went.

He read in order to get the facts. But he did more than this, and again I am telling a family story. Our younger son, as many teenagers do, at one point flirted dangerously with transcendental meditation. He was talking endlessly about it, of course, discussing it with everybody, and saying he had been reading these marvellous books that would set the world right, and it was all great, from the standpoint of 15 years old. So my father said, 'Well, now, what are these books?' This is the great thing about grandparents, isn't it, they have time to talk. And so Jonathan produced a book by a man called Lobsang Rampa, and my father said, 'I'll take that book and read it.' So he took the book with him, and went off to preach in Manchester, actually in the Free Trade Hall.

They had a great service on that particular evening, and as he came home in the train that evening he thought he would read Jonathan's book. And he read it from cover to cover. He did say that he had a slightly uncomfortable feeling while doing so. It was a little paperback, with a picture of a sort of Chinese face on the cover. The book was called *The Third Eye*, and in the Chinese face there was an eye in the middle of the forehead—a most bizarre-looking cover, hideous with this eye glaring out. He had an uncomfortable feeling that if any of the people who had heard him preach in the Free Trade Hall were sitting opposite him, they would wonder quite what was going on! However, he read it. He read it with care. He read it seriously. He took notes on it, and when he came back he went through it with Jonathan.

In other words, our tendency so often with young ones is to say, 'For goodness' sake, that's all rubbish, you'll forget about that. That's nothing, you'll grow out of it.' This was not at all true of my father. He wanted to know just exactly

what it was that was getting hold of this boy, and so he went
through the book. He said where the points were good, and
pointed out where they were dangerous. And because he
had read it, he knew the book far better than Jonathan. And
as a result, the information that he had acquired made him
able to deal with this kind of situation.

But reading for information was only a part of his reading;
he read widely and he read generally. He read biography,
detailed rich biographies, and of a very interesting variety.
For instance, he had greatly enjoyed reading the biography
of that great, brilliant and tragic figure of the 19th century,
Cardinal Newman. The whole story fascinated him. He
also kept in touch with the thinkers of the 20th century. He
believed in reading widely, explaining his reasons as, 'It
will be good for your mind; it will preserve resilience and
freshness. I have therefore always tried to do this, and to
take certain journals which deal with general affairs and
literary matters, and where there are good, well-written
articles and *good book reviews* [my italics] which will suggest
other books for reading.' Reviews, you see, not only made
him enjoy his own reading and gave him further ideas, but
they enabled him to join enthusiastically in other people's
reading as well.

A friend of ours was thinking of doing a Ph.D. theology
thesis. He had decided upon his subject and my father
suggested a long reading list of suitable books. He had read
his reviews, he knew the kind of book. He had read half of
them himself, and he knew thoroughly the field in which the
man moved. And, in a way, even more remarkable, I think,
were his various pieces of advice to our daughter, Bethan,
who was doing an esoteric thesis on a very particular literary
subject of language in poetry involving people like Edward
Thomas and the old early Welsh bardic poets. He said to
her, 'You know, along this line you are discussing, there are
some interesting developments in Cambridge at the
moment.' This was about three or four years ago. He had

read of the structuralists in Cambridge and commented, 'There is going to be some sort of problem there, I think.' Well, of course, two or so years later, the whole balloon blew up in Cambridge; but he had seen it coming. Or he would say to Bethan, 'There is a book you should read by Frank Kermode, exactly along your line'; or, 'I read a poem by one of your tutors, Tom Paulin, in *The Times Literary Supplement* this week.' Not only in general knowledge but in specific little details of research he would know what was going on, and as a result he was able to help us enjoy what we were reading.

He was a tremendous enthusiast. And he enjoyed sharing other people's enthusiasms as well. With the grandchildren, he would enjoy discussing the finer points of a wrestler with Adam, or school problems with Elizabeth and Rhiannon, or American politics with Jonathan. When I myself was a very little girl, I used to collect cigarette cards. Now, as you can imagine, it was rather a hard job for me to collect cigarette cards, because nobody around me smoked. There were very few members of the church in Aberavon that smoked either, and I really laboured my way through a collection of film stars in cigarette cards. Anyhow, by cadging from my friends, by borrowing from school friends' fathers, by using all sorts of devices, I got them all except Norma Shearer, and Norma Shearer hung over me for weeks. I couldn't get her. I kept on getting all the ordinary ones like Errol Flynn and all these others, but not Norma Shearer. I can't remember now what number she was, but I was getting depressed about this—I suppose I was about seven or eight at the time.

Then one morning—I remember it to this day—I got up and there at my breakfast place, on my plate, was Norma Shearer. My excitement was tremendous. Apparently what had happened was that my father had been preaching somewhere up the valleys. Someone had been driving him and they were out to tea together. After tea was over the man who had been driving him pulled out a packet of cigarettes and took a cigarette out. My father leaned across the table and said, 'Excuse me, have you got a card in there?' Somewhat surprised, the man said, 'Well, I'll have a look.' 'I have,' he said. My father said 'Can I see it?' 'Good!' he said, 'It's Norma Shearer,' and pocketed it for me.

Now you see what I mean. I am off my point now, but it was part of the quality that made him such a great reader. He joined in with us. That is why ministers have said so often how much they loved him coming to preach for them; he would join in with their enthusiasms. It didn't matter what it was. Whether you were reading great tomes of philosophy, or whether you were a little girl collecting cigarette cards, he would join in with you, and he would enjoy it with you, and your pleasure was as much to him as his own pleasure in finding it.

Then, and this is very significant of him as a reader, he believed, of course, in relaxation. Now, on the whole, if people do a lot of reading they are told, 'When you get tired go out and have a walk, play a game of tennis or watch television or something.' Not my father. He has a sentence which I think is very revealing. He says, 'The mind must be given relief and rested. But to relieve your mind does not mean that you stop reading; *read something different* [my italics].' Now this is what he did himself. He read for relaxation, and the funny thing is that his real relaxing was reading his medical journals. He read medicine, as Fred said, right to the end. He enjoyed them and often you would find him in the evening reading them and, as I have said, he sometimes read them to the most marvellous effect. He didn't just read them to relax, he took them in. Again he masticated his medical reading as well, and sometimes it was invaluable. He would have read something in some medical magazine somewhere that was just the answer that somebody somewhere needed. So he read for relaxation. He also read apologetic works of course. The Rev Hywel Jones of the LTS has said that he thought the great thing about my father was that he was always about ten years ahead of everybody else in reading. He had read Hans Küng long before anybody else had heard of him. He knew what Hans Küng was saying. Not only could he see the problem arising in the English faculty in Cambridge, he could see the philosophical and theological developments of the world, and he was slightly amused at the sort of wild rush that a lot of speakers had to get hold of a copy of Hans Küng to read him, because they did not know him. He had read him and had understood him, and saw how the man's thought was going and the problems that were going to arise.

Again to quote my mother, she has said that he often used to say to her that he felt that when he did his general reading like this—philosophy, as I say, and general religious thought—he always wanted to know the other man's point of view better than he knew it himself. And because he read these writers so thoroughly he always advised us, and I am sure you all remember this, to be quite certain what a man *didn't* say as much as what he *did*. You know, one would read, and get taken over by, a certain writer. 'My goodness,' we would comment, 'he says A B C D E.' 'Yes,' my father would reply, 'but he doesn't say F G H I J.' So he would read these philosophical books, and he would read all the journals; theological journals of every shade and colour would arrive in the house. He would read them and, reading the reviews, he would have ideas for his own reading. Not only that. He felt that it was important for us all as Christians to know what was going on in the world around us.

But he said too that one always needed to be careful about one's general reading. It's the same point that I was making earlier. General reading is good, but it must never take over. You must know yourself, he would say. If you find you are spending too much time reading something, stop it and get your balance back again. He believed in balance, and not only was he balanced himself, he was helpful to others. He said 'You have to know what to read for yourself, and also for others.' And he certainly did. It is interesting to me always, looking back over the last 30-odd years, to remember what a help he was to those of us who read literature back in the '40's and '50's. You see, this was the time before the whole interest in art had taken over in the Christian world, before Dr Schaeffer had become well known, with all the help that Dr Schaeffer's books have to give. I was reading English at Oxford at the time, and I remember quite well getting myself into terrible trouble by attacking Chaucer for writing some story that I felt he shouldn't have written, and more or less calling him a dirty old man. I didn't quite, but I very nearly did. And of course the wrath of the tutor came upon my head, and I remember telling my father this, rather thinking that I had been suffering as a Christian, as it were. 'Not at all,' he said, 'you are not handling your literature properly.' He believed in this balance; you looked at literature as literature, and as a Christian he helped you to handle it, to see what the style did, what the content was, what the purpose of the man was in writing it. I learnt far more from him than from the tutor how to handle literature itself. And he was very good at giving the right book to the right person. He tempered the wind to the shorn lamb. He has a marvellous passage in *Preaching and Preachers* where he says that if somebody is introspective and slightly given to depression, you do not give him a book that is thundering out the message of conviction of sin and the total depravity of man and so on; otherwise, he says, you may well drive him mad. He knew his people, he knew how to help; and, as I say, from literature students through to those who were suffering, there was always something that he could find to encourage them.

And now I must quickly consider the last three things, the reading he loved best. He read theology. 'A preacher,' he said, 'should continue to read theology as long as he is alive; but it must be biblical theology.' He did not like this arid reading and discussion of theology, where you tossed one doctrine around from one to the other. It had to be theology that arose out of the Word of God. This was theology at its greatest to him. And when he read a book of theology, again he could see what the man didn't say. I remember when he was in hospital having some very unpleasant treatment, for the whole of one hour when the treatment was really at its worst he sat talking to us about a person who is having a great vogue at the moment in the States as an evangelical theologian. 'You need to watch his writings,' he said. 'He is not quite right.' In other words, my father's theology was great. It was so much a part of him that he could almost feel what other people were or were not saying.

Then there was his devotional reading. I use this word carefully, because he said at one point, 'I abominate'—and it is a very strong word—'I abominate "devotional" commentaries. I do not want other people to do my devotion for me.' He didn't like that sort of sentimental devotionalism at all. What he meant by something devotional was a type of reading which, he says, 'will help you in general to understand and enjoy the Scriptures.' He helped a lot of people in this. Of the Puritans he said, 'You will find, I think, in general, that the Puritans are almost invariably helpful.' He told the story of how, when he himself was at a low ebb, 'the heavenly Dr Sibbes' had helped him through his *The Bruised Reed* and *The Soul's Conflict*; this heavenly pastoral figure had given him a great blessing. And then, of course, how often have we heard him say, 'I am an 18th century man.' Jonathan Edwards was a particular favourite. He kept telling Fred and me, 'You must read Jonathan Edwards. In the middle of your political life and all your travelling around, read Jonathan Edwards. He is the one that can keep you with your feet solidly based on the rock. Read him and learn from him.'

In the Thanksgiving Service Dr Caius Davics and the Rev Omri Jenkins had a kind of debate about my father as a human being, whether he was essentially a doctor or essentially a preacher. Now, not speaking about the greatness of the calling at all, but about him as a personality and of his temperament, we in the family think that probably both were right. But there is one other thing that one must add, and that is that he was a *Welshman*. This was a very important part of him. It is interesting how many people were surprised that it was in Wales that he was buried. He couldn't have been buried anywhere else. He was a Welshman through and through. He loved the other nations—sometimes with a sardonic smile—but he was a Welshman, and at the very end he only read two things, and one of those was his book of Welsh hymns. These men, you see, these transcendental poets (transcendental in the right way), with their marvellous imagery, their great grasp of doctrine, the wonder of their love for God, the tenderness of their application of the gospel message to the soul—he loved them. And, as I say, at the end it was that book, the one of the two, that was by his side. Always the Welshman.

Then, of course, he loved church history and biography. Now this is so obvious that I really needn't go on. What was the Westminster Conference doing, what was he always telling us to do, but to read church history and biography? He loved it for itself. Again, it had to be detailed biography, none of these potted things. That is why he always enjoyed big ones, like Arnold Dallimore's book on Whitefield, or some of the earlier ones with their great concentration of detail and so on. He also felt, I think, that reading biography provided a balance. He said, 'The best way of checking any tendency to pride—pride in your preaching or in anything else that you may do or may be—is to read on Sunday nights the biography of some great saint.' And all I want to do, really, is to illustrate this by two short stories.

First of all, this reading on Sunday nights. At the beginning of 1954 he was reading through D. E. Jenkin's three-volume life of Thomas Charles—some of you probably know it. Big tomes again! And for several weeks in January and February he would read bits of this to us on Sunday evenings; as we were going round getting the supper and so on, he would be sitting there in the chair reading bits aloud. And over these two particular months Thomas Charles was having terrible trouble with the lady whom he subsequently married. I don't know how many of you have read it, but she dithered for ages. She would come right up to the point, and then she would suddenly become afraid of 'launching upon the troubled seas of matrimony.' Back Thomas Charles would go again into a depression. On and on this went, week after week, with the letters—he loved the letters in biography—going back and forth, and in the end, one glorious Sunday night, she said 'Yes.' And I assure you we were all really rejoicing in this. In fact, if I am to be honest, I have to confess that the Sunday night before Fred and I were due to be married, he was reading bits out of Thomas Charles, and I actually found myself thinking to myself 'Oh bother, I won't be here next Sunday night'! You see, so great was his enthusiasm that it had got hold of us all. That was one story.

The other story is a marvellous occasion when we climbed up to see the great memorial to the Covenanters at the Communion Stones. I don't know how many of you have been there, it is up in the hills in South West Scotland. You remember the great story of the Covenanters and how they used to have to go and have their communion up in the hills in case they were caught. Well, we had a dire journey up there. We had to go through fields of bulls, over ditches, under barbed wire, but we got there in the end, to this really lyrically beautiful spot, a sort of amphitheatre in the hills where there is this high monument with a communion cup on the top. It is a wonderful monument to those great men

of God, the Covenanters. And my chief memory is of my
father, when we arrived there, standing looking at it and
taking off his hat. You see, he not only loved them, he was
such an enthusiast about these great men of God, he revered
them as brothers in the Gospel. They meant so much to
him. And the gesture was exactly indicative of how he felt
about them.

And then last of all, of course, the Bible. I have left this
until the very end because everyone knows it. 'Read it,' he
said, 'because it is the bread of life, the manna provided for
your soul's nourishment and well-being.' He followed the
Robert Murray McCheyne scheme of daily Bible readings.
He believed in reading the Bible from beginning to end,
through and through, not just reading one's favourite
passages. You studied certain passages when you needed
them, but you read the Bible consistently time and time
again. I think mother worked out that they must have
followed this scheme for at least 53 or 54 years. So, you see,
he would have read the New Testament at least 110 times
through following the scheme, let alone all his own studies
for his sermons. It is a remarkable fact to me that he died on
1 March, and that on 28 February the last chapter of the
daily reading he would have read was 1 Corinthians 15. It
was as if the Lord was pointing him on to the resurrection of
the body which was to come.

He read his Bible regularly. He knew it and he loved it. At
the very end, when he couldn't speak, he would point to
verses out of it. He pointed Ann to the one about being
content in all things, not to be anxious. He pointed me to
the one about this earthly house of our tabernacle, and the
far better reward that was waiting for him. He just pointed,
or he tried to write them down on a piece of paper. It was
the Bible, the Welsh hymns and the Bible, that were his
only reading. One of his sermons in Aberavon said this: 'On
your own deathbed [he was about 28 at the time] you will be
confident in the love of God and the knowledge that you

have that Christ has died for you and your sins, and that you shall be with Him in the world to come.' Now he proved that. You see that was true of him because great, enthusiastic, wide-ranging, fascinated reader that he was, as far as he was concerned the only act in the whole world that really mattered was the truth to which the Word of God, his greatest reading, pointed him, the old story of Jesus and His love.

And to finish, I would like to read you a passage out of this little book, *The Force of Truth*. I think it really expresses the kind of way that we all saw my father at the very end. It is written by the Rev John Scott, who wrote about Thomas Scott, and this is what he said:

In the concluding years of his life he was, as it appeared to me, obviously ripening for heaven. He had fought a good fight, he had finished his course. He had kept the faith. So that at the last his genuine humility before God, his joy in Christ Jesus, his holy zeal for the diffusion of the gospel, his tender affection to his family and all around him, his resignation to the will of the Heavenly Father, and his exclusive trust in the merits and grace of his Saviour, seemed to leave little more to be done but for the stroke of death to bring him to his grave in full age, like as a shock of corn cometh in its sheaf.

Chapter Nine

THE THEOLOGIAN

by

Philip Edgcumbe Hughes

Dr Philip Edgcumbe Hughes is Visiting Professor at Westminster Theological Seminary in Philadelphia, USA, where Dr Lloyd-Jones gave the series of lectures on preaching that became his classic work *Preaching and Preachers*. A friend of the Doctor over many years, Dr Hughes is also Professor Emeritus at Trinity Episcopal School for Ministry, and Associate Rector of St John's Episcopal Church, both in Pennsylvania, USA. He is best known for his commentary on Hebrews and more recently for his book *Christian Ethics in Secular Society*.

There was nothing that interested Martyn-Lloyd Jones more than theology. It was his absorbing passion and the key to the understanding not only of his mental and intellectual preferences but also to the manner both of his preaching and of his living. Though as a young man he set out with such brilliant success on the career of a physician, he told me that he found that his aspirations to meet and minister to the needs of others were not being satisfied. There was a fundamental core of human need to which the skill of the physician or surgeon, however dedicated and efficient, could not penetrate. And so, early on, he went off to South Wales to preach. In preaching he found and fulfilled his true vocation, and he became the outstanding preacher of his day; but the point to be emphasized here is that his preaching was essentially *theological* preaching, and, more particularly, *biblically* theological preaching. His was not the speculative or idiosyncratic kind of preaching. He was well aware of his rhetorical powers of persuasion, and, as he said to me on one occasion, he was even afraid lest by an exaggerated use of these powers he should manipulate the minds and wills of his hearers and thus offer an obstacle to the convicting work of the Holy Spirit. Accordingly, he practised restraint in the pulpit. The message was all-important. The authentic power belonged not to him but to the Holy Spirit working through the Word.

What a famous preacher said of himself in the pulpit 500 years ago might just as truly have been said by Martyn Lloyd-Jones: 'When I am up here I am always well, and if I could be as well out of the pulpit as I am in it, I should always be well.'

It was theology that drew us together. Personal affinities of course cannot be left out of account, but it was theological accord that gave depth and strength to our friendship which lasted some 40 years until his death in 1981. It was in December 1935 that I first saw and heard him. The occasion was the great meeting in the Royal Albert Hall, London, under the auspices of the Bible Testimony Fellowship. Of a distinguished platform he was the concluding, and the most youthful, speaker. Though he was as yet not known to London audiences, there was considerable interest in him as reputedly a rising luminary in the British evangelical firmament. I was captivated not simply by his wonderful gift of communication and the force of his intellect—which won the rapt attention of that vast concourse—but especially by the exceptional and single-minded intensity of his personality. His address was essentially theological as he appealed for a return to the proclamation of the great evangelical doctrines which form the central message of Holy Scripture. More than two-and-a-half years would elapse before he left Wales to come to Westminster Chapel in London; and my first meeting with him took place some six years after the Albert Hall meeting. I had been away from England during most of this intervening period, but following my ordination and my appointment to a curacy in a London parish an unexpected opportunity occurred for me to encounter in person this man who had so strongly impressed me. I was a member of a group of young ministers who met together periodically to read and discuss papers on theological subjects, and Martyn Lloyd-Jones had been invited to come and comment on a couple of papers that had been given and then sent on to him. I happened to be one of the two authors involved, and to my relief he spoke very favourably of what I had written. That was the beginning of our friendship, and it could justly be described as a beginning that was founded on theology.

The Doctor was a voracious reader. Most of all he enjoyed theological works which dealt with the great doctrinal themes and biographies of devoted men and women whose lives illustrated the sovereign power of God in the history of His church. And his reading was wide-ranging; it was not limited to evangelical or even Christian authors. His really extensive knowledge of literature in general, both classical and modern, was apparent, though never obtrusive, in the allusions and quotations that served to press home points in his preaching. He liked to remind his hearers of the valuable lessons that can be learnt from the study of history. 'It is our ignorance of church history,' he declared, 'and particularly of the history recorded in the Bible, that so frequently causes us to stumble and to despair'; adding that 'the Bible does not merely record history' but also 'helps us to understand the meaning of history,' and above all to see that all history is sovereignly controlled by God.[1] His daughter Elizabeth remembers his being absorbed in Emil Brunner's *The Divine Imperative* on the beach at Borth in the midst of a summer vacation.[2] There were important issues on which he strongly disagreed with Brunner, but he did not therefore shut himself off from the theological thought of a notable contemporary scholar. As iron sharpens iron, so his mind was sharpened by his familiarity with other able minds (Prov 27:17). Thus in a letter of March 1949 he told me: 'I listened to Emil Brunner give a lecture at King's College on Tuesday evening on "Predestination and Human Freedom." He was very stimulating. He came to listen to me on Sunday morning and came in to see me at the close of the service.'

The evidence of the theological character of his sermons and expositions is readily apparent in the numerous volumes that are now available, which are, apart from some minor adjustments, printed verbatim as delivered. He was unwavering in his persuasion that because the Bible was the revealed Word of God its teaching was absolutely reliable and the indispensable source of our knowledge of God and of ourselves. He had a superb logical faculty, which made him formidable in debate but added great cogency to his preaching; and he had a quite exceptional ability to analyse attitudes and situations in a methodical and almost clinical manner, though always in the light of the scriptural revelation. His use of this gift attracted and riveted the attention of great numbers of thoughtful persons who had looked elsewhere in vain for the presentation of the Christian faith that did not bypass the mind by soliciting a merely emotional response. His method, as displayed, for example, in his expository studies of Psalm 73 (*Faith on Trial*) and the prophecy of Habakkuk (*From Fear to Faith*), was a penetrating form of psychoanalysis which, since it was at the same time a biblically based spiritual analysis, went to the deep heart of the problems of both believers and unbelievers in a way that was altogether beyond the competence of secular psychotherapy.

The Doctor used to insist that it was important for Christians to think, to use their minds, to be logical. He drew a distinction between 'rational thinking' and 'spiritual thinking,' meaning, by the former, thinking that is governed by finite and fallen human reason, and by the latter, thinking that is enlightened and controlled by the knowledge of God's revealed truth. 'I am not for a moment suggesting that spiritual thinking is irrational,' he said. 'The difference between them is that rational thinking is on the ground level only; spiritual thinking is equally rational, but it takes in a higher level as well as a lower level. It takes in all the facts instead of merely some of them.[3]

Nicodemus, theologically literate though he was, could not understand what Jesus meant by the necessity of being born again because he was trying to understand spiritual things with his natural understanding. Spiritual rebirth relates to our being in its entirety. As much as any part of us, our minds are in need of redemption. God's thoughts are not our thoughts (Is 55:8) and only the reborn are able to think God's thoughts (see 1 Cor 2:6–16). 'The first thing that happens to us when we become Christian is that we find that we are thinking in a different way. We are on a different level. In other words, as soon as we start thinking spiritually miracles are no longer a problem, the rebirth is no longer a problem, the doctrine of the atonement is no longer a problem. We have a new understanding, we are thinking spiritually.[4] To judge things by our fluctuating feelings is to reverse the true order of understanding, so much so that our doubtings and misconceptions are 'ultimately due to the fact that we are governed by our feelings and our hearts and sensibilities instead of by clear thinking and the honest facing of things before God.'[5] Nothing, then, could be more false than to equate Christian belief with mindlessness and irrationality. Hence the admonition that 'we must never give the impression that people become Christian by ceasing to think and by just responding to their hearts';[6] on the contrary, 'one of the hallmarks of the Christian should be the capacity to think, to think logically, clearly, and spiritually.'[7] Not surprisingly, Martyn Lloyd-Jones had a liking for 'the logic of the New Testament.'[8]

He had little patience with the type of Christianity that is thoughtless or irrational or easy-going, that is to say, untheological Christianity; nor could he view with complacency the facile kind of evangelism that invites people to believe in Christ because of all the benefits they would gain, without stressing the exceeding sinfulness of sin and the absolute necessity for repentance. These represented distortions and caricatures of the real thing. Popular evangelism with its emphasis on human happiness and satisfaction all too often leaves out the mention of sinful depravity and the holy righteousness of God, and in doing so deprives the Gospel of its proper background. Our need for salvation derives from our sin which separates us from our Creator. If sinfulness is omitted, there is no understanding of the incarnation; 'for the incarnation would never have been necessary were it not for sin.' Consequently, 'the only way to understand the New Testament doctrine of salvation is to start with the doctrine of sin.'[9] And this means, further, that 'there is no true evangelism without the doctrine of sin, and without an understanding of what sin is.' Superficiality, it could be said, is the bane of the church. This was something about which Martyn Lloyd-Jones was deeply concerned, as the following passage shows:

> I do not want to be unfair, but I say that a gospel which merely says 'Come to Jesus', and offers Him as a Friend, and offers a marvellous new life, without convicting of sin, is not New Testament evangelism. The essence of evangelism is to start by preaching the law; and it is because the law has not been preached that we have had so much superficial evangelism. Go through the ministry of our Lord Himself and you cannot but get the impression that at times, far from pressing people to follow Him and to decide for Him, He put great obstacles in their way....This means that we must explain that mankind is confronted by the holiness of God, by His demands, and also by the consequences of sin....So evangelism must start with the holiness of God, the sinfulness of man, the demands of the law, and the eternal consequences of evil and wrong-doing. It is only the man who is brought to see his guilt in this way who flies to Christ for deliverance and redemption.[10]

Superficial evangelism can of course be expected to lead to superficial Christianity. The Bible is treated as a kind of lucky-dip from which to draw comforting verses when we are feeling discouraged, instead of being systematically studied so that its teaching can be consistently applied to the living of disciplined Christian lives. Martyn Lloyd-Jones could refer trenchantly to 'many people who use the Psalms like drugs,' telling you 'that they always find in trouble or perplexity it is a good thing to read one of them.'[11]

Feeling good is no substitute for right thinking. He warned that 'religion should not act as a drug on us;' and he observed regretfully that 'there is often, far too often, justification for the charge that religion is nothing but "the opiate of the people"', since 'to many people it is a form of dope and nothing else, and their idea of the house of God and worship is just a place where they can forget their troubles for the time being.'[12] His sounded at times like a lone voice challenging the church to recover the seriousness and discipline of the Christianity of the New Testament. He had good reason to be critical of the 'glib, superficial view of Christianity which holds that so long as a person has signed a decision card he is a Christian and must, therefore, be perfectly happy';[13] for this, again, is that mindless brand of Christianity which is productive of 'that inane grin upon our faces that some people think is essential to the manifestation of true Christian joy.'[14] It tends to be self-indulgent rather than glorifying to God. 'Is not our ignorance our main trouble?' he asks. 'We talk so much about our decisions and what we are doing. We must learn to think in this other way and to see that it is God who has done it all. You never decided for Christ, it was He who laid His hand upon you and, to use Paul's term, "apprehended" you. That is why you did decide. Go beyond your decision. What made you decide? Go back to the beginning, to the grace of God. It is all His grace, and if it were not, though you decided for Christ you would very soon decide otherwise, and you would fall right away and go right out.... You must realize that "it is God which worketh in you," from beginning to end. Thank God for His amazing grace—saving, restraining, wonderful restoring grace.'[15]

A deficient view of the true nature and importance of holiness is another consequence of a deficient emphasis on the seriousness of sin. This was a connection that the Doctor saw very clearly. 'Not only has our evangelism been superficial,' he charged, 'our conception of holiness has been superficial also.'[16] It was because he was profoundly concerned to reaffirm the New Testament doctrine of holiness or sanctification that he was critical of what was known at that time as 'Keswick teaching.' This was the distinctive teaching annually propounded and heeded by his fellow Evangelicals at the Convention for the Deepening of Spiritual Life (commonly referred to as the Keswick Convention because of its venue at Keswick in the Lake District). For large numbers of Christians 'Keswick' was (and no doubt still is) a yearly fixture on their calendar. Once, when we were travelling together by train (from London to Oxford, if I remember rightly) Martyn Lloyd-Jones described 'Keswick' as 'the Evangelical Ascot'—a nice example of his sense of humour, which was zestful without being malicious.

There was of course no disagreement about the need for holy living. He was most emphatic that 'the eternal purpose of God with respect to His children' is, in the words of the Apostle, 'that we should be holy and without blame before him in love.'[17] He insisted that the sanctifying work of the Holy Spirit in the believer is constant and progressive, and that the active cooperation of the believer is involved; whereas 'Keswick' laid stress on sanctification by a sort of passivity, the receiving of holiness by faith, without effort on our part. 'It is not just a question of being converted, and then remaining like that for years, and then going to a convention and getting a second blessing,' he asserted. 'Not at all! From the moment you become a Christian this "working" begins, and it goes on and on, leading, prompting you "to will and to do." '[18] He opposed the notion that sanctification, like justification, is a gift to be received, and that all that is required for us to receive it is to 'surrender,' to 'be willing to be made willing,' and to stop struggling. Such a doctrine, he maintained, 'makes the second half of most of the New Testament Epistles entirely unnecessary.'[19]

Still less acceptable to Martyn Lloyd-Jones, if anything, was the teaching of Christian 'perfectionism' which, according to its advocates, is the result of 'baptism of the Holy Spirit,' and of the 'total eradication of sin' attained by 'the second experience.' 'Are we to be guided by Scripture, or by an idea or theory that came to someone?,' he asked. 'The Apostle does not say that sin can be suddenly taken out of us and completely eradicated. Neither does he say that the risen Lord will do it all for us if we but "hand it over" to Him. He shows, rather, what we have to do, and to continue to do, in the light of his teaching.'[20] Interestingly enough, despite his objections to the 'Keswick' doctrine of sanctification, he was repeatedly invited to be a speaker at the Keswick Convention. Characteristically, however, it was an invitation that he felt unable to accept. I remember telling him that I thought he should regard such overtures as an opportunity for him to go and propound the truth as he saw it, and thus perhaps to influence 'Keswick' away from the error he discerned. I believe that now the emphasis of the Convention has in fact changed, and that its leaders no longer believe themselves to be solemnly committed to the teaching that he found so disturbing. Perhaps this would have happened sooner had he agreed to join the Keswick platform.

The Christian's supreme desire should be not simply to be forgiven and to be blessed but to know and rejoice in God Himself. This was Martyn Lloyd-Jones's intense desire. He sought it earnestly. 'We desire the blessings and we do not stop to enjoy the blessed Person Himself,' he warned. The author of Psalm 73 (which he was expounding) 'had been through all that, and now he has come to see that the greatest of all blessings is just to know God and to be in His presence.' The passage that follows opens a window into the Doctor's own soul and shows that he had progressed far along the road of true holiness and godliness:

There are many examples of this in the Bible. Psalm 42:1, 2 expresses it perfectly, 'As the hart panteth after the water brooks, so panteth my soul after thee, O God.' That man is crying out for this direct knowledge of God, this immediate experience of God. His soul 'panteth,' he is 'thirsting' for Him, the living God. Not God as an idea, not God as a source and fount of blessing, but the living Person Himself. Do we know this? Do we hunger for Him and thirst for Him? Are our souls panting after Him? This is a very profound matter, and the terrible thing is that it is possible to go through life praying day by day and yet never realizing that the supreme point in Christian experience is to come face to face with God, to worship Him in the Spirit and in a spiritual manner.... Is the greatest desire of our hearts and our highest ambition, beyond all other blessings and experiences, just to know that we are there before Him and that we know Him and are enjoying Him?[21]

This earnest longing for personal holiness before the face of God Himself was accompanied by the deep desire of Martyn Lloyd-Jones to see a mighty spiritual work of revival, a sovereign manifestation of divine power, in which the church would be aroused and revitalized by the irresistible force of the Holy Spirit. He was an eager student of the accounts of the great revivals by which the church had been blessed in the past. He rejoiced in his work, which was being remarkably blessed; but he was never complacent; there was a healthy spiritual dissatisfaction as he longed and prayed for God to rend the heavens and come down in overwhelming power (Is 64:1). 'I can say quite honestly that I have never enjoyed preaching so much,' he wrote to me in March 1945. 'The Word and its message grips me more and more and the joy of preparation has never been so great. I am conscious also of freedom in speaking and of authority. And yet I feel that these are but days of sowing. I long for revival comparable to that of the 18th century. More and more am I convinced that there and there alone lies our hope....Oh! how I long to know exactly what Paul means in 1 Corinthians 2:1–5 and to experience it in my ministry. I have become tired of all else and when I read of Whitefield I feel that I have never really preached in my life.'

A little over a year later (April 1946), in another letter, he deplored the 'levity and carnality' associated with certain large evangelistic rallies then being held in London 'which I simply cannot reconcile with the New Testament'. 'Nothing but an unusual and signal manifestation of God's power through the Holy Spirit can possibly meet the present need,' he wrote. 'I pray daily for revival and try to exhort my people to do the same.' Again, in a foreword which he wrote in 1947 for a small book of mine, in which a number of brief studies on the subject of revival were brought together, he said: 'There is no subject which is of greater importance to the Christian church at the present time than that of revival. It should be the theme of our constant meditation, preaching, and prayers. Anything which stimulates us to that is of inestimable value. At the same time it is the finest spiritual tonic. At a time when the greatest danger is to rush into well-intentioned but nevertheless oft-times carnal forms of activism, it is good to be reminded forcefully of the essential difference between an organized campaign and the sovereign action of the Holy Spirit in revival'.[22]

In the early days of the contemporary charismatic movement both the Doctor and I had watched its rise with interest and indeed with a measure of hopeful expectancy. But such hopes as we had, failed to be realized, except to the degree that it has been a route that has brought many to a living faith. But the marks of genuine revival have failed to appear, especially solemnly powerful preaching, a sense of

the awful majesty of Almighty God and the abject wicked-
ness of sinful men and women in the presence of their holy
Creator, and in consequence a deep abhorrence of sin and a
grateful reception of the mercy and grace of God in and
through our Redeemer and Lord, Jesus Christ. The movement, moreover, is characterized by a widespread uncon-
cern about theology. Its emphasis on being 'one in the
Spirit' has encouraged silence about theological issues that
might be divisive of this unity. Its preoccupation with
spiritual phenomena and feelings has led not only to much
spiritual superficiality but also to emphases that are clearly
unbiblical, such as the insistence that 'receiving' the Spirit
is always accompanied and authenticated by speaking in
tongues, and even that it is open to a person to receive and
exercise all the gifts of the Spirit. And as a variation of the
'second blessing' scheme of Christian experience it is con-
ducive to the 'higher level' notion of Christianity which
lends itself rather readily to divisiveness. I mention these
things because on various occasions Martyn Lloyd-Jones
and I discussed them at considerable length together. The
theological insouciance of the charismatic movement was
particularly uncongenial to him.

The Doctor was undeviating in his insistence on the
doctrine of the New Testament as the sole standard for
Christian truth, the absolute authenticity of which flows
from this fact, that the truth the apostles communicate to us
in its pages is precisely the truth they themselves received
from the Lord, who is Himself the Truth. 'The test of truth
is its apostolicity,' he declared. 'The gospel of Jesus Christ
as announced and taught in the New Testament,' he added,
'claims nothng less than that it comes with the authority of
the Lord Jesus Christ Himself who gave it to these men
who, in turn, preached it and caused it to be written. Here is
the only standard. And it is still the only standard.'[23] As a
theologian, his aim was always to be faithful to the teaching
delivered to us in the New Testament. It was his 'first

principle' that 'every teaching is to be tested by the teaching of the New Testament, not by feelings, not by experience, not by results, not by what other people are saying and doing.'[24]

Wrong doctrine, he asserted, was generally attributable either to a diminishment or to an expansion of apostolic truth, and was recognizable by the insistent emphasis it placed on one particular idea or practice. He mentioned the Jehovah's Witnesses and the Seventh Day Adventists as 'obvious examples' of erroneous teaching, but held that it is found also in the notion 'that adult baptism by immersion is essential to salvation,' in the insistence on 'the absolute necessity of speaking with tongues if you are to be sure that you have received the Holy Spirit,' and sometimes 'in connection with physical healing in the teaching that no Christian should ever be ill,' and in the Roman Catholic cult of Mary and the saints—though he stated that 'from the sheer standpoint of orthodoxy and doctrinal beliefs I find myself nearer to many a Roman Catholic than to many within the ranks of Protestantism.'[25] Here, too, this theological judgment was bolstered by his knowledge of history, as the following quotation shows:

These wrong teachings are subtle and attractive and you feel that that is what you need, that it must be right. Then you suddenly remember this argument about experience and it holds you. You remind yourself, for instance, of men like George Whitefield and John Wesley who were undoubtedly filled with the Spirit in an astounding, amazing, mighty manner by God, outstanding saints of God and among God's greatest servants; yet you find that they observed the first day of the week and not the seventh, you find that they were not baptized in a particular manner, you find that they never spoke with tongues, you find that they did not hold healing meetings, and so on....Cannot you see that these new teachings which claim so much are denying some of the greatest Christian experience throughout the ages and the centuries? They are virtually saying that truth has only come by them and that for 1,900 years the church has dwelt in ignorance and in darkness. The thing is monstrous.[26]

Martyn Lloyd-Jones was a very private individual. To have been admitted to the intimacy of his friendship was in itself an immense privilege and blessing, and to have enjoyed fellowship with him in his devotion to the apostolic theology of the New Testament, and above all to the Master who is its source, was a benefit for which I can never be sufficiently grateful. Those who desire the knowledge of his theological thought have but to turn to the books which contain his expositions of Romans and Ephesians and many other great scriptural texts, for in them the most notable preacher of our day is revealed as the passionate theologian.

NOTES

1. *Faith on Trial* (London, 1965), pp.54, 55. See also *From Fear to Faith* (London, 1966; 1st edn. 1953), pp.21ff. 'If we read right through the Bible and note its message, instead of just picking out an occasional Psalm, or the Sermon on the Mount, or our favourite Gospel, we shall find that it has a profound philosophy of history and a distinctive world view. It enables us to understand what is happening today and that nothing that occurs in history fails to find a place in the divine programme' (ibid., p.9).
2. Frederick and Elizabeth Catherwood, *Martyn Lloyd-Jones: The Man and his Books* (Evangelical Library of Wales, 1982), p.15.
3. *Faith on Trial*, p.34.
4. Ibid., pp.35f.
5. Ibid., p.72.
6. Ibid., p.76.
7. Ibid., p.80.
8. Ibid., p.102.
9. *Studies in the Sermon on the Mount*, Vol.1 (London, 1959), p.234.
10. Ibid. p.235. Similarly, e.g., *Spiritual Depression: Its Causes and Cure*

(Grand Rapids, 1965) p.28: 'You must be made miserable before you can know true Christian joy…. There is no rising again until there has been a preliminary fall…. Ultimately, the only thing which is going to drive a man to Christ, and make him rely upon Christ alone is a true conviction of sin.'

11. *Faith on Trial*, p.22.
12. Ibid., p.43.
13. *Spiritual Depression*, p.65.
14. Ibid., p.14.
15. *Faith on Trial*, p.94.
16. *Studies in the Sermon on the Mount*, p.236.
17. *Romans. An Exposition of Chapter 6: The New Man* (Grand Rapids 1973), p.137. Eph 1:4 is the passage quoted.
18. Ibid., p.140. Many, it might be said, went not just for a second but for an annual blessing.
19. Ibid., pp.155–157.
20. *Romans. An Exposition of Chapter 8:5–17: The Sons of God* (Grand Rapids, 1975), p. 98; also pp.91ff.
21 .*Faith on Trial*, pp.111f.
22. *Revive us Again* (London, 1947), p.5.
23. *Spiritual Depression*, p.183.
24. Ibid., p.184.
25. Ibid., pp.181, 187.
26. Ibid., p.188.

Chapter Ten

GOD'S GIFT TO A NATION

by

Elwyn Davies

The Rev Elwyn Davies is general secretary of the Evangelical Movement of Wales, an organisation with which the Doctor was closely involved from its earliest days. This article first appeared as a tribute to the Doctor in the special Martyn Lloyd-Jones memorial issue of the EMW's magazine (in 1981). Elwyn Davies was one of the ministers who took part in the Doctor's funeral service in Wales in 1981.

The task of attempting a brief assessment of Dr Lloyd-Jones' ministry, and in particular of his influence on church life in Wales, is well-nigh an impossible one. The impact of his life and ministry, extending over more than half a century, has been so profound that one is truly at a loss to know where to begin. The words of the Welsh hymn, sung with such fervour by the company of relatives and friends who were gathered around his grave at Newcastle Emlyn, say it all. It is from the vantage point of 'heavenly Jerusalem's towers' alone that we shall be able with any measure of certainty to trace the path along which we have been led through 'the desert' of this life.

To attempt to do this is incumbent upon us, however, if only to enable us to return thanks to God for all that He achieved through the ministry of His servant.

And we would be doing a gross injustice to that story if we failed to start with his remarkable period of ministry at Sandfields, Aberavon. In a very real sense the 11 years he spent there served to shape and to determine his lifelong convictions. His subsequent ministry at Westminster Chapel with its world-wide ramifications—through the publication of his sermons and the many thousands of foreign students and others who worshipped there over the years—could so easily dazzle our eyes to the remarkable years of his first period of ministry. Most certainly, no account of his impact and influence on the Welsh religious scene could ignore this formative period in his life.

No one who knew Dr Lloyd-Jones would be left in any uncertainty as to his love for Wales and for its people. Thus, when he felt called to leave the field of medicine and to devote his life to the work of the ministry, it seemed right to him that he should offer his services to the Forward Movement of the Presbyterian Church of Wales. But there was a further reason why he chose to do this. In a television interview with the late Aneurin Talfan Davies he once explained that his father's radical views and his concern for the poor and underprivileged had had a profound effect upon him. This is why he was particularly anxious to minister in the kind of areas that were then being served by the Foreward Movement.

That the hand of God was upon him, inclining him in the direction that was eventually to bring him to the church at Sandfields, Abcravon, was made evident by the many tokens of blessing and favour that attended his labours there. From the working-class community of that town and neighbourhood, through his anointed labours, God called and redeemed many remarkable trophies of grace. Soon a sizeable congregation of men was to gather regularly on a Saturday evening to attend the Doctor's 'brotherhood discussion session.' And before he left, 11 years later, the congregation had grown to such proportions that an annexe had to be built alongside the church building, enabling the overflowing numbers to follow the services through the open windows of the chapel.

News of Dr Lloyd-Jones' call to the ministry and the fame of his preaching spread far and wide, and it was from that town, so strategically placed in South Wales, that God sent his servant, in what became a regular mid-week ministry, bearing the message of salvation to all parts of Wales and beyond. It may be difficult for us today to imagine what it was like. Those were days when, in Wales at least, the chapels were full and the entire population, it seemed, was in membership in some chapel or other. To a young lad in his early teens at the time it also seemed as though everyone went to hear the Doctor, wherever he preached.

Looking back over those years, Dr Lloyd-Jones was well aware that there were Christians in Wales at that time who were disappointed that he felt unable to identify himself wholeheartedly with their testimony. And it is true to say that the Doctor himself could not fully explain at the time why it was that he could not bring himself to be associated with, for example, some of the Pentecostal and Keswick traditions which had emerged in Wales following the '04–'05 Revival.

These were the years when he was possessed with one consuming passion—to tell men that in and through the Lord Jesus Christ they could know God. They were also the years when for the first time, following upon his distinguished medical career, he was able to give himself avidly to the study of theology and Christian doctrine. There is the famous story of how he was challenged at the close of a service in Bridgend by a minister who commented provocatively, 'I cannot make up my mind what you are. I cannot decide whether you are a hyper-Calvinist or a Quaker.' On being asked why the comment was being made, he was told, 'You talk of God's actions and God's sovereignty like a hyper-Calvinist and of spiritual experience like a Quaker, but the Cross and the work of Christ have very little place in your preaching.' Assuring him that he was not a hyper-Calvinist, the Doctor's response was to ask the Rev Vernon Lewis—later to be made Principal of the Memorial (Congregational) College at Brecon—when he called the following Monday morning, what he could read on the Atonement. He was referred to the works of P.T. Forsyth, R. W. Dale's *The Atonement*, and Denney's *The Death of*

Christ—such was the dearth of truly evangelical literature at the time.

Commenting on this incident in later years the Doctor explained that in his early preaching he was like Whitefield. First and foremost he preached regeneration: man's own efforts were useless; he needed power from outside himself, 'I assumed the Atonement but did not distinctly preach it or justification by faith.'

A little later, in a second-hand bookshop in Cardiff he came across the two-volume edition of the works of Jonathan Edwards, and later still, to his great delight on a visit to the United States, the entire works of Warfield. Years afterwards the Doctor was to explain that what kept him from identifying himself with the traditions to which we have referred was his knowledge of what God had done in the past through men like Daniel Rowland of Llangeitho, Howel Harris and others. He was looking for those who shared their view of doctrine, but, more, their view of experimental religion and of revival.

And such people were at a premium in the denomination to which he was attached, as they had been. To us today it seems so regrettable that Dr Lloyd-Jones was ordained a minister of the Presbyterian Church of Wales when it was too late even for a person of his gifts and convictions to influence the issue of whether the denomination should adopt a Shorter Confession, and thus to all intents and purposes relegate the old Confession of Faith to the status of a historical document. Such was the case, however, and even though at one time Dr Lloyd-Jones had reason to hope that the common people, in response to his preaching, would reject the arrogant views of the vast majority of liberal and modernist preachers who by then were occupying the pulpits of our land, this was not to be.

On one occasion he was given what seemed to him a most promising portent for good. He had been invited to preach in the same Association meeting as the Rev Tom Nefyn

Williams, probably the most radical of all the liberal preachers of the day, a man of considerable talent and charm. The Doctor would recount the story of how he came down to breakfast on that occasion, only to sense as soon as he entered the room that an uncomfortable silence had fallen upon all those who were at the tables. Upon making discreet enquiry, he was asked chidingly, 'Don't you know what's happening? They are all debating who will get the bigger congregation, Tom Nefyn or yourself.' At the first of the two services at which they were to preach, each man's congregation had been more or less equal. But at this first service Dr Lloyd-Jones was given remarkable liberty in preaching, so that by the second service his meeting was full to overflowing, while the Rev Tom Nefyn's congregation had been considerably reduced.

But it was not to be. A few years later Dr Lloyd-Jones was given incontrovertible proof that if the common people were prepared to hear him gladly, a good number of the religious leaders of his denomination had been considerably irked by his uncompromising adherence to the evangelical faith. They were prepared to resist quite openly a proposal which, if accepted, could have meant his sphere of influence within the denomination being very considerably enhanced. After 11 years of intensive work at Port Talbot it was suggested that he be appointed, in a year's time, to the staff of the Theological College of the Presbyterian Church of Wales at Bala, under the Rev David Phillips as Principal. Although the proposal was favoured by the Associations in the South and East, the North Wales Association kept deferring a decision—a deliberate ploy, on the part of some of the leaders at least, to avoid the opprobrium of an outright rejection, whilst at the same time making it obvious to the Doctor and others that his services were not welcome.

In the meantime, while his own heart was very much inclined towards the Bala vacancy, Dr Lloyd-Jones had been invited to assist Dr Campbell Morgan at Westminster

Chapel. Within six weeks of going there he had been invited to continue on a permanent basis. But from October 1938 until after Easter 1939 he refused to commit himself, still waiting for a firm invitation to the College at Bala—an invitation which never came. The Doctor had persuaded the friends at Westminster Chapel to await the decision of the North Wales Association's meetings to be held at Chester. Three ministers had fully intended going to those meetings and pressing for a favourable response, but for different reasons all three were unable to be present, and the matter was once again left on the table. The Doctor had no alternative but to accept the invitation to become co-pastor with Dr Campbell Morgan and thus to commence his 35 years of ministry at Westminster Chapel.

As is so often said on such occasions, 'Wales's loss was surely England's gain.' In the hindsight of close on half a century we now know that that step, which to some might have seemed so regrettable at the time, proved to be possibly the most far-reaching and consequential development this century in the history of the evangelical cause in Britain, if not throughout the world. However influential the Doctor's ministry might have been in a finishing college devoted primarily to pastoralia, how can one begin to compute the influence for good of this prince among preachers, this wise counsellor and spiritual leader, through his pulpit ministry, his Friday evening lectures, his meetings for ministers, the Westminster Conferences, his wider preaching ministry, his availability at all times for counsel and advice—a ministry which is to continue through his printed works and through the kind Providence that has enabled his spoken word to be preserved, so that to an uncanny degree we are able to hear the Doctor as though he were yet with us? All these things, we now know, hinged upon his ministry at Westminster Chapel. We can only say with the Apostle, 'How unsearchable are his judgments, and his ways past finding out!' (Rom 11:33).

It proved to be Wales' gain also, despite the fact that after the 1939–45 war, when it was evident that Nonconformity was losing its grip on the people, Dr Lloyd-Jones would occasionally be criticized for forsaking Wales in its hour of need. One writer even suggested that he had done so for a more lucrative and comfortable ministry in a big church in London! Nothing, of course, could be further from the truth. He never lost touch with the situation in Wales, nor did he ever show any sign of rancour or bitterness as a result of what had happened. He continued to preach to vast congregations in many centres in Wales. In 1977, for example, he celebrated his 50th consecutive annual visit to preach at Carmarthen. There were many similar instances. His sermons too had a wide circulation.

But it was in the years after the war that his links with Wales assumed a completely different role and significance. Prior to this his ministry had been that of a visiting preacher, preaching to vast congregations. Now it assumed more that of a friend and counsellor to a body of young men whose labours were eventually to lead to the emergence of faithful evangelical ministries in churches of all denominations in Wales; to the emergence also of what became known—on the Doctor's own suggestion at the Annual Welsh Conference held in Denbigh in 1955—as 'The Evangelical Movement of Wales', and, later, to the establishing of avowedly evangelical causes free of all denominational entanglement.

The Doctor's interest was first alerted to a movement of the Spirit that occurred in the colleges of Wales in the years 1945–50. It seemed to have two focal points—one in the south, which because of a strong Presbyterian background was more doctrinal in its thrust, and one in the north which had a more experimental emphasis. In the providence of God, Dr Lloyd-Jones was brought into close touch with both streams at the very outset and, in ways which today we can see were graciously ordained of God, was able to assert from the beginning a most salutary, formative and unifying influence.

As a consequence of his remarkable preaching ministry at Westminster Chapel, he had by now been greatly used by the UCCF (or the IVF as it was then known). In his own words, 'I became the theologian of the IVF.' When it was suggested that the work in the recently reinvigorated Welsh Christian Unions would benefit from meeting together in an annual conference, Dr Lloyd-Jones was the obvious choice as speaker. For the first three years he took the main conference addresses, each year taking one major tenet of the Christian faith as his theme. His ministry had a profound effect on the students. One student, who later succeeded to his pulpit at Sandfields, Aberavon—the late Rev. J. B. E. Thomas—would often remark that he had learned more of Christian theology in those conference addresses than in all the lectures he had ever attended at his theological college.

No sooner had the blessing broken out in the north than Dr Lloyd-Jones was to speak at a student mission at the University College, Bangor. There he learned with immense satisfaction of the spontaneous work of the Spirit among the students. Later he was to give his full endorsement to an experience of a further enduement of the Spirit which some of the students had known—an endorsement which coincided with his own renewed interest in the subject of the sealing of the Spirit and revival.

When some of these students came to realize a little later that there was not a single publication in the Welsh language committed to the evangelical faith, Dr Lloyd-Jones was asked to write in the first issue of a new Welsh-language magazine which they published. When, later, they decided to invite the readership of the magazine to a conference, his daughter Elizabeth attended the first, held at Bala in 1951, and Dr Lloyd-Jones was the main speaker at the second, held at Caernarfon the following year. When, a little later, the need was felt for an equivalent provision in English, Dr

Lloyd-Jones was once again the main speaker, returning, to the delight of many friends, to his pulpit at Sandfields, Aberavon. When some of the students from both North and South Wales were to attend the National Eisteddfod for the first time to sell the new Welsh-language magazine and to witness to their people, Dr Lloyd-Jones met them twice and addressed a late-evening gathering in one of the local churches.

Finally, when some of those students had themselves become ministers, Dr Lloyd-Jones was able to offer invaluable advice which led to the emergence both of the Ministers' Fellowships associated with the Evangelical Movement of Wales and also of its Annual Ministers' Conference. Barring periods of ill-health, the Doctor attended that conference without fail, and every year would lead the two discussion sessions and deliver his memorable closing addresses. Had Dr Lloyd-Jones not been with us at that time, there is little doubt that the work of the gospel in Wales would have taken a very different form.

Some of the evangelical ministers in South Wales were anxious to meet in a monthly ministers' fellowship restricted to brethren of a Reformed persuasion. They were anxious to invite the Doctor to the first of what would become an annual gathering of ministers of the same persuasion from all part of Wales. Dr Lloyd-Jones agreed to be present on condition that they widened the basis of their fellowship—a step which was to lead to incalculable gain and benefit to the cause of the Gospel in Wales, and of the Reformed faith in particular.

And so the story continued. Throughout the 30 years that followed, the Doctor's interest and support were unfailingly available to all who sought his counsel; his presence and ministry were a source of strength and encouragement to all who knew him.

Our comfort is surely that of the pastor's wife who, as she glanced at the congregation that sang the hymn at his graveside, suddenly noticed how many ministers were present. Dr Lloyd-Jones had been pastor and friend to them all. With the support and constant encouragement of his dear wife and partner Mrs Lloyd-Jones, he had while physical strength remained preached in their pulpits and attended all their conferences. In him the words of our Lord had been gloriously fulfilled: 'Whosoever will be great among you, let him be your minister; and whosoever will be chief among you, let him be your servant.' In many things he excelled, but in this most of all.

Wales had never lost one of its ablest sons. Allowed to function freely in a church unfettered by any element of compromise or apostasy, he had continued to serve his people. And now, taken to be with the Lord on St David's Day, 1981, he had come home again, to rest awhile—till He come.

Chapter Eleven

A MAN UNDER THE WORD

by

Leith Samuel

Leith Samuel is the former pastor of Above Bar Church in Southampton, and an ex-president of the Fellowship of Independent Evangelical Churches, with which Dr Martyn Lloyd-Jones was involved towards the end of his life. Leith Samuel was a regular summer preacher at Westminster Chapel during the Doctor's ministry there. Both men were for many years active in the student work of the IVF (now UCCF).

I was based on Chester during the early part of World War II, so I heard nothing about Dr Martyn Lloyd-Jones until 1943, when I began to preach in the London area and speak at hospital Christian Unions. Some medical students in these CU's became concerned about what they felt was a somewhat inadequate presentation of the Christian faith at Speakers' Corner, Marble Arch in those days. Would I lead them in a witness team at Easter and Whitsun? The first meeting lasted eight hours!—such was the barrage of questions following the enthusiastic testimonies.

As at Athens in Paul's day, some listeners were hostile, some sceptical, and a few wanted to know the truth about Jesus Christ. The question arose, where do we send these people to get good biblical teaching? The students were in no doubt. 'Send them to Dr Lloyd-Jones at Westminster Chapel. He has taken the place of Dr Campbell Morgan and he's terrific!'

So began a long-sustained habit of recommending people to 'go and hear the Doctor,' though I didn't hear him myself until another four or five years had gone by.

It was at a conference of the Theological Students Fellowship just after Christmas in 1947 or 1948 that I first saw and heard the Doctor in action. By this time Dr Douglas

Johnson had persuaded me to become University Missioner for the IVF (now UCCF), an appointment I held for five years. One of the perks was many visits to Swanwick conferences of various kinds. On this occasion Alan Stibbs and others gave first-class Bible expositions and addresses. But the highlight of the conference came when the Doctor chaired a free-for-all. The Scottish theologians were to the fore in hurling their questions at him. The sharpest minds included James and David Torrance and James Barr, all three of whom became well-known professors. James Barr waxed eloquent, apparently trying to tie the Doctor up in knots about the inspiration of Scripture. He and his friends suggested the Bible was like a regenerate man, with something from God which was holy and true, bound up with something that was still sinful and far from perfect. On this analogy we could expect to find true and wonderful things in the Bible, but also errors.

The Doctor's answer was a firm 'No! You have the wrong model. The Bible is like Christ, with the divine and human elements united. As the human nature of Christ was without sin, so the human element in the Bible as originally written was without error, whether in geography, history, scientific allusion or any other aspect. In His providence God has allowed some copyists to make an occasional and remarkably rare mistake, for example in some numerals. But there are no textual mistakes that put any important truth at risk.'

Judging by his book, *Fundamentalism*, James Barr was one of the minority present who was not persuaded by the Doctor's argument, which he backed up by the many Scriptures he drew out of the theologians listening to him.

Like many others, I came away from that conference with a stronger conviction than ever that the Scriptures are one hundred per cent inspired, God's Word in God's words which are also the words of the men He chose to record them. Therefore these words not only have divine authority

but are infallible in their teaching about God and inerran
in their details.

The infallibility and inerrancy of Scripture were the
burning issues then. Those questions are still vital, bu
today the battle seems to be raging round the sufficiency o
the Scriptures. Do we need modern prophecies as well as
the Scriptures? The Doctor left his hearers in no doub
about his view of the finality and sufficiency of the Word o
God in the Old and New Testaments.

On one occasion only the Doctor shared in an ecumenica
mission. This was run by the Student Christian Movemen
and/or the Chaplains at Oxford in 1941 or 1942. He sharec
the platform with William Temple and one other man no
known as a conservative Evangelical. Needless to say there
was no soft-pedalling in the message he brought to the
students. *The Plight of Man and the Power of God*, sermons
published for the first time around this period, gives a goo
idea of what he taught about man's fallenness and helplessness to save himself, about Christ's deity, His atoning death
and His power to regenerate and transform.

I believe it was during this mission rather than the late
Oxford mission he shared in, that a student got to his fee
after the address and said in a rather bored voice, 'Sir, we
have been listening to what you have to say, but what have
you got for us?'

The Doctor took up his question with great relish! Wha
right had an Oxford undergraduate to think that there wa
one way of salvation for ordinary mortals, reaching righ
down to the dregs of society, and another, distinctive anc
superior, for those privileged to study among Oxford's
dreaming spires? 'You, sir, are common clay like anybody
else . . .' and the Doctor proceeded to tell him he had human
birth, human sin, an unregenerate human nature and the
certainty of human mortality in common with every other
human being, whether at Oxford or not. And unless he
repented of his sin he would surely perish like anybody else

I heard the late Bertie Rainsbury tell this story on several occasions in other universities.

Dr Oliver Barclay was chairman of the National Executive of the IVF at this time and he tells me he had the difficult task of telling the Doctor that this student executive found it embarrassing that their national president was sharing in a mission sponsored by non-Evangelicals! The Doctor never did it again and, as most readers will know, became one of Britain's leading critics of the idea that you can get anywhere with a doctrinally-mixed platform.

The Doctor was involved in one other mission in Oxford. The other speaker was the Anglican Prebendary (later Australian Archbishop) Hugh Gough, who spoke for the first three or four days. Dr Oliver Barclay was present as an assistant missioner and was virtually aide-de-camp to the Doctor, who arrived after the week-end and heard at the assistant missioners' meeting about people unable to sleep at night because of conviction, and of a few very clear cases of conversion. Quite a lot was going on.

'At that point,' says Dr Barclay, 'Dr Lloyd-Jones took over and preached some masterly sermons in the Union Debating Hall. I remember the thrust of some of these and it was very penetrating, but the immediate effects were slight. Dr Lloyd-Jones said he hoped he had not spoiled the obvious work of conviction of sin that was going on. The fruits of his preaching were a little disappointing though the attendance was good and people came back again for more. My impression,' concludes Dr Barclay, 'is that Dr Lloyd-Jones decided after this not to take part in missions because it was not his particular gift. This is not to say he didn't communicate the Gospel effectively. Some students were deeply touched. But his kind of preaching took time to sink in. At Westminster Chapel many people were converted only after hearing him preach several times, taking in truth gradually.'

As an example of this last point I will never forget hearing of an Oxford graduate, Elizabeth Braund, going to see the doctor in his vestry after listening to him for some weeks. 'I would like to become a Christian,' she said. 'Good,' said the Doctor. 'Keep coming.' He wasn't prepared to give her a push into the kingdom of God. He was relying on the Holy Spirit to do His own work in His own time. He wanted genuine demonstration of the Spirit's power in deep conviction and unmistakable new birth, not statistics to impress a somewhat gullible evangelical public!

In his history of evangelical student witness in Wales, 1923–1983 (*Excuse me, Mr. Davies—Hallelujah!*: IVP Evangelical Press of Wales), the Rev Geraint Fielder speaks warmly of a mission led by Dr Lloyd-Jones in Bangor in 1949. All sorts of men went to see him. They didn't know where they stood or what they believed and this included theological students. (p.40 op.cit) At some point he asked them all the same question, 'Have you been on your knees before God thanking Him that Christ died for sinners?' The impact was enormous as students listened to the Doctor's message. The editor of the weekly college newspaper devoted most of his space to the mission. 'We were compelled to discuss our ideas about religion . . . Is it not a good thing to have more important matters than life's trivialities being discussed in the Students' Union these days?'

To quote Geraint Fielder again: 'It was a rare thing for Dr Lloyd-Jones to lead a university mission. The nature of his ministry was a cumulative one. Its effects in people's lives tended to show over the long term rather than in the immediate context of a mission . . . one can but wonder what might have happened if his ministry had continued longer.'

Rare though it may have been after that to get the Doctor involved in university missions, the leaders of the London Inter-Faculty Christian Union, with over 700 members in the constituent colleges at the time, prevailed upon him to give the addresses at the central meetings in both 1950 and 1953. An old friend of mine, Dr (now Sir) Eric Richardson, then principal of Northampton College of Engineering took the chair for the first meeting in the Great Hall of King's College, Strand. Seeing among those present quite a number of his own engineering students it occurred to him, so he told me recently, to introduce the speaker not only as the well-known minister of Westminster Chapel but as an excellent technician. This allusion was not intended to refer to the Doctor's handling of the Word of God but to his massive knowledge of the mechanics of the human body. The Doctor did not take it as a compliment as had been intended!

As much at home in King's Great Hall as in Westminster Chapel, he expounded the first four verses of Hebrews 1. We all sat gripped by the power and eloquence of his preaching. I happened to be the missioner in King's, so it was a particular thrill to me to see the impact of plain straightforward exposition of Scripture on some of the students from King's who were sitting near me. There were no gimmicks, no quips, no funnies, no drawing attention to himself.

I forget whether there were two or three main addresses from the Doctor that week, but I well remember Professor Tasker, then professor of New Testament exegesis in the University of London, taking the chair at the closing meeting. The Doctor spoke with great power on the Second Coming of Christ. He proclaimed the great certainties, so different from the trivial and speculative details so popular in some evangelical paper-backs of the 1930's and 1940's.

Three years later I was invited back from my ministry in Above Bar Church, Southampton, to be missioner again at King's. The Doctor was, for the last time, giving the main addresses. Once again Professor Tasker was the chairman and I will never forget the electrifying effect of his opening remarks: 'I don't know who else heard Dr Lloyd-Jones speaking in this hall three years ago on the Second Coming of Jesus Christ. But I know one man whose whole life was revolutionised by that address. That man is your chairman tonight!'

The Doctor had noticed a middle-aged man slipping into Westminster Chapel late on many a Sunday evening. Eventually he identified him as Professor Tasker, who was also Rector of Chenies, Bucks, coming to get more and more of this powerful Biblical preaching such as neither he nor I nor thousands of other theologs ever had in our student days.

Two significant consequences came out of this spiritual crisis in the life of Professor Tasker. He forsook liberalism and took a stand in the theological faculty at King's College on the complete trustworthiness of Scripture. This led to considerable isolation from the other members. He once told me he felt as if he had been sent to Coventry! The other consequence was that he approached the Inter-Varsity Press and asked if they would publish his next monogram. He hoped thereby to burn his theological bridges and be identified with the then rather despised and small group of conservative theological writers in the theological world. Ronald Inchley, for many years publications secretary of IVF, gladly co-operated with him and a copy of *The Gospel in the Epistle to the Hebrews* is one of my treasured possessions. Later on, he became general editor of the whole series of Tyndale Press commentaries on New Testament books.

It must be rare for a professor in a theological department to be converted in a university mission. Would to God that more such men would become servants of the Word of God instead of pontificating as though they were masters of it.

*   *   *   *

A very depressed student, a fringe member of a Christian Union, took her own life. Her family approached the Doctor. Could he take the funeral? He wasn't sure because of his very heavy commitments, so I was asked if I would stand by. Thankfully he was able to fit it in, and I went along, partly out of sympathy for her family and friends and partly eager to learn how an evangelical pastor would handle such a situation.

He said nothing about the tragic circumstances, her state of mind, or the shock to all concerned. He just majored in the certainty that we must all die, a favourite theme which I heard him mention so often, and the certainty that Christ has died for sinners and has conquered death by His own death and by His glorious resurrection. The lesson has stayed with me for life: 'Make much of Christ at *any* funeral.'

*   *   *   *

I can still visualize the spot where I sat in Westminster Chapel while the Doctor expounded the doctrine of election. I had been brought up to believe that because God knows everything He knows which way we are going to jump by the exercise of our own free-will. And here was the Doctor demolishing that idea for all he was worth. I boiled with indignation! Gradually I saw my problem was not with the Doctor and his apparently new interpretation, but with the very words of John 17. Did I really believe Scripture was the Word of God? Indeed I did. Then I must submit my mind to all its truth and abandon my ill-thought-out ideas. I must acknowledge I was a Christian because God had chosen me in Christ before the foundation of the world. This didn't mean I was no longer responsible for my actions. I must exercise the renewed will He had given me, freely and intelligently, for His glory and according to His Word. But it did mean that *all* the credit for my salvation could and would go to a gracious and loving God who had laid hold of me long before I dreamed of laying hold of Him. My indignation was replaced with gratitude for the Doctor's merciless logic.

*   *   *   *

Billy Graham's visit to Kelvin Hall, Glasgow, in 1954 had sparked off a fresh interest in evangelism in Scotland. Many ministers under the leadership of the Rev Tom Allen, then at St George's Tron, got together and combined with BBC Scotland to present the Christian message north of the border under the slogan *'Tell Scotland'*. The British Council of Churches noted the impact of this, as well as the effect of Billy Graham's visit to Harringay, and came up with the idea of a matching programme for south of the border, which could be called 'Tell England.' But where would they get the preachers for this evangelism?

It was at this point that they recognized that the conservative Evangelicals, previously denounced as heretics by Kenneth Slack in the *Presbyterian Messenger*, must be drawn into the project if there were to be any impact. Maybe these Evangelicals could get people converted and then the mainline BCC folk could teach them a better theology? The key man to get hold of was obviously Dr Martyn Lloyd-Jones. If they could draw him in, together with the Rev John Stott, recently-appointed Rector of All Souls, Langham Place, the rest would surely fall in line behind these two.

I believe it was at the Doctor's instigation that I was invited to join what was to be known as the Group with Differing Biblical Pre-suppositions. George Duncan gave an opening address typical of his devotional touch. That was a good start. Dr John Huxtable, Principal of New College, London, shortly to become the first president of the newly-formed United Reformed Church, was the chairman. The underlying question was, could liberals and high churchmen already in the British Council of Churches work together with conservative Evangelicals to present a united front to the whole nation in evangelism? Did we hold enough basic doctrine in common to speak as one man on the radio, for example?

I remember asking the Doctor at the outset, 'Why don't we deal with Scripture next time we meet?' I was eager to discuss this as being the key to our distinctive separate stands. 'No,' he said, 'We'll leave that till last. They think it is the only thing that divides us. We must show them it isn't. We part from them on nearly every fundamental doctrine.'

So we started with Romans 5:12–21 and the doctrine of man. Quickly we saw how divided we were over Genesis, the Fall as history. One doctrine after another was dealt with in subsequent sessions and it was nearly always the Doctor who put his finger on the nerve that produced the reaction, making clear how impossible it was for us to speak with one voice. To most of the BCC folk the idea of a substitutionary atoning death of a sinless Saviour was unacceptable. We, for our part, could not accept the doctrine of salvation by sacraments.

One session remains vividly in my memory. After we had discussed the doctrine of the Atonement, a leading liberal Evangelical said, 'I don't go with these conservative Evangelicals in their attitude to Scripture, but I'd rather have their preaching of the Cross than what we get from our wishy-washy liberals!'

We met frequently over a period of a few years. The Doctor only missed one session. When Dr Jim Packer was brought in, he was present every time. But in the end the liberals lost interest and the series was wound up. There was no way that conservative Evangelicals could be harnessed as the evangelistic wing of the British Council of Churches.

*   *   *   *

One of the most influential of the Doctor's ministries sprang out of a suggestion from his old medical friend, Dr Douglas Johnson, first General Secretary of the IVF (UCCF). A small group of some 40 ministers were brought together at the end of the war in what was called the parlour of Westminster Chapel, to thrash out theological and pastoral issues

under the Doctor's sharp biblical eye. The Revs Alan Stibbs
Ernest Kevan and others were later joined by the Rev John
Caiger.

Dr Johnson came to the first two. Then, sensing that
ministers would take part more freely in discussion if only
men in pastoral charges were present, he sensibly withdrew
leaving Alan Stibbs as secretary. Later on John Caiger
filled this role with his typical graciousness.

Woe betide any man who made a senseless statement or
asked a stupid question! The Doctor could be devastating
with those he thought could take it. But often he caught my
eye with a wicked twinkle as he gave some man an answer
he wasn't expecting. Some men seemed to take pleasure in
becoming his chopping blocks! His summing-up statements,
often brilliant, always pithy and lucid, took us to the biblical
heart of every issue. Men who had to make long journeys
early on Monday mornings to get to Westminster always
felt it was worthwhile.

So many men eventually packed into the parlour that it
was sometimes called the Black Hole of Calcutta as the air
got so thick, even without pipe or cigarette smoke. This
gathering became open to anyone in pastoral charge who
could be vouched for by existing members as being truly
evangelical. The Westminster Fellowship was nicknamed
the Westminster Confession because so many ministers
unburdened their hearts to the Doctor about the problems
they faced in their churches. From these private sessions, as
well as the main gatherings, hundreds of pastors like myself
went back to their work with renewed confidence and clearer
minds to face pastoral and theological problems. He was
pastor of so many pastors for most of the years he was at
Westminster. Well do I remember his patient listening as
on various occasions I went through my latest list of things
about which I sought his advice. And how I appreciated it
when often he said to me, 'Bring your lunch into the vestry.'
I was 15 years his junior but he never made me feel inferior

He was always warm and understanding in personal conversation. People who only saw him in the pulpit might be surprised to learn how gentle and sensitive he was to know personally as a man.

In 1966-67 the basis of the Fellowship was tightened to preclude any who were not prepared, whatever happened in their denominations, to consider secession. The turning point was the assembly of Evangelicals convened by the Evangelical Alliance in October, 1966. It troubled the Doctor deeply to see Evangelicals so fragmented. He saw in this rally a great opportunity to invite them, in his own words, 'to come together in a loose affiliation or federation of churches, the looser the better.'

I believe I am right in saying that all the Doctor had seen of the Church of Wales in his youth had made him instinctively suspicious of the established church. How could Anglican leaders be in anything but the same mould as their Welsh counterparts? The (understandable) rejection by most of the Anglicans at the conference, followed by their conference at Keele, coloured the Doctor's thinking even more and inevitably made him feel that maybe no good thing could come out of the Church of England except by the drastic act of secession.

In personal counselling, however, he never sought to precipitate a crisis in men's lives. In fact he advised some who consulted him not to leave their denominations unless and until they were quite sure it was right to leave, and wherever possible not to move until they could see where they were going in the interest of spreading the gospel.

A number of sincere and godly Anglicans and Baptists ceased to meet at Westminster following the 1966 watershed. Other ministers kept coming. Where could they find a sharper mind to analyse problems and evaluate situations? Or a greater enthusiast for preaching the Gospel in all its fulness? Many of us were enthused for the consecutive systematic exposition of the scriptures in our own churches.

For many years the Doctor longed to see revival. He urged people to pray for a divine visitation of heavenly blessing, of 'God rending the heavens and coming down in power among His people.' 'Are you not disappointed?' asked an interviewer for the Evangelical Movement of Wales magazine two or three years before the Doctor's promotion to glory. He admitted he was disappointed but still hoped to see a real move of the Spirit before he died, and I gather this hope stayed with him right to the end.

But in October 1979 I heard him say he was now persuaded there was one objective even more important than revival, namely our personal godliness. I can still recall the warming of heart I felt when I heard this. It rang all my bells. Here is no far-off, may-or-may-not-be-reached target. Here is a New Testament norm for every believer to aim at. As Robert Murray McCheyne said over a century ago, the greatest need of every minister's congregation is his own personal holiness, true godliness in his home and in all his relationships. This the Doctor exemplified. He was at his best in family situations, his own and other people's. The solemn preacher knew how to relax.

What more can I say? Perhaps a couple of personal allusions. In December 1952 my wife and I stood before the morning congregation at Westminster Chapel as the Doctor dedicated our first-born child, Margie, now married to Rupert Bentley-Taylor and serving the Lord in the ministry. On that occasion he commended me to the prayers of the congregation as I was about to leave London for the pastorate of a church in the main street of Southampton, Above Bar. Two months later he preached at my induction there. Little did he or I dream that I was to be there for almost 30 years and that he would preach at the church anniversary time and time again.

No-one in Britain could draw a weeknight congregation as he did! It was not our habit to encourage our children to go to weeknight meetings while they were still at school. But

I remember urging our son John, also now entering the ministry, to come to those occasions during his teenage years. All of us have unforgettable memories of the Doctor's preaching.

Is it any wonder that some people have called him the Spurgeon of the 20th century? No preacher ever moved me more than he did. No Bible teacher ever taught me more!

Chapter Twelve

AN APPRECIATION

by

John Stott

Dr John R. W. Stott is president of the London Institute of Contemporary Christianity. He was Rector of All Souls, Langham Place, from 1950 to 1975, during most of which time the Doctor was serving as Minister of Westminster Chapel, a short distance away. Many people would attend a service at the one church in the morning and the other in the evening. John Stott is also the author of many books and, like Dr Lloyd-Jones, held the post of president of the IVF (now UCCF).

With the death of Dr Martyn Lloyd-Jones, the most powerful and persuasive evangelical voice in Britain for some 30 years is now silent. He will be remembered chiefly as a biblical expositor. In his heyday in the '50's and '60's at Westminster Chapel, Buckingham Gate, he would hold a congregation of 2,000 people spellbound for an hour to an hour-and-a-quarter. He combined the analytical prowess of a scientifically trained mind with the passion of a Welshman. 'What is preaching?' he asked himself in his influential book *Preaching and Preachers*, and replied 'Logic on fire! Eloquent reason!' Although one needed to hear him in order to feel the strength of this combination, it continues to be communicated through his multi-volume expositions of *Romans* and *Ephesians*.

Dr Lloyd-Jones could give an impression of sternness in the pulpit, and of shyness in his correspondence. Even letters to his friends began 'My dear Sir', and he would seldom sign himself by his Christian name. Yet, when counselling individuals in his vestry or study, he could not have been more sympathetic and affectionate. He kept up his medical reading since his early days as Lord Horder's assistant, and he confronted the foibles and frailties of human beings with the insights of both physician and pastor. One of his most popular books, *Spiritual Depression, its Causes and Cure,* is full of practical, biblical wisdom.

In his view of the church he was a strong independent, and could not understand how any Evangelical remained a member of a 'mixed denomination' like the Church of England. For years he continued to argue that consistent Evangelicals should secede. At the National Assembly of Evangelicals in the Central Hall, Westminster, in October 1966, he issued a stirring appeal to us to come out and form a faithful evangelical 'remnant.' I was in the chair and, when he had finished his address, felt it right to disassociate myself from his position. I did so in the hope of dissuading some ministers from writing precipitate letters of resignation before the matter had been discussed (as it was to be) in the following days. But later I called on Dr Lloyd-Jones to apologize—not for what I had said (which I still believe) but for misusing the chair and almost turning the meeting (as he put it) into a 'debate.' He told me that he had scarcely restrained himself from answering me and developing the debate.

But we continued to have a warm personal relationship. I always had a strong affection and admiration for him. In an era of theological flux he stood firm for historic, biblical Christianity. And although he was a polemical speaker, he always distinguished between principles and personalities, and was at heart a man of love and peace. 'The Doctor' was a spiritual father figure to many of us. His death has created a serious vacuum.

(This piece was originally intended for publication in *The Times*).

Chapter Thirteen

THE PASTOR'S PASTOR

by

Hywel Jones

The Rev Hywel Jones is principal of the London Theological Seminary, a training institute for preachers which the Doctor was instrumental in establishing. A former pastor in London and in Wales, Hywel Jones now serves on the committee of the Ministers' Fellowship which Dr Lloyd-Jones led for nearly 40 years. He was also one of the participants in the Doctor's funeral service in Wales in 1981.

To many, myself included, there was someone who needed no other designation than 'The Doctor.' By such a singularity of reference no offence was, or is, intended either to those who adorn the profession of his choice—for, as he delighted to remind us, he had not chosen to be a preacher—or to those who hold a research degree in some aspect of academic study. While the noun 'doctor' was an accurate designation of him in both the senses just mentioned, the definite article was and still is expressive of the profoundest respect and affection. His passing from us is still mourned, but not without hope—and he would want that hope to grow clearer and glow brighter as the days go by.

In Westminster Chapel he held what I am going to dare to call 'a finishing school' for ministers. I say 'dare' because I know, and others will also, how he would have abominated such a description being applied to his beloved Fellowship, and also the great likelihood that even if he had been told that the term was not only going to be most seriously qualified, but even reinterpreted, he would still have repudiated any possibility that the Fellowship could be fairly represented in such a way. I can imagine hearing him say 'poise and polish', the words reverberating with explosive scorn because, in his view (and how right he was!), nothing could be further removed from the rough hewn dynamism of the prophets of the Old Covenant and the preachers of the New than sophistication and professionalism. On one occasion he charged evangelical churches and their preachers with 'dying with dignity!'

However, I am still adhering to my description and my reason lies in the fact that I am using the expression 'finishing school' analogically. As young ladies (if that term is acceptable anywhere, any more) having thus completed their education are regarded as being 'ready for life,' so the Doctor sought to make those who had the irreplaceable privilege of being members of the Westminster Fellowship *ready for life*. There was, however, one massive and all-pervading difference and it was that the life he had in view was one of reality, not unreality. The meeting focussed on the reality that is the existence and nature of the spiritual as well as the physical world, or the physical as well as the spiritual (for each can be minimised or denied). Yet the Doctor saw to it that the pre-eminent position was given to the spiritual because, without that dimension, complete sense could neither be made of the physical nor could there be any solution to its problems.

For a meeting with such scope and aim extraordinary gifts were necessary, gifts not commonly found and certainly not found in combination. We had such a leader in *the* Doctor. His intellect *and* spiritual understanding is, in my view, what merits the use of the definite article. Of course, it was the man who preceded the meeting, not only chronologically but also causally and the meeting took its shape and character from him. But it was the Lord who prepared him for this great part of his life's work.

The Westminster Fellowship resulted from a request made by Dr Douglas Johnson that the Doctor would hold a study meeting for ministers at Westminster Chapel. It commenced in early 1941, soon after the Doctor began there as an associate of Dr Campbell Morgan. It grew and soon occupied a full day. In 1967 it underwent an important change—in fact, the Doctor closed it down and was requested to restart it. This was on a significantly altered basis because of what resulted from the Doctor's call upon Evangelicals at the National Assembly of Evangelicals in 1966 to secede from their doctrinally mixed denominations, a call which he repeated the following year in the Luther Commemoration Rally held by the British Evangelical council.

The Westminster Fellowship continues to meet, but its founding father is sorely missed. Perhaps it can be said that it is in the Fellowship and other similar meetings, for example the Evangelical Movement of Wales Conference for ministers held at Bala every June, that his passing is most sorely missed. In the ministers' meeting he was with his fellow preachers of the 20th century of the glorious Gospel of the ever blessed God. He was glad to be alive in this godless and lifeless age, which is so decadent and despairing, and to have a gospel to preach to it, and time and again by the Holy Spirit he made us feel the same. We looked up to him, but he never looked down on us. He made us realise that we were brothers in the same noble family, fellow labourers in the same great work and fellow soldiers in the same stern conflict. It was there, many of us feel, that, outside the circle of his own particular family (and how grateful we are to them and especially his wife for sparing him to us) that he was at his most free and open.

There was an element of preparedness and control in all his public ministry, and even when at his most liberated in preaching, but in the Fellowship he was at his most unpredictable and versatile. In the discussions he was at times humorous, even on occasion outrageously so; sarcastic, but never savage; uncomfortably challenging; at times elusive and deliberately vague, at other times dogmatic and immovable on one point, while being quite open—infuriatingly so to some—on another matter. He did us the honour of expecting us to understand that however he spoke, it was in order to make us think.

For all his culture, there was something essentially rough hewn about him. We were glad that it was so, for preachers should not be colourless, though he did not approve of their being flamboyant. He abhorred the prejudice which frequently went with rank and the weakness which manifests itself in being trendy. To him, and he often quoted it, 'The rank is but the guinea's stamp, a man's a man for a' that.'

Similarly, cant and the stock-in-trade approach or reply fell under his disapproval, which was at times unmistakably expressed. To evade a question or an issue, in Cabinet fashion, was anathema. In doing so we knew we were dodging and we knew that he knew, too—the twinkle in the eye, the puckering of the corner of the mouth and sideways shake of the head said it all— though sometimes we had to bear more—much more! But it was all in love and for our good. Someone with such perception of truth and experience of God was caring for us and wanting us not only to be better and more useful than we were, but even better and more useful than he had been. And because of the God he knew, he believed that even that was possible.

From its beginning the Fellowship had been open only to ministers and from 1967 only to those ministers who had seceded from the doctrinally mixed denominations and those who were convinced that secession was inevitable and were waiting on God to know what steps they ought to take. In both phases, the meeting was closed for the sake of the profitableness of the meeting itself. In the first place this was so that open discussion might be encouraged in an atmosphere of mutual trust and confidentiality, and in the second place so that there should be the agreed basis necessary for useful discussion. Just as the evangelical view of the Bible and the Gospel were, albeit in an unwritten way, factors which limited attendance at the Fellowship in the first era of its history, so in the second era, and this time in written form, the evangelical view of the church that is in opposition to and distinct from the ecumenical movement was an additional limiting factor. This was quite proper because the Bible and the Gospel demanded it.

The fact that the meeting was a private one was not allowed to breed exclusiveness in our thinking. We were jolted out of our complacency on many occasions by questions which erupted or flashed, such as 'What difference did being at the Westminster Fellowship make to us in our ministering—that is, our preaching, our conduct of public worship and the prayer meeting, and in our dealing with people? What difference did it make to us in our personal communion with God—praying secretly for oneself and others and not publicly as a church official, and reading the Holy Scriptures for food for our own souls and not for sermons for others? Further, were we aware of the need of the age, the darkness of the hour which had deepened since we last met? Were we crying to God and urging our people to do so, as well as calling on men and women to repent? Were we serious? Were we in earnest?'

Such questions were presented and re-presented, applied and re-applied, and many a time we were brought to lament our own condition, our prayerlessness and consequent powerlessness with God and men. But never were we sent away in despair. While others were invited to open the sessions in prayer, the Doctor always closed them and the Lord was always there in the closing prayer in the afternoon. He drew near and was invoked not just as our Lord, but the Lord of our brothers, many of whom were in need; the Lord of our wives and children; the Lord of our churches, their officers and members, at home and world-wide; and the Lord of our nation and even the world, who could again arise, shake terribly the great ones of the earth and revive His people.

The pattern usually followed in the meetings was quite open. Any member could raise a question for discussion and it was the practice for a theological subject to be taken up in the morning and a pastoral one in the afternoon. Such an arrangement had many benefits. First, the need for ministers to be continuing students of theology was underlined, yet the need to be truly pastoral was not minimised. In addition, discussion imposed upon us the necessity to do some work ourselves rather than just have information, as it were, doled out to us. In this way we had to speak to each other, listen to each other, correct and be corrected by each other. He made us learn how to cope with each other's adjustments to or even disagreements with our positions without our feeling personally attacked. He inspired us to submit our views to the scrutiny of the meeting and did this himself too. The meeting was bigger than any of us. We were there to confer. He made many of us 'men.'

The chief benefit of such a pattern to the meeting, however, lay in having the Doctor's responses to the matters raised. These would be given at the beginning, in the course of and at the end of the discussion. They would vary in length according to their position and, of course, in content in accord with the subject under discussion. The Doctor's approach was, in its basic features, both scientific and spiritual. The uniqueness of his methodology lay in the combination of these factors. There was something of his mentor, the great Jonathan Edwards, about him.

There are people who, claiming to be scientific, are consequently at best agnostic about the spiritual world. On the other hand there are those who feel that to be spiritual means of necessity they must be anti-scientific. Such a divide is but another indication of how far our nation has departed from God and His Word. Who believes any longer that theology is the queen of the sciences? The Doctor did and he taught us to do so too. As he refused to believe in a necessary conflict between the two, he refused to sacrifice either on the altar of the other. To crown theology was to give science its proper place as well as theology.

Therefore the spiritual was not to be discarded merely because it was denounced by someone in the name of science. An attempt had to be made to discover whether it was real science, i.e. theory without facts. Similarly a false spirituality which consisted of an other-worldliness coupled with asceticism was to be opposed because it lacked the support of Scripture. The Doctor, not only as the physician but also the theologian, believed in the sanctity of facts and would not knowingly deny *one* for the sake of any theory. All facts, whether in the world or in the Word, were true. They, therefore, stood in harmonious relationship with each other because they all stemmed from the God who cannot lie.

It is impossible to convey what relief this brought to many a mind troubled by theories and conclusions ranged against Scripture teaching, and how it nerved the spirit for one's work of studying and preaching. We had nothing to fear, quite literally. As *all* truth was on God's side, our side, we did not need to fear truth. Why then should we need to fear error, ignorance, scepticism and unbelief? How foolish we had been! To demonstrate how foolish and arrogant scientists can sometimes be, he quoted to us some words of J. S. Haldane who in 1931 wrote in his book *Philosophy of a Biologist*, 'It is inconceivable that there should be a chemical compound with the properties of DNA.'

But though urged to unbounded confidence in the veracity of the Holy Scriptures and to the unreserved application of our minds to their study, we were also repeatedly warned against the subtle danger of trusting our own reason and its ability. The long history of the church of Jesus Christ, beginning in the New Testament and continuing to our own day, was too full of examples of believers, preachers and theologians (particularly the latter) misinterpreting the Word, teaching error and leading others astray for us to think of ourselves but with all our resources more highly than we ought to think.

When a question was raised, the Doctor would first of all

set about opening it up for consideration. This he used to do
in one of two ways. Sometimes he would ask the questioner
to say a little about the matter which he had raised, for
example, how he had met with it or why had he raised it. By
this means, some aspects of the subject might appear and
some stimulus to discuss it might be provided. On other
occasions, he would himself take up the question and rephrase it and in so doing broaden what otherwise could
never have provided sufficient basis for a morning's discussion. It was not unknown for him to do more than rephrase
the question; he would on occasion provide us with one of
his own about something which was pressing upon him.

Both these approaches were instructive. The first impressed on us the need to discover as much as we could about a
subject before proceeding to form views about it by analysis,
and then conclusions. The Doctor would invite others to
add information to this stage of the discussion and try to
keep suggestions as to how to respond to it out of the
picture. This was truly the scientific method—observation
and the gathering of data came first in the consideration of
any question and no fact which seemed to complicate was to
be excluded. How often we felt reproved at the slender and
partial basis on which we made our judgments!

The second approach taught us the importance of the
indirect method. We were repeatedly reminded of the need
to be general in one's approach to a subject before concentrating more narrowly upon it. The method followed in
discovering what elements were present in a chemical was
urged upon us, namely, one began with tests to discover
which large category it fell into before using more specific
tests to determine its precise nature. To rush at a problem
and face it directly was dangerous folly. This was (and is)
particularly the case in the area of exegesis of biblical texts
where often they became pretexts for some hobby-horse
because they were not seen in their contexts. Similarly,
areas of theology or eras of history with their predominating

features, were of immense importance in dealing with subjects. It was also the case that one needed to bear in mind
certain generalities regarding nature and human-ness, male
and female, before concentrating on more narrow details.
In this way, what was complex and difficult in Scripture,
history and contemporary life was almost half resolved.
Perspective was crucial, but it had to be valid, i.e. supported by data, to be truly helpful.

Of special relevance in this whole area was the treatment
of biblical texts. The Doctor not only taught us the importance of being accurate in exegesis of words and terms, but
of discovering the *principles* of truth contained in them. We
were not to make connections between texts in terms of
words used, concordance-wise, but in terms of those principles of truth which were enshrined and expressed in them.
This instruction was massive gain, for one was taught to
think doctrinally and biblically at one and the same time.
One's doctrines were not to be culled from a tome on
dogmatics, but were to arise from the words of Scripture. In
this way the danger of being theoretical in one's doctrine
was guarded against and also the danger of being inaccurate
and contradictory in one's teaching from Scripture.

The Doctor was not more concerned for principles than
for people. His sensitivity to them and their conditions was
as keen as his perception of principles. While it is true that
he refused to let personalities cloud his thinking, whoever
they were, he insisted on considering people, whoever they
were, in his expression of those principles. In him there was
but a single step between being a scientist and a theologian
and also between being a preacher and a pastor. He grasped
truth; declared it; but also sought us with it.

What we looked forward to was his summing up. On so
many occasions he would have the conclusion in mind
before the discussion had really started and he would be
guiding it accordingly. He would in concluding always have
something to say which was both clarifying after our

meanderings and stimulating for further thought. One occasion stands out clearly in my memory. The question raised that morning was whether Evangelicals could be fairly charged with being adolescent. In the lively discussion which followed it was obvious that the Doctor saw substance in the charge. The time came for him to sum up. He did so by specifying the symptoms of adolescence which he saw around him. These were that the 'evangelical adolescent'

1. Does not think he needs to grow
2. Tends to be easily impressed and credulous
3. Confuses excitement with spiritual life
4. Is prone to be unstable and go off at tangents
5. Lays great value on the gregarious element

Are not these worth pondering still?

So many subjects were raised at meetings at the Fellowship. They included: Apostasy and Backsliding, Missionary Societies and the Church, the Missionary and the Church, Counselling, Visiting, Demon Possession, The Supernatural, Mental Illness, Healing, Acupuncture, Abortion, Euthanasia, Homosexuality, Cremation and Burial, Marriage, Music, Tongues, Prophecy, Laying on of Hands, Apostles, the Prayer of Faith, Law and Love, Tithing, Should an Evangelical only be positive and not negative, Bible Translation, Evangelism, Prayer, Worldliness, Church Discipline and Politics.

Though the meetings covered a wide range of topics— and the Doctor with his voluminous reading always had something to say on each—he had certain major concerns to which he frequently returned. He knew that ministers' time was often threatened (he urged us to keep the mornings free, even on holidays if we could) and that the pressures of modern life coupled with the perplexities of the ecclesiastical and social scene could have a diverting as well as a disturbing effect. He therefore repeatedly gave us our bearings and kept us to the main things with regard to the work of the Christian ministry. We often left the Fellowship being able to say to ourselves with regard to some development which was making us uneasy that we were right after all. It was also often the case that we were, if only in our minds, brought back on course again.

What were these emphases? First and foremost was the importance of *spiritual life*. This was asserted in relation to the individual Christian, the minister and the church. The essential place of truth, i.e. the truth of the written Word of God, in spiritual life has already been stressed but to the Doctor life included more than truth. Meetings were given over to a consideration of the question 'What is wrong with us today?' or, 'Why is there a lack of life in our churches?' The short and most serious answer which the Doctor urged on us was our lack of realisation that God was the *living* God. This showed itself in our preoccupation with what he called 'our greatest enemy,' namely religion, and our being immersed in our own plans and actions which we then presumed to baptize by special prayer. We praised the Gospel instead of proclaiming it, defended it by apologetics instead of declaring it by assertions, and we had become exhibitionist theologians instead of ambassadors with a message from the King. We were more concerned about the application of Christianity to society than to the soul, and about relationships than the spirit. We were more concerned with a horizontal plane, i.e. man to man, us to people, the church to society, than with the vertical dimension, i.e. us and all and each one to God. Though repudiating and ridiculing the 'God is dead' theology, Evangelicals knew and spoke very little about the living God 'who deals familiarly with men.' The Doctor said on this score, 'Brethren, we are mad, mad!'

The reality of the *living* God, the Doctor maintained, was the centre and circumference of the Bible. God was living and revealed Himself. He did so irrespective of the circumstances of time and place in the Bible. He could intervene and not be kept out; He could overturn and set to rights again individuals and nations, and do so by His own sovereignly chosen means or without any. It was in relation to the greatness of the variety of His activity, but also its necessity, that the Doctor said: 'The study of the Scriptures *alone* would have finished the church long ago.'

So, when this element of spiritual life which was the result of the working of the Holy Spirit was under consideration, the Doctor could become a critic of orthodoxy, even Reformed orthodoxy. He did so not only because of the heady effect which the (re)discovery of Reformed theology was having, but also because some exponents of that theology were overlooking or excluding the immediate works of the Spirit in addition to regeneration, viz. the baptism of the Spirit, the bestowal of spiritual gifts, and revival. He pointed out repeatedly that Charles Hodge omitted any reference to revival in his three-volumed *Systematic Theology* and that B. B. Warfield regarded the gifts referred to in 1 Corinthians 12–14 as having ceased with the age of the apostles. This the Doctor described as 'a new form of dispensationalism.' For him, Jonathan Edwards was right when he distinguished between excesses and the spiritual, though the latter would have varying, even striking, physical phenomena. He declared: 'We must learn to draw the line between the essential and the indifferent on the one hand and on the other between the indifferent and the wrong.'

The Doctor was interested in anything which appeared to display signs of spiritual vitality, wanting all the information about it and urging us to have the same interest. In the Fellowship he would bring details of incidents which he had heard about and members would raise matters related to house church groups and the charismatic movement in their areas. We discussed tongues, prophecy, miracles, healing, music and dancing and the use of the body in worship. In all these, the Doctor was most careful. He would not dismiss all such phenomena as psychological or demonic as some would have preferred. But he did not hesitate to say that those elements could be present. On the other hand, he would not and did not endorse the charismatic movement. He urged careful observation and evaluation in the light of what the Bible taught of the spiritual effects on an experience of God—awe and reverence, a sense of personal sin and unworthiness, love to the Saviour and the brethren, concern for the perishing and a spirit of prayer. His most emphatic charge directed against us was 'Why do we not have problems associated with spiritual life?' The answer was obvious.

He did not urge us to adopt the practices of the charismatics. Rather he called on us to seek the Lord without setting limits to what He might do or what we would allow Him to do, asking Him to turn to us and visit us in gracious revival. Meanwhile, we were not to follow any human methods for obtaining the Spirit because none were laid down in Scripture. God gives the Spirit in the name of Jesus Christ to those who ask Him.

The second feature is the primacy and importance of preaching. His views on this have rightly been published and need not be repeated, but two or three things can be said. The first is that the Doctor's own story is one of a commitment to preaching. What could he have become in the medical world? In Aberavon he could have become involved in politics, locally and from there even on the national level. He could have become a theological teacher in the Calvinistic Methodist church—the church which he loved for all the right reasons. If Howel Harris, Daniel Rowland and William Williams could, as some one has said, have ruled a kingdom between them, what might have been the upper limit of the Doctor's abilities? But having been called to be a preacher of the glorious Gospel of the ever-blessed God, he would not stoop to be a king.

By what he did as well as what he said he underlined to us the importance of the calling which he and we shared. To

continue to give ourselves to the work of preaching in an age
of counsellors, mass evangelists, guitarists, song leaders,
film operators, overhead projectionists, and story-tellers
was not easy. He provided us with the support we needed.
He would come to preach for us and refer to us as his friend.
At times he would come to listen to us, concealing himself if
he could in the back row, and would go away happy if he
had been given a sense of God.

He was apprehensive about the effect which the various
gifts practised by charismatics would have upon preaching
and preachers. While urging the restoration of meetings like
the society meeting of the 18th century, he contended for
the retention of public worship in the nonconformist
pattern, led from the front by the minister in a raised pulpit
who integrated the service. He did not regard this as either
grieving or quenching the Spirit. He gave himself to the
preaching of the Word, 'the highest and the greatest and the
most glorious calling to which anyone can ever be called',
and God exalted preaching through him.

As the Spirit gave birth to the church by means of the
Word and by the same instrument sustained, protected and
promoted its life, the Doctor saw the preaching of the Word
as crucial to the church's well-being. Nothing was more
important than that the Lord would call men to preach and
equip them for that ministry. This was why he took the lead
in the formation of the London Theological Seminary and
became the first chairman of the board. While not denying
that prediction may still occur, he regarded the prophecy
referred to in 1 Corinthians 14 as the kind of thing which
can happen in preaching when new thoughts and unpre-
pared words are given from above. He urged us always to be
open to that dimension in preaching and never to adhere to
our prepared sermons so rigidly as to refuse to follow such
leading.

The third feature was his concern for the church. While
thankful for the good work which had been done by organi-

zations, societies and movements, it was the church which
he found to be at the centre of the outworking of the pur
poses of God and His chosen instrument for the furtherance
of the Gospel. It was the Doctor's complaint that prior to
1966 he had found great difficulty in getting Evangelicals to
discuss the doctrine of the church. Further, at a time when
non-Evangelicals were eager to take a fresh look at the
church and the churches, Evangelicals were to be found
defending their denominations with the same fervour as
they engaged in evangelistic work. This saddened him
because he believed that, of all people, Evangelicals should
be ready to examine everything in the light of Scripture, and
that included the church. But he saw more than this. He
saw that:

1. Whatever creed or confession they had on paper, they
were fostering a denial of the Gospel and Evangelicals were
unconcerned about their church involvement in such sin.

2. Evangelicals were guilty of the sin of schism because
they were joined to people on matters of secondary impor
tance and separated church-wise from people who believed
the same Gospel as they did. He maintained that non
Christians could not actually be guilty of schism though
they spoke much and lamented greatly that the church was
in schism. To be guilty of schism people had to be in Christ.

In the National Assembly of Evangelicals in 1966 all this
came to the fore in the Doctor's address and he called on
Evangelicals to leave their denominations and form a loose
fellowship of evangelical churches for the defence and con
firmation of the Gospel. The rightness of this call was
confirmed by subsequent events in Anglicanism and Baptist
nonconformity. The Keele Congress and the publication of
Growing into Union showed that Evangelicals were accepting
the right of non-Evangelicals to be in the church and accep
ting the role assigned to them of being a wing in it. At the
Baptist Union Assembly the same position was in fact taken
by not disciplining the Rev Michael Taylor who denied the

deity of the Lord. The Doctor knew that the situation was such that heretics could not be disciplined and for Evangelicals to say they would leave only when excommunicated was to stipulate an impossibility, so alien is it to the spirit of the time.

After the Westminster Fellowship was re-formed, we were often required by the Doctor to do two things. The first was to look at the situation to see if there was any material change in it. Nothing was further removed from the truth than the claim that having seceded we retreated into an isolationist ghetto, continuing to persuade ourselves that we needed to stay there to give credibility, in one's own eyes at least, to the step already taken. Frequently we looked around and not only saw no reason to change our mind or repent of the act, but were confirmed in the step, the costly, agonising step, many others had taken—and the Doctor in particular.

But the issues of principle remained. The questions 'What is a Christian? What is a church?' were still not being answered univocally in the churches and by their leaders.

The second requirement presented to us was to look at ourselves and to face the question 'Were we closer—and closer to each other as churches?' Was there a church fellowship in existence outside the church groupings to which we belonged? Were we committed to the British Evangelical Council? Secession was the road to unity, the Doctor taught us, and not the path to isolationism and exclusivism. We saw that we could not go back without denying principles of truth which could not be more closely bound up with the Gospel, but I wonder whether we saw as clearly that we must go on. The Doctor impressed on us that we had been brought out in order to be brought in. Unless we went on to show the glory of the Gospel in the churches, how could we expect any to join us?

Those who attended the Westminster Fellowship regularly during the Doctor's chairmanship had a privilege second to none. Many of us found in that meeting what we had not gained in university or theological college. To have been a member of the Westminster Fellowship is to us far more important than the degrees we possess. But the meeting was more than a context for instruction. It was a *fellowship* between him and us and we felt the bond. The same relationship existed even over the telephone and better still in our homes. He listened to us and soon one knew one was talking to a valued, trusted and beloved friend. Now that is over—for a little while. When we meet again we will not need to ask him any questions. We will be before the Lord; the ultimate answer to every problem will be provided and we shall know as we are known but we shall together share in 'wonder, love and praise' for ever.

Chapter Fourteen

TRANSATLANTIC LINKS

by

Warren Wiersbe

The Rev Warren Wiersbe was a pastor in the USA for many years, and is the author of over 30 books, published mainly in America. He is now the general director of the Back to the Bible radio broadcast.

My first 'meeting' with Dr D. Martyn Lloyd-Jones was in the pages of Jill Morgan's biography of her father-in-law, *Campbell Morgan: A Man of the Word*. That was in the mid '50's when I was pastoring my first congregation, a young seminarian who thought Campbell Morgan ranked somewhere near the Apostle Paul. (The fact that Morgan died on my 16th birthday made me feel even closer to him.) I figured that anyone Morgan chose to be his associate, and then his successor, had to be a remarkable man.

My second encounter was also in the pages of a book, this time one written by the Doctor himself. I was at that time associated with Youth for Christ International, editing their literature and ministering to churches and youth meetings throughout America. As I was leaving for a weekend of ministry, I dropped volume one of *Studies in the Sermon on the Mount* into my briefcase, thinking I might be able to 'scan it' and write a review for one of our publications.

Scan it! The very thought was almost blasphemous!

As I began to read those masterful sermons, I simply could not put the book down. The more I argued with the Doctor's logic, the more convicted I became! It was not long before I was on my knees, broken before God. In fact, I read most of the book on my knees, so penetrating was the message of the Word that it conveyed to me. It is the only one of his books that I ever asked Dr Lloyd Jones to autograph for me, and I treasure that volume dearly.

I met Dr Lloyd-Jones personally in June, 1969, when I was serving as a senior minister at the Calvary Baptist Church, Covington, Kentucky, just across the river from Cincinnati, Ohio. Dr and Mrs Lloyd-Jones were at that time the guests of their friends Mr and Mrs A. M. Kinney in Cincinnati, and the Doctor was working on the manuscript of his series on Romans.

My wife and I knew the Kinneys quite well so it was inevitable that we should have the privilege of meeting the Lloyd-Joneses. By that time I had read several of the Doctor's books and was anxious to get to know him personally. When Mr Kinney asked me if I wanted Dr Lloyd-Jones to preach in our church, I immediately said 'Yes!' and we arranged for a Sunday morning in June.

The Wednesday before he was to preach, the Doctor asked Mr Kinney to take him to the church so he 'could get acquainted with the pulpit and the speaking situation.' I was in my study when they arrived, but I hastened to meet them (volume one of *Studies in the Sermon on the Mount* in hand), though I did it with some fear and trembling. After all, the Doctor was called 'the last of the Puritans,' and I imagined a man like John Owen or perhaps John Manton—severe, stern, penetrating, perhaps unapproachable.

'Penetrating', yes. 'Unapproachable'—in no way! His greeting and handshake were warm and sincere, and we two 'hit it off' from the very first meeting. He autographed my precious book and then asked me to show him the church sanctuary. We had recently completed a new building with a sanctuary that seated nearly 2,000. As we walked through the building, Dr Lloyd-Jones made some interesting comments.

'Most churches are not built for preaching,' he said. 'They are designed to be monuments to some architect or committee. I can see that you people have built this one for preaching!' I should have realized that *preaching* was the great passion of his heart and purpose of his ministry. Now I know better what he meant.

He stood in the pulpit and surveyed the empty pews, testing the sound system. The pews in that building are arranged so that the congregation is right before the preacher; he is not speaking to an empty centre aisle.

'Good, good!' said the Doctor. 'You can look right at them!'

He wanted to tour the rest of the building, so I took him from room to room, ending up at the baptistry. I must explain that the baptistry in this building is quite large, with the water always kept in it, circulated by a system of pumps. The tank was so new and the water so clean that you could not see the water at all—and Dr Lloyd-Jones stepped right into the water! I was so embarrassed that I wanted to dive in and drown myself right then and there!

The Doctor laughed and put me at ease. 'Don't fret about it, not at all,' he said with a smile. 'It will dry off in time.'

(I must add at this point that the next week he sent me a lovely 'thank you' note, and added as a postscript, 'Sometime I'll come back and you can baptize the rest of me!')

The next Sunday morning Dr Lloyd-Jones arrived in my office, ready to preach.

'Is there a pulpit Bible?' he asked. 'I didn't bring my Bible.'

I had to admit that there was no pulpit Bible, but I offered to go to my study and get a Bible for him.

'Why, here's a Bible right on your desk!' he said. 'I'll use it.'

'Doctor,' I said with some hesitancy, 'that's a Scofield Bible.'

He smiled and replied, 'Oh, it can't hurt my sermon too much!'

I then explained to him that our service would probably

not be like a worship service at Westminster Chapel. The atmosphere was probably more 'casual,' I did not pray for 20 minutes, and we always closed with a hymn of response. I tried to avoid using the word 'invitation.'

'My brother, this is *your* church!' he said. 'I'm a guest here. You just do whatever you always do; I'll preach the sermon and sit down.'

And what a sermon he preached! Over the years, the Calvary Baptist congregation had heard some of the world's greatest preachers, both from America and Great Britain; but this was a new voice, that they immediately recognized as declaring the Word of God with clarity and authority. He gave the most exciting exposition of 1 Thessalonians 1 that I have ever heard or read, and the congregation listened with keen interest.

When he finished the message, I simply asked the congregation to sing the hymn of response; and I invited any who wanted to make a spiritual decision to come forward and meet at the front. Several people stepped out to trust Jesus Christ! I sensed that the Doctor was happy that God had used the Word to reach hearts, even though the giving of a public invitation was foreign to both his theology and his practice.

My wife and I joined the Kinneys and the Lloyd-Joneses for dinner at a local restaurant, and the conversation was all that a young preacher could want. Dr Lloyd-Jones talked about Campbell Morgan and told us some stories that have never appeared in print. We discussed books (it seemed that he had read every book I mentioned!), British preachers and churches, and the ministry in general. The good Doctor was so patient with me, answering question after question and trying to eat his dinner.

Privately, he confessed that he was not feeling well.

'I have a bilious feeling,' he said. 'I think it's from drinking Kinney's coffee. He makes it too strong. It's as thick as treacle!' (I explained to my wife that 'treacle' was British for 'molasses.' At that time she was not bi-lingual!)

I was glad that our first meeting with the Lloyd-Joneses had been so pleasant, because a few weeks later I had an experience with him that was not so pleasant. I stood up to deliver the Sunday morning message, looked at the congregation, and there sat Dr Martyn Lloyd-Jones! With a mischievous smile on his face, he was desperately trying to hide behind the lady sitting in front of him and not succeeding at all.

'Do I see Dr and Mrs Lloyd-Jones in the congregation?' I asked in a stern voice.

The good Doctor looked up, lifted his hand and waved it, and then sat back to listen to my sermon! It was unnerving enough that he was in the congregation, but that morning I was preaching from—Romans!

'Why didn't you warn me you were coming?' I chided him after the service. 'At least I could have escaped from Romans!'

There was that warm smile again, a hearty handshake, and some gracious words about the message that made me feel that I had just been given a Pulitzer Prize for preaching. How encouraging he was!

We had dinner with the Kinneys and the Lloyd-Joneses several times before the Doctor and his wife returned to Britain, and each experience was enriching. 'When you visit England, be sure to let us know!' the Doctor said as we parted, and he gave me his telephone number.

In the early summer of 1971 my wife and I made the first of several visits to Britain. We were accompanied by our friends Dr and Mrs Howard Sugden. Howard and I share an enthusiasm for British history in general and British preachers in particular, so we planned to visit as many historic sites as we could cram into a three-week itinerary. Once settled in our London hotel rooms we telephoned the Doctor.

'Welcome to England!' he almost shouted. 'By all means,

we must get together!'

The Doctor and Mrs Lloyd-Jones joined us at our hotel for dinner, and then we retired to the Wiersbes' hotel room for a chat. The Doctor was in an especially blithesome mood and there was a good deal of laughter. For one thing, he was lecturing to us about the beauties of the Welsh language, and giving us numerous examples. 'It's a great language for preaching,' he said. I told him that we thought he did quite well in English.

As I recall, he had just recently addressed a conference of a Christian medical group, so he gave us a digest of his message. He presented us with some helpful insights on 'faith healing' and the influence of the mind on the human body. Then he asked, 'What are you planning to see in London?'

We gave him a sketch of our itinerary—it was quite 'touristy' to say the least—and he then began to make suggestions. 'Be sure to visit Bunhill Field. That's where all the great Puritans are buried. And right across the street is Wesley's Chapel; you must go there. And be sure to see the Foundry Chapel as well, and Wesley's house.' He named some other historic sites that would interest an evangelical Christian, each of which we visited without regret.

In 1976, the Sugdens and the Wiersbes returned to Britain for another visit, and this time we met the Lloyd-Joneses at the Cambridge Arms Hotel. They were staying with their daughter who lived near Cambridge, and were gracious enough to motor over to lunch with us and then give us a short 'evangelical tour' of the famous university city. I was then senior minister of the Moody Church in Chicago, and the Doctor was quite interested in how the work was going.

It was a very warm summer day, but Dr Lloyd-Jones was dressed like a 17th-century Puritan divine: black suit, black tie, and black hat.

'At least there's no chance of losing him in this crowd!'

Howard whispered to me.

He led us to King's College, and then to Charles Simeon's church. He was most anxious to show us the very place where Simeon's disciple, Henry Martyn, dedicated himself for missionary service. He gave a running account of Simeon's life, Puritan preaching, and anything else that he thought would enrich our store of evangelical knowledge. From Holy Trinity church he led us to 'one of the greatest bookstores in the world'—Heffers; and there Howard and I (both book-lovers) revelled in the experience of being surrounded by tens of thousands of volumes.

I must add that the women somewhat lagged behind us and chatted about whatever pastors' wives chat about. At one point, Mrs Lloyd-Jones said to my wife, 'Now, my dear, you must not let your husband work too hard!'

'How do you manage that?.' my wife asked.

Mrs Lloyd-Jones smiled and replied, 'My dear, I really don't know!'

In the years that followed we kept in touch with the Lloyd-Joneses but did not see them again until June 1980 when my wife and I visited Britain with our daughter Judy and a dear friend, Beverly Smith. The Doctor suggested that we dine at the Paddington Station dining room which was close to our Baker Street lodgings. (That sounds like a sentence Conan Doyle would write.)

None of us felt that the Doctor looked well that evening, or acted as we were accustomed to see him act. He graciously autographed a copy of *Preachers and Preaching* for our pastor son, and I gave him a copy of my latest book, *Listening to the Giants*. He had written some nice things about the previous volume, *Walking with the Giants*, so I wanted him to have the sequel.

We discussed preachers, from John Henry Newman to George Morrison, and had a good time doing it. He was upset that I enjoyed Morrison's sermons. 'Nothing but poetry!' he said. 'No doctrinal substance!'

Had I known that we would have our last meeting on earth with the Doctor that evening, we would all have walked Dr and Mrs Lloyd-Jones to their train and lingered as long as possible. But we never know when our farewells are final. When we returned to London a few weeks later we telephoned their home, only to discover that the Doctor was in the hospital at Shepherds Bush and would be undergoing surgery. Apparently this was the beginning of the condition that finally took his life.

As I review our friendship with Dr Martyn Lloyd-Jones, and evaluate its impact on my own life and ministry, I am amazed at how so few personal contacts resulted in so much spiritual enrichment. However, it is my guess that my own evaluation will not be much different from that of others who have had the privilege of longer and deeper friendships with the Doctor.

My first impression was one of amazement that he should pay any attention to a young preacher and even agree to preach in our church. More than that, why should he even come to hear *me* preach? And why should he and his wife agree to dine with us? But we never felt that he was 'condescending'. He always showed a keen interest in young preachers and did all that he could to encourage them. He made you feel 'at home' with him, even though in your own mind you felt like a midget trying to make contact with a giant. This said to me, 'Wiersbe, if you ever get the opportunity, be an encouragement to other pastors. Don't get so "big" that you haven't time for the fellow who is just getting started.'

Another thing that impressed me was his amazing breadth of knowledge. It seemed that every book I mentioned was one he had read, and he could give me a digest of its contents. And yet all of this knowledge was under the discipline of the Word of God. He subjected everything to the light of the Word. I read widely (though not as widely as he did), and I am trying to follow his example of testing everything by Scripture.

The Doctor was first and foremost a student of the Bible and a preacher of the Word. 'This one thing I do!' could certainly be applied to his life and ministry. This has helped me tremendously, because I have a tendency to get too involved in too many good things, at the expense of weakening the best things. As I read his masterful expositions today, I sense anew the 'thrill of preaching.' If ever a preacher taught me to magnify the Word of God and the preaching of the Word, it was Dr Martyn Lloyd-Jones. By his example and his teaching he has encouraged me to take preaching seriously. Surely he agreed with Spurgeon's admonition to his students, 'Brethren, avoid anything like trifling over sermon-making.' Or with the old Puritan who said, 'Thou art a preacher of the Word: mind thy business!'

This does not mean that I have always agreed with him, and I said so when I reviewed *Preachers and Preaching* for one of our leading Christian periodicals. It is tragic to see young ministers imitating the Lloyd-Jones approach but lacking the Lloyd-Jones ability. It takes a gifted man to preach verse-by-verse (almost word-by-word) through a book, and hold his congregation spellbound. Not every preacher is supposed to do that. I agree with the Doctor that expository preaching is the best way to preach, but every man must be true to his own gifts.

The Doctor encouraged me to trust the power and authority of the Word of God, and to get from the Word the message God wanted me to bring. He helped me to see that an outline is not necessarily a message, and that the development of the message must come from the text itself and not be forced on it from without. A preacher with 'a gift of gab' could find a sermon in almost any text, but would it be an authoritative message from God? I find that my own standards for preaching have been raised much higher because of my contact with Dr Lloyd-Jones.

I know that at one time the Doctor declared that all

Evangelicals should leave the liberal denominations and unite in one witness. Others know more about this matter than I do and I will leave the judgment to them. What I do know is that Dr Lloyd-Jones helped to teach me to have a heart big enough for all of God's people, no matter what 'label' they might wear. I recall one discussion we had about John Henry Newman, whom Lloyd-Jones called 'the most brilliant preacher in Oxford at that time.' Certainly the Doctor did not agree with Newman's theology (he called his *Lectures on Justification* 'abominable'), but he saw what was good in his life and ministry.

From all my contacts with the Doctor—our intermittent personal visits, hearing him preach, reading his books—the one thing that stands out is his great ambition and desire to glorify the Lord. To him, preaching was a solemn act of worship, not an opportunity to display knowledge or ability. I must confess that there are times when the awesomeness of preaching God's Word just overwhelms me. I am sure that part of that attitude has come from my friendship with Dr Lloyd-Jones. I hope I never forget the lesson.

If during his lifetime, I had dared to dedicate one of my books to Dr Lloyd-Jones, I would have borrowed a dedication that Dr John Hutton penned for Campbell Morgan years ago:

To
Dr D. Martyn Lloyd-Jones
Known of all men
as a preacher;
Known to his friends
as the kindest of men.

Chapter Fifteen

THE ENCOURAGER

by

Henry Tyler

The Rev Henry Tyler served for many years as a Baptist pastor in north-east London and Felixstowe. He is now an elder at Clarendon Church in Hove, and through his membership of the Coastlands team has a wide ministry in India, Hungary, Mexico and the USA. He is also a speaker at the annual Downs Bible Week.

I was in my late teens when I first met Dr Martyn Lloyd-Jones. I had seen him from afar on a number of occasions in the pulpit. The first time I heard him preach was on the disciples' question to Jesus, 'Why could we not cast him out?' After 40 years I can still remember the masterly way he expounded this section of God's Word. Now, introduced to him personally, I was an over-awed and tongue-tied teenager before the 'great preacher.' But there was one thing the Doctor never ceased to be. He was to the last a kindly physician and, sensing my fears, he sought to put me at ease. That earliest recollection left me with the impression of his genuine love and concern and, at the end of it all, I felt I had found a friend.

The introduction had come about because the Doctor had become president of the mission in south London which I had attended as a child, where I had been taught the Scriptures and learned the way of salvation. It was one of a number of missions that were affiliated to Spurgeon's Tabernacle and the superintendent at that time was Mr A. Waghorn, who had become a member of Westminster Chapel. He was a forceful, if somewhat strange, character and he managed to persuade the Doctor to become our honorary president.

I think there were two factors which must have helped the Doctor to agree to this. In the first place, the mission was situated in a very poor locality and Dr Lloyd-Jones, like the Lord Jesus, had an innate compassion for the poor, utterly divorced from any condescending manner or attitude. Secondly, it was a mission that taught the doctrines of grace, so it was from my Sunday school teacher there that I learned that God had given a people to His Son in the eternal covenant; that all the elect would certainly be saved: that those who believed are justified and God would so work in them by His indwelling Spirit that they would be enabled to walk in holiness and at last be glorified, conformed to the image of God's Son. These truths have never ceased to thrill me, for thrilling they are indeed. So thoroughly were these truths taught that for years afterwards I was under the impression that this was common teaching among all Evangelicals! But good teaching can be wrongly applied. The doctrine of election has been sadly distorted by some, leading to a failure to evangelize or to engage in fervent prayer for the salvation of the lost. Not a few have fallen into this sad error, forgetting the principle enshrined in God's word to Abraham, 'I will bless you and make you a blessing.' God blessed Israel that she might be a light to the nations. Christ builds His church that we may go into all the world and preach the Gospel. This was the balance which obtained at the mission. It was a Spurgeonic ethos and we know that the Doctor felt very much at home in such an atmosphere.

The duties of the mission president were not onerous, but it did mean that every year he appeared either to preside or to preach at the annual meeting. These visits also provided opportunities for the workers to meet him and so, being a Sunday school teacher at that time, I was introduced to the Doctor. Another annual event was the visit to the circus at Olympia in London. Each year at Christmastime the Bertram Mills circus sent a batch of tickets for the deprived children of London to have an evening at the circus. Those who knew the Doctor will not be surprised to hear that he excused himself from this presidential duty, sending Mrs Lloyd-Jones to deputise for him!

In my early '20's I entered theological college to train for the ministry and, on completion of my course, received from the mission workers a token of their love. This was presented by the Doctor with loving words of commendation and prayer for blessing upon my future ministry. From that point on the Doctor took an unfailing interest in me and the various churches I was called to serve. Within a year or two of beginning my first ministry I was asked to preach at the mission annual meeting, the Doctor to preside. If I was over-awed at our first meeting, I was petrified at the thought of preaching before the Doctor in the place where I had been 'brought up.' But again his sympathetic and sincere welcome calmed my fears and afterwards his words of encouragement were all the more appreciated, because I knew he would not say anything he did not sincerely mean. Many a time afterwards I was to be blessed with his counsel and encouragement, never failing to be impressed with his ability to speak the truth in love.

Early in my ministry I became a member of the Westminster Fellowship. In those early days we met on Tuesdays in one of the vestries at Westminster Chapel, and when I joined there were no more than about 25–30 members. The standard of debate was very high indeed and the Doctor relished the cut and thrust of debate with men like the Anglican, Alan Stibbs, and Dr E. F. Kevan of the London Bible College. Over the years the number of ministers attending rose to hundreds, and I sensed that the Doctor was in his element in this scene. Next to his pulpit and preaching, this was the place where he loved to be—among men who were called to the ministry, loved the Word of God and were seeking to understand it.

It was the practice to begin the day with some biblical theme, some question of exegesis or doctrine. The second section would be devoted to pastoral or practical issues. Needless to say, there was a certain amount of overlap here because the Doctor never ceased to remind us 'every scripture and doctrine has its practical application.' In these sessions we were made to think, and think deeply, about the implications of what we believed and what we were preaching, so the Doctor would be known to interject and question the speaker on any point that he had made, throwing him back upon what the Bible said and not what the contributor *thought* it said. Woe to the man who misquoted the scripture. The Doctor never let that pass unchallenged. When he thought that a man was on the wrong track or had misunderstood the biblical teaching in question, he would probe and question, eliciting from the man his answers. Then he would face him with the implications of his teaching in order to make him *see* where he had gone wrong. The Doctor referred to this as the Socratic method of teaching, which he had known and used in medical training. In south London, where I had been brought up, we used to call it 'giving a man enough rope with which to hang himself.' I have seen many a ministerial Haman build a gallows only to hang on it himself! We learned the hard way—but we learned!

The Doctor took a great personal interest in the men who attended the Westminster Fellowship, and made himself available to them. Many took the opportunity to seek from him counsel for some personal or pastoral troubles. These were valuable times because, however many men were waiting to see him, he never gave the impression of being rushed or hurried but liberally gave of his time and counsel.

In the early years of the Fellowship we would go on an annual outing to Welwyn Garden City with a rich repast for lunch prepared by the church there. This gave us the opportunity to fellowship in less formal surroundings, and it was an added insight to discover the Doctor's weakness for ice-cream on these occasions!

Having access to the Doctor placed one in very good stead to invite him to preach. He was always willing to accede to requests of this nature when his diary allowed. The usual procedure was to write and then perhaps he would phone and, with a little juggling of the dates, the arrangements would be firmed up and secured. Dr Lloyd-Jones preached in each of the three Baptist chapels which I pastored. On the last occasion when he did this, he ministered on 2 Peter 1:1 from the words 'like precious faith.' It was, in every sense, an outstanding sermon preached with a rich anointing of the Spirit. Two men who were present that evening told me a week or two later that they had been so blessed by the Word of God that, on the way home and for some days afterwards, they had tried to analyse why it had had such an impact upon them. They had come to the conclusion that, and I now quote, '...he had made God to be so great and glorious that (they) were foolish not to trust Him more.' When I recounted this to the Doctor he was greatly encouraged in God that those men had been blessed by his ministry and was delighted that they had expressed it in that particular way.

I was present on several notable occasions when the Doctor's preaching ministry was outstanding. I vividly remember an Evangelical Alliance meeting where the Doctor was the only Evangelical on the platform. He was the closing speaker; the other main speaker was the late Sir Stafford Cripps, Chancellor of the Exchequer in the post-war Labour government. The size of the congregation was enormous, every seat being taken and people standing in every available space they could find. We had been treated in the meeting to a mixture of humanistic platitudes with a veneer of religion. The Chancellor had urged us to pray harder, for then we would work harder and, as we worked harder, our national production would rise, exports would increase and our economic problems would be solved and, with them, all other national ills too. One sensed, in listening to all this, that the Doctor could not wait for his turn to speak! When he did, his message was like a thunderbolt from heaven. With tremendous courage and clarity he enlarged upon the need and necessity of new birth. With a passion reminiscent of Whitefield, he pressed home the truth upon all present, both in the pew and on the platform—'you must be born again.'

Another memorable occasion was also under the auspices of the Evangelical Alliance, at the Central Hall, Westminster. By this time the Alliance had reverted to its original evangelical basis and this was the occasion of the historic call by the Doctor for Evangelicals to leave their doctrinally mixed denominations and work together as evangelical churches, 'one in faith and doctrine, one in charity.' This call once again showed his immense courage. Although it largely fell on deaf ears I believe there was a prophetic element in his message, which God will vindicate in His time. It is interesting that today many are seeing how denominations effectively divide the one body of Christ and the fact that they have no basis in Scripture is causing many to sever their connections with denominational bodies. I believe that this is a movement which will accelerate and grow.

Over the years the Doctor came on several occasions to the Baptist Revival Fellowship annual conference. All his ministry on these occasions was of a very high level, but one year in particular excelled them all. He ministered to us from Romans 14:17: 'For the kingdom of God is not meat and drink but righteousness and peace and joy in the Holy Ghost.' We were treated to a session on each clause, each session rising higher and higher in faith and joy. It was exhilarating ministry, giving us an experience like that of the two who walked with Jesus on the road to Emmaus. Our 'hearts burned within us as he talked by the way and while he opened to us the scriptures.' The Doctor followed closely the efforts of the Baptist Revival Fellowship to maintain an evangelical witness within the Baptist denomination. When a Principal of one of the Baptist colleges gave an address at the annual assembly which cast reflection on the deity of Christ, a protest was mounted, spearheaded by the committee of the Baptist Revival Fellowship. But to no avail. The Baptist Union refused to censure or remove the Principal from his post. As a consequence a number of ministers— all too few, alas—felt obliged to sever their connection with the Union. The sympathy and help afforded by the Doctor at this time was of enormous benefit.

Some of my best memories of the Doctor are of private conversations held with him in various places at various times. I remember one morning meeting him in the Evangelical Library. He had come to stock up with books for his annual holiday and I had come because my books were overdue! We sat for hours as he reminisced of men and movements in church history. His anecdotes about preachers were spellbinding—memories of some he had heard in Wales and comments on preachers from settings and generations other than his own, such as the older Methodists like Dinsdale Young and Samuel Chadwick. His fund of stories seemed limitless, concerning his predecessor, Dr Campbell Morgan, or other preachers as diverse as Jonathan Edwards and D. L. Moody—all this with enlivening comments upon the evangelical scene past and present.

In the late '60's I had become involved much more with what is commonly known as the charismatic movement, and I never ceased to marvel at how informed the Doctor was about this. When we met he would ask me endless questions about what was happening among the various 'house churches' that were springing up in many places, and when communes and communal living became the fashion among some he wisely pointed out the dangers of breaking the natural family unit, illustrating this with examples from church history. On one occasion he asked me if I had heard or met an Anglican minister who had received some prominence in the press for his healing ministry. He knew all about him and how he had come into that new measure of the Spirit in his ministry, and he urged me to go and hear him for myself.

The Doctor had some reservations about the charismatic movement in general—for instance the tendency of some charismatics to compromise with Rome; in no way would he ever countenance that. He felt too that the time given to singing in charismatic meetings was inordinately long. I tried to explain that this was not mere singing for singing's sake but prolonged worship and delighting in God. I don't think I ever quite succeeded in convincing him on this point! On one occasion, thinking that it would please him, I told him how the charismatics were now singing many psalms and portions of scripture. He gave me a wry smile and said, 'Good. Perhaps they will now stop singing those awful choruses.'

But, these apart, the Doctor was glad of the renewed emphasis upon the baptism in the Holy Spirit. He welcomed the gifts of the Spirit but needed to be assured that they were genuine and not spurious. He told me of his pleasure in reading an article by Arthur Wallis which appeared in *Theological Renewal*, where the writer had argued scripturally and cogently for the baptism of the Spirit as a distinct and separate work of the Holy Ghost coming upon the people of God. Arthur Wallis had written this article to counteract teaching which sought to explain the baptism of the Spirit as the release of the Spirit which we received in first coming to Christ, or, as the Catholics believed, at baptism. This was a view that the Doctor felt to be unscriptural and he was greatly encouraged to see such a view refuted in print by a leading figure among the charismatics.

I think back upon the many times that the Doctor encouraged me in my ministry among charismatic churches, urging me to go on expounding the Scriptures, emphasising the need to maintain the balance between the Word and Spirit. From time to time he graciously told me that he had heard of my ministry in various parts of the country. He had also heard adverse reports and frequently he said to me, 'Do not pay too much attention to the criticisms—Press on with God and work for His glory.' This was a tremendous encouragement at a time when many former friends seemed to be less friendly!

In the later years of the Doctor's life my colleague, Terry Virgo, and I had reason to visit him in his home in Ealing. We shared fully with him our vision to see the church restored. He made some very significant comments upon the state of the church and concluded with this statement: 'Evangelicalism is dead. God must do a new thing.' His conviction that the only answer for the church was the Holy Spirit sent down from heaven in revival grew increasingly and never faded in any way. Right to the last it was his hope, his prayer and his desire.

I cannot conclude this article without referring to the Doctor's intense interest in my physical health. At my last pastorate in London I was dogged with periods of illness—it was literally one thing after another. I recovered from one malady only to succumb to something else. Dr Lloyd-Jones was wonderfully solicitous of me, exhibiting that extraordinary blend of pastor and physician. I remember how he telephoned me one morning to enquire how things were with me. At that time I was suffering from a slipped disc; the pain had steadily increased and the treatment given at the local hospital (carefully charted by Dr Lloyd-Jones) had left me feeling like the woman in the gospels of whom it was said 'she had suffered at the hands of many physicians and was nothing bettered, but rather grew worse.' On this particular day I informed the Doctor in answer to his question that I was standing speaking to him in agony and did not know what to do to get relief. He immediately said that obviously the treatment was not right for the condition and suggested that I obtain another opinion. This he undertook to arrange for me and within half an hour had made an appointment for me with a consultant in Harley Street. The consultant told me that I needed to be hospitalized for complete bed-rest. On learning this, Dr Lloyd-Jones in co-operation with Dr Marjorie Blackie, a member of Westminster Chapel, obtained a hospital bed for me. All the arrangements were made by the Doctor. It was characteristic of him to take such pains, fulfilling the law of Christ and bearing another's burden.

I remember, too, the last conversation I had with the Doctor after a session of the Westminster Fellowship, when he was again enquiring after my health. I told him that I had been having problems with my hearing and he himself had known the same affliction. He counselled me to go back to my men and get them to anoint me with oil in the name of the Lord and seek the Lord for my healing. Such was this man of true sympathy, of faith and of fidelity to the Word of God. As I look back over my life I count it to be one of the greatest privileges to have known the Doctor. I thank God for the many blessings that came to me through him. Many will speak, and rightly so, of the Doctor's gifts, his amazing abilities as a preacher and teacher and his world-wide influence, but for me he was a true friend and one who always left me with the impression that he genuinely loved me. For that I thank God with all my heart.

Chapter Sixteen

THE FRIEND

by

G. N. M. Collins

Professor G. N. M. Collins is the Professor
Emeritus of Church History at the Free
Church of Scotland College in Edinburgh. A
friend of Dr Lloyd-Jones for over 40 years, he
was a frequent preacher at Westminster
Chapel during the Doctor's ministry there.

When I say that I was introduced to Dr Lloyd-Jones before I had actually met him, I had better explain myself. Some time in early 1936, while attending a conference in London, a fellow-member of conference told me with great enthusiasm of a Bible Testimony Fellowship which he had attended in the Albert Hall, London, in December of the previous year. The Marquis of Aberdeen had presided, and the principal speakers had been the Rev E. A. Carter, Mr Lindsay Glegg and Dr D. M. Lloyd-Jones.

'Their addresses are all there,' he remarked, handing me a brown booklet. 'You can read it on the train tomorrow, and I'm sure you'll enjoy it.' (He was right. I did.)

The chairman and the first two speakers I had heard on more than one occasion. The last was a complete stranger to me. Of course, I had heard of the medical consultant who had thrown everything away—as some judged his action— to become a preacher in a relatively obscure township in his native Wales. Naturally, he had become a centre of interest in religious circles; the strangeness of his decision would make sure of that.

But would the euphoria last? Wasn't it rather impulsive and imprudent on the part of the Sandfields people to enlarge their church buildings to accommodate the growing

252

congregation? Sensation-seekers in church movements are notoriously fickle. Better wait and see.

This was the background of my thought when, the following day, as my friend had suggested, I took up the brown booklet he had given me. I went straight to the address delivered by the preacher who had become such a centre of interest. It gripped me at once and, as I read on, the grip tightened. This new voice in evangelism had the authentic accent of apostolic teaching. This was the kind of thing he was saying.

> Our business, our work, our first call is to declare in a certain and unequivocal manner, the sovereignty, the majesty, the holiness of God; the sinfulness and the utter depravity of man, his total inability to save and to rescue himself; and the sacrificial, expiatory, atoning death of Jesus Christ, the Son of God, on that cross on Calvary's hill, and His glorious resurrection, as the only hope of human salvation.
>
> We must go back to the old position and declare the justice and righteousness of God as well as the love of God. We must go back and emphasise once more the wrath of God as well as the mercy of God; and we must picture salvation, not merely as something that makes people feel nice and happy and comfortable, but first and foremost as the one and only means of saving them from hell and from the wrath of God and sin's punishment. At any rate, as I read my Bible, that is the only method of evangelization I find there, as it is the only method of evangelization that you find in the patristic, evangelical fathers, as it was the great evangelical method of the Protestant Reformers, as it was the great method of George Whitefield and John Wesley, and all the great leaders of the evangelical awakening of the 18th century.

And that was how, as the Flying Scotsman thundered its way to its Scottish terminus on a day in January 1936, I was introduced to Dr D. Martyn Lloyd-Jones. Three years were yet to pass before I met him personally. In the interval he had left Sandfields and taken up the challenge of a pastorate in London, as minister of Westminster Chapel.

It was in 1939 that we first lured him to Edinburgh. A local committee had engaged him for a week's meetings in the Usher Hall, and there, night after night, he held forth to the crowds who came, and kept coming, to hear the Gospel of saving grace preached as few of them had ever heard it preached before; the very message that, in Scotland's past, had reared a race of spiritual giants who, at the counted risk of persecution, imprisonment and even martyrdom, had set their hands to bonds which ranged them on the side of Christ and His church in the period of the covenants.

Personally, I remember those meetings in Edinburgh as marking the beginning of a friendship that I prized more and more with the passing years. There was a racial affinity, of course; we were both of Celtic strain. There was a community of interests; we were both lovers of history and Christian biography. In theology, we were Calvinists.

We had him back in Edinburgh in 1941 to lecture in the Free Church College. It had become the custom of the Senate to invite outstanding Reformed scholars from overseas to deliver short courses of lectures in the college from time to time; but during the war years the usual sources of supply were cut off. So it came about that in 1941 Dr Lloyd-Jones was the visiting lecturer. The meetings were made open to the public who, from the outset, packed the presbytery hall to overflowing. Seats and chairs were set in adjoining rooms, as far as the voice could be expected to carry, and many of the audience had to be content with hearing the speaker's voice and not seeing his face.

The lectures were later published under the title *The Plight of Man and the Power of God*. They were based on the second half of Romans 1—a passage which, as the speaker said, seemed to be written 'specially and specifically for our day.' Men today were exposed to the wrath of God for sin, and the prophets who were crying 'Peace, peace' and presenting their followers with a Gospel that made no mention of repentance were thereby demonstrating their own falsity. Not until men learned to look to the Cross through tears of repentance would they see the glory of the grace that meets the sinner at the very lowest level of his need, and enter into the new hope which the Christian Gospel alone presents. The times were serious. The plight of man on the moral and spiritual side was truly alarming, and it presented the church with a challenge which she must not minimise nor try to evade. The trivial message of the 'Liberal' pulpit had been proved totally inadequate to meet the existing situation. A bewildered society was asking, as in the days of Zedekiah, albeit incoherently, 'Is there any word from the Lord?' And again the answer came, 'There is.' It was a message that would not charm the ear until it had first stabbed the conscience. But it had to be spoken, 'whether they will hear, or whether they will forbear.' It was 'criminal,' said Dr Lloyd-Jones, 'to look at life through rose-coloured spectacles...The time has arrived when the situation of the world must be dealt with and considered in a radical manner....We must be prepared to be cruel to be kind.'

It is no exaggeration to say that such strong, forthright preaching, so Biblical in character, so relevant to the contemporary situation and delivered with such passionate conviction, put new heart into the praying people of all denominations who gathered to hear him. The plight of man was indeed desperate, but the power of God is sufficient to 'save to the uttermost' all who come to Him by Christ.

In his vestry, one evening, as we talked of former ministers of the Chapel, Dr Lloyd-Jones referred to Dr John A. Hutton, who was minister there for a short time before becoming editor of *The British Weekly*. Dr Lloyd-Jones had often gone to hear Dr Hutton in earlier London days, he said, for he reckoned him a man of great pulpit gifts. After he himself became minister at the Chapel, Dr Hutton sometimes went to hear him. On one of these occasions, as they talked together in front of the pulpit, John Hutton looked up and remarked reminiscently, 'Ay, it's a great pulpit, *when you've got a sermon to match it.*'

And Martyn Lloyd-Jones always had, for he invariably dealt with great themes of Biblical revelation, and especially the one in which all the rest are comprehended, 'Jesus Christ and Him crucified.' The first Free Church of Scotland pulpit that Dr Lloyd-Jones ever preached from was Free St Columba's, Edinburgh—the former Free St John's, built in 1845 to accommodate Dr Thomas Guthrie and his congregation who had broken with the establishment at the Disruption of 1843.

When we decided on the ways in which we were to celebrate the centenary of the Church in 1945, the man I most wanted as the special preacher for the occasion was Dr Lloyd-Jones. When I broached the matter to him he wondered why my choice had fallen on him, and, as a lead-in to my reply, I told him a story relating to Thomas Guthrie's ministry. Guthrie's son, David, became minister of Liberton Free Church in 1856 while his father was still in St John's. A woman who frequently dropped in to hear Thomas Guthrie decided to hear David for herself and see how he compared with his father. Now David, it would seem, was a solid doctrinal preacher, but entirely lacking in the spell-binding eloquence of his father; so this was how she compared them. 'Ah weel, Tammas has mair diveersity than Dauvit; but Dauvit has mair diveenity than Tammas.'

So, I said, I wanted both ingredients, in the proportions that make for good preaching! Would he come?

He smiled, and shook his head deprecatingly. But he came, and was in his very best form. At the morning service he preached on Peter's deliverance from prison (Acts 12:5); and, in the evening, on entering in by the strait gate... (Matt 7:13, 14). It was superb preaching, and even after 40 years it is easy to recapture the thrill of that memorable day.

He had to return to London sooner than he had intended

on that occasion, cutting out an engagement at Newcastle
by the way. The war in Europe was in its closing stage, and
he had made it known before leaving London that he would
be holding a service of thanksgiving in the Chapel on the
evening of the day after the cessation of hostilities was
announced; and the announcement might come any day. It
came on 9 May. The following evening a service was held in
Westminster Chapel as planned.

I was in London, preaching at the quarterly Gaelic service in Crown Court Church the following Lord's Day, and
I worshipped in the Chapel that evening.

'What text did you take at your thanksgiving service?' I
asked the Doctor when I joined him in his vestry afterwards.

'Hitler's text,' he replied.

'Which was—?'

He quoted Psalm 37:35, 36: *I have seen the wicked in great
power, and spreading himself like a green bay tree. Yet he passed
away, and, lo, he was not: I sought him, but he could not be found.*
'Could anything have been more prophetic?' he remarked.

It was the Doctor's visit to Edinburgh in connection with
our church centenary services that gave us the privilege of
having him as our guest at the manse. And a privilege it
indeed was, notwithstanding that, at that time, he was a
complete faddist in his food! Cereals and porridge were at a
discount, but milk sprinkled with bemax was an acceptable
alternative—only we had no bemax! Fresh salmon we had,
but he would not eat *fresh* salmon; it had to be canned! Jams
too were under his ban at the time, but not honey. And if
honey was not available, golden syrup was an acceptable
substitute! It all added to the fun of the occasion as we
amended our menus!

Alex B. Murdoch—his friend and mine—told me of his
wife's regret when they learned, too late, on his first visit to
them, that he was very fond of apples, for it so happened
that at the time they had no apples in the house! When next
he was to stay with them they saw to it that they had apples

in plenty and variety. But by that time he was off apples!

He liked to have a packed lunch, with coffee, on long railway journeys, but when he proceeded to squeeze the cream for his coffee out of a tube, he noticed with concealed amusement that questioning glances were being furtively directed at him by fellow-passengers. 'I got the impression,' he said, 'that they thought I was squeezing toothpaste or shaving cream into my cup.'

As time went on, his eating habits became more normal. But, whatever the circumstances, his visits were always occasions of great joy. He entered fully into the family circle and was immediately at home with everybody. A fascinating conversationalist, he was a host in himself, and we loved to draw him out on subjects of common interest. His grave and even severe cast of countenance gave little hint of his keen sense of humour, but it was always there and ready to call. When we were alone in the study we invariably talked shop. Deeply versed in Puritan theology, his fuller study of Scottish theology opened to him a new vein of gold. He had early acquired a copy of Dr John Macleod's *Scottish Theology in Relation to Church History Since the Reformation*, and it was always at his hand for reference. At his request I did some book-hunting for him in Edinburgh in search of the more notable books that Dr Macleod had referred to, and quoted from, in his book. In this I had some success, but our biggest breakthrough came in Wales. We had gone to address some meetings in Bala under the auspices of the Evangelical Fellowship of Wales when a message was sent to us that the Theological College in Bala was closing down, and its library was being sold. We were offered the first pick from its shelves if we cared to go along.

The result was predictable! The programme for the next day was re-adjusted for the convenience of book-hungry ministers and students. Enough to say that a good time was had by all! The Doctor concentrated, for the most part on the Scottish section; and there we found most of the spiritual classics that I had been unable to procure for him from Scottish sources. By the time we finished, his heap of acquisitions, quantitatively and qualitatively, was truly impressive. He had come to share Principal Macleod's high admiration of Professor John ('Rabbi') Duncan, and in the Bala library he found copies of the two books relating to the 'Rabbi' that I had not been able to pick up for him—David Brown's fine biography of Dr Duncan, and William Knight's *Colloquia Peripatetica*.

William Knight was not of the same theological school as his Hebrew Professor, but he was a scholar whose keen mind and retentive memory made it easy for him to retain and recall the epigrams, aphorisms and pithy definitions that every now and then, like shafts of light, broke through the heavy prose of the set lecture, irradiating and epitomising the topics dealt with. I can hear the Doctor still, as he sat that evening reading out some of Knight's quotations:

'Augustine was greater than Calvin. Calvin is the more complete; no thanks to him for that, for Calvin was standing on Augustine's shoulders, Augustine on his own feet.'

'Hyper Calvinism is all house and no door. Arminianism is all door and no house!'

'God will neither take the blame of sin, nor alienate or split the praise of grace.'

'I preach a free Gospel to every man, or I don't preach the Gospel at all, but I know that its acceptance without the help of the Spirit is an impossibility....Calvinism is not inconsistent with a free Gospel.'

This was all grist to the Doctor's mill.

Dr Macleod's *Scottish Theology* brought home very forcibly to Dr Lloyd-Jones that there was very much more behind the Disruption of 1843 than the question of church and state relations. Incipient Liberalism was finding a willing ally in the Moderatism that had precipitated the conflict. The very constitution of the Reformed Church in Scotland was at stake and Dr Lloyd-Jones revered the men who rallied to its defence in the hour of crisis—especially Dr Thomas Chalmers and Dr William Cunningham. At a time when he was dealing with the doctrine of the Holy Spirit in his Friday evening lectures at the Chapel, I introduced him to Professor George Smeaton's Cunningham Lectures on the subject, with the result that they were reprinted by the Banner of Truth Trust with whom the Doctor's recommendations were almost mandates. 'Smeaton on the Holy Spirit,' he writes, 'provides in many ways the best practical teaching on this subject that I know.'

For Dr John Kennedy of Dingwall also—another of the Free Church leaders—he had a profound admiration, and when the Dingwall Free Church Presbytery invited him to address a series of meetings for them, he was genuinely thrilled to know that he would be preaching from the pulpit that Kennedy had made famous, and that had been occupied by C.H. Spurgeon at the opening services of the church in 1870. The Dingwall congregation were in the throes of building a new manse in 1970, and some had expressed their disappointment that it was not ready for occupancy by the time of his visit. 'But I had no regret in that connection,' he remarked to me afterwards. 'I shall always be glad that I slept under the roof that, for so long, sheltered John Kennedy, and where so many men of God gathered around him.' He loved to tread 'where the saints have trod'—the holy places where, in pre-Reformation days, the Scottish martyrs sealed their testimony with their blood; the grey buildings in Edinburgh and Glasgow where, in the second Reformation, the Covenanters gave their solemn oath to be loyal to 'Christ's Crown and Covenant,' whatever the cost; and to cast his eyes over the moors of the south-west Borders, and to 'hear about the graves of the martyrs the peewees crying,' and realise once more, as one is specially enabled to do in such surroundings, how truly Tertullian spoke when he said in the stormy dawn of Christian history, 'the blood of the martyrs is the seed of the church.'

The Doctor's critics sometimes alleged that he lived too much in the past, but the criticism fell flat. This remarkable man's life was completely dedicated to the service of God in the contemporary world. Like Bunyan's Christian, he liked his thoughts 'to wax warm about whither I am going,' and the recalling of the past had much to do with the warming. 'Whosoever desires to build a future may not neglect the past,' wrote Paul Kruger to Louis Botha. and Martyn Lloyd-Jones would have agreed. The voice of history—the 'word behind thee'—was a constant source of guidance for the present, and into the future, insisting 'this is the way, walk ye in it.' His optimism for the future arose from the fact that he believed the promises of God. And, like the Apostle, because he believed, he spake, and in such wise as to confirm the faith of others.

'Dr Lloyd-Jones is a man I greatly admire,' Professor Daniel Lamont once remarked to me as I drove him home after an evening spent with the Doctor. 'To be in his company for any time is always an inspiration. He makes my heart warm to the faith of our fathers.'

Many preachers could have borne similar testimony; young men especially, confused by the cross-currents of the Liberal theology in which they had been trained. Some said that he created a cult. If he did, it was not by intention. And it was justified by its results. 'Many young men,' writes Dr Douglas Johnson, former general secretary of the Inter-Varsity Fellowship, 'have felt that in him they had the support of the Rock of Gibraltar in their lonely stations.' The *Westminster Record* found its way into many Scottish manses and brought spiritual blessing and direction to its subscribers and the congregations whom they served.

Sometimes, during the Doctor's visits to Scotland, arrangements were made for informal meetings for the special benefit of these younger men, where they might address questions to him on matters that were causing them concern. His attitude to the modern ecumenical movement was well known but not always understood, and it frequently happened that requests were made for fuller elucidation.

On one of these occasions the chairman of the meeting invited him, as an experienced and far-travelled evangelist, to give an assessment of the church's work and witness today, as he saw it. In an age when iniquity abounded and the church seemed to be in the doldrums, was there any 'sound of a going in the tops of the mulberry trees' to suggest that the armies of heaven were mustering to regain lost territory and extend Christ's Kingdom?

Dr Lloyd-Jones gave a lucid and balanced account of the situation as he saw it, making special mention of the undoubted renewed interest in the Reformed message that was becoming so evident in various parts of the world. But the church must bestir herself and lay hold upon God in prayer. It was when Zion travailed that she brought forth her children.

When he finished, a local minister, not of his outlook, rose to suggest that the Doctor had passed over the most promising sign of all, the ecumenical movement. Why was that?

The Doctor replied that the relation of the modern ecumenical movement to the spiritual revival was hard to discover. It paid but scant respect to true unity in the faith and to the Biblical doctrine of the church. Rather it represented man's attempt to revive the church by his own methods.

'But surely,' persisted his questioner, 'when so many churches are coming together in a World Council of Churches, revival must be on the way.'

'You seem to be arguing,' came the reply, 'that if you succeed in bringing together a sufficient number of dead bodies they will come alive!' Ezekiel's vision of the dead bones in the valley suggested otherwise. There was motion; there was a coming together; but there was no 'breath'. Not until Ezekiel 'prophesied as He commanded me' did the dead bones live. There must be, on the part of the church, a humble submission to God's command, an unquestioning acceptance of His way as revealed in His word, before we can look for spiritual revival and Christian unity. Yet of the ultimate triumph of the church he had no shadow of doubt. 'I am not interested in times and seasons,' he declared at a great meeting which he shared with Professor Daniel Lamont in Glasgow at one of the darkest moments in the second world war. 'What I am interested in is that God has His plan as He has always done in the past. "How soon?" says someone. My reply is that with Him "a thousand years are as one day and one day as a thousand years." Yet in His own time God will act, in spite of sin and evil and Satan and hell, and "the kingdoms of this world will become the kingdoms of our God and of His Christ."'

In the journeys which took him to the Highland regions of Scotland Doctor Lloyd-Jones preached, on one or two occasions, in places where Gaelic was still the local language of worship. This meant that the sermon was in English and the rest of the service in Gaelic. Such an exercise in bi-lingualism presents its own difficulties, but the Doctor came through with ease. His facility for getting on to the wave-length of his audience, whoever they might be, was always quite remarkable. I once heard him preach an English sermon to a vast Afrikaans congregation in the Groote Kerk of Pretoria, to the evident appreciation of the people from first to last, although the discourse was up to the full West-minster Chapel measurement! I commented afterwards on the obvious ease with which he had fitted into a bi-lingual service and had held the interest of people accustomed to worshipping in another tongue. 'Perhaps,' he quipped, 'the tie helped.' The reference was to the flowing white tie of the Dutch predikant that he was wearing—the only concession to clerical usage that I ever knew him to make, except for the simple Geneva pulpit gown that he wore in the Chapel.

He owed nothing to the meretricious appeal of vestments or liturgy, or to the cheap novelties that too often disfigure modern evangelism. Resplendent personal gifts he had in abundance, but these were never paraded. Never have I known a man who could more fittingly join Paul in the great claim that the Apostle made for his own ministry: 'For we preach not ourselves, but Christ Jesus the Lord; and ourselves your servant for Jesus' sake.'

*　　*　　*　　*　　*

I was to preach in my old pulpit of St Columba's, Edinburgh on 1 March, 1981, and was in the vestry before the morning service when the church officer came in with a letter addressed to me. It was to inform me that the home-call had come to Dr Lloyd-Jones in the early hours of that morning. The news was not unexpected yet, for a moment, I felt stunned and numb. And then the room around me seemed to brighten with a light that was not of the sun, and my grief became tinged with a strange elation. The Doctor was not dead! His ministry was not ended! 'Blessed are the dead which die in the Lord from henceforth: Yea, saith the Spirit, that they may rest from their labours; and their works do follow them.'

It was this thought that came uppermost again in the closing words of the brief tribute that I paid him at the great memorial service held in Westminster Chapel a few weeks later when, speaking for the multitudes of Scottish people who mourned his passing, I concluded, 'We mourn with you the falling of a great standard-bearer; but we rejoice in his triumph, and in his ongoing ministry.'

AFTERWORD

by

Christopher Catherwood

'Logic on Fire!' This great phrase of my grandfather, Martyn Lloyd-Jones, 'The Doctor,' sums up in many ways what made him the outstanding man of God that he was, both as a man and as a preacher. It was the unique combination of these two things, so often separated today, that provides the key to a true understanding of him.

It could certainly be said to be true of him as a grandfather. He was more than simply the world's best grandfather, though he was, of course, that as well, both to me, his eldest, and to the other five. The logic came in around the meal table, especially when he came to stay with us in Balsham for several months of the year. Since his visits usually overlapped considerably with school and later university holidays, we used to see a lot of him. He would have spent much of the day busily at work on his manuscripts. (Now that I help to edit them, along with others in the family, I know how hard a task that must have been.) Quite possibly he would have taken a short break, immediately before the meal, in which time he and I would have played croquet against my mother and grandmother. He would apply his logic to getting the ball through the narrow metal hoops, working out the tactics with great skill, and giving me, his slightly erratic partner, the benefit of his advice. But logic, however powerful, could not usually defeat the 60 years and more experience of my grandmother, so that the ladies frequently won.

It is perhaps appropriate to add here that, humanly speaking, he would never have been the man he was but for my grandmother, Bethan. They were married for 54 blissfully happy years, and she was in every way the perfect wife for him. She was practical in everyday things in a way that he was not—often to the immense amusement of the family. We, the six grandchildren, knew them by the Welsh affectionate diminutives—Dadcu and Gu. When we were asked who was the leading partner in the home, we had to say, of our own parents, that they were evenly matched. But with our grandparents there was no doubt—'Gu' ran the home. My grandmother, a loving woman with strong character, is highly educated—she qualified as a doctor at University College Hospital in London in an age in which women seldom studied beyond school.

Yet she selflessly devoted those 54 years of her life to what she felt God had called her to do—support and look after her husband, the man she loved and, as she said, to 'keep him in the pulpit!' She would always give her opinions within the family circle—my grandfather esteemed her common sense very highly as well as her shrewdness and considerable knowledge of the Old Testament. She was— and remains—a fine judge of character. But in public she kept carefully in the background. Along with my mother she would in later years spend hours a day helping him to prepare his manuscripts for publication. A few years after his death she wrote a moving account of their early days in South Wales, which she never intended for publication. When *Memories of Sandfield* came out, she was amazed to see herself as an authoress for the first time, aged 85! With her innate modesty, she was genuinely astonished when it became a bestseller. But it was a fitting reward for her, as well as being a heartfelt tribute to all God had done through her and her husband in their first years together.

But once around the table, with all the family, my grandfather resumed his normal place as the centre of our attentions. He would raise a topic, which had struck him while preparing a sermon for publication or in the course of reading a book, and say something to provoke us into discussion. He would often have a mischievous twinkle in his eye as he egged on his three Catherwood grandchildren. Each one of us would respond with a vigour that no-one else dared in debating with him. We were, as my father has so aptly pointed out, like cubs around an old lion. We were also, of course, not his descendants for nothing! He had been raised in an atmosphere of discussion, despite his own father's lack of formal education, and he was determined, rightly, that we should be too. The same applied, although they were much younger, to family discussions in his London home with his three Desmond grandchildren, the children of his younger daughter Ann.

For his aim was also to make sure that each of us learned to think for ourselves. He was always most concerned that we should hold opinions not because he thought them— that would have been abhorrent to him—but because we had reasoned them out for ourselves, in a clear and logical manner. We should know why we believed what we did and be able to defend our view, especially against so formidable an adversary in debate! (He was, of course, very loving, including even towards some of our dottier opinions). This applied to all spheres of life; above all, naturally, to the spiritual. How biblically could we justify a particular interpretation? He would take us to the logic of our position and see where that left us.

In so doing he was using, as others have pointed out, the Socratic method instilled into him in his student days by Lord Horder. As he was deeply concerned to help each of his family with any problems that they might have, he was always available to give us his wisdom whenever we requested it. In retrospect this was an immense privilege. Here was this great and internationally distinguished man, whose advice was sought by countless Christians across the world, yet who would sit and listen to the personal problems, of no earth-shattering consequence in wider terms, of student and school-aged young people such as his grandchildren. He did so, of course, out of the deepest affection, sorting out our teenage traumas or heartaches in the way that often only a grandfather can. But he would deal with them in exactly the same way as those of the great. He would ask us questions, in a caring but always logical manner, so that in the end we had as often as not seen the solution to the particular problem for ourselves. Now that he has gone, he has left all of us who knew him, family, friends and followers alike, better equipped as Christian individuals to face the world into which God has put us.

The 'fire' applied to us as well. As I have mentioned, he was totally devoted to all his family circle. Nothing was too good for any of us and we all knew the great love that he felt for each one—a love that was fully reciprocated by oldest to youngest alike. Family gatherings were effortlessly enjoyable occasions as a result, Christmas included. Every Christmas morning he would be with us at Balsham, and with my grandmother would come down, before we went to church, into the dining room, where all the presents would be laid out. Here he would show one of his greatest qualities—that of enthusiasm.

He was genuinely interested in what each one of us received, however young we might be. He led me, from a very early age, to share with him his very deep love of history. As a teenager he had come to be fascinated in politics, spending hours in the gallery of the House of Commons listening to giants such as Churchill and Lloyd-George engaging in debate. For me, this was history, and I often used to receive books on that period as Christmas presents. So he would peer over to see which particular books I had chosen, adding his own reminiscences of the personalities and issues about which I was reading. When I went to Oxford to read Modern History his joy was all the greater. He always looked at the book reviews in the learned weeklies and Sunday quality papers, and would often draw a particular biography or study to my attention—maybe sometimes in the hope that I would have it for Christmas, so that he could discuss it with me. Now that he is no longer alive, Christmas has, in a very real sense, never been the same.

Through his warmth and enthusiasm he made himself irreplaceable in the lives of all of us, whether in discussion around the kitchen table, debating the issues of the day, or in playing lexicon, his favourite word game, when he used to joke with us and indulge his penchant for puns. The same applied to him as a croquet partner (I have yet to find another) or when giving advice. But the keys to what made him great are all revealed in these different facets of him as a family man, and it is to this that we must now turn.

'Logic on fire,' then, can be said to contain the secret of Martyn Lloyd-Jones. From where did it come? My grandfather was known, affectionately, to the wider world simply as 'The Doctor' invariably without any other qualifying phrase. Most of the contributors to this book refer to him by that name, and it is entirely right that they do so. For he was indeed a doctor—an M.D. of Barts hospital, London University. The fact that he was a *medical* doctor is the key to an understanding of his whole personality, along with his Welshness, with which I will deal later. It made the entire difference to the way in which he preached and also to the way in which he dealt with people and issues.

For, as I wrote earlier in this chapter, his medical studies at Barts under Lord Horder trained him in logical thinking, through the use of the 'Socratic method.' Horder taught his pupils how to think, and to his star pupil, Martyn Lloyd-Jones, he gave his copy of Jevon's famous work *Principles of*

Science: A Treatise on Logical and Scientific Method. Anyone
could see, after cursory examination, what a patient's outward symptoms might appear to be. But it often took
painstaking, careful diagnosis to discover what was *really*
wrong with the invalid and what the right treatment ought
to be. Illnesses could sometimes have a deeper cause than at
first met the eye, as the Doctor frequently found out when
he lent a hand to the perplexed physicians in South Wales
back in the 1920's.

The same principles applied, of course, to his preaching.
The world either failed to see that it was spiritually sick or
mistook the symptoms for the real disease. In his sermons
the Doctor would show the truth about the malady that
afflicted the human race. He would demonstrate, in a logical
way, the hopeless condition of people without a real knowledge of God and the sheer futility of all their remedies. But,
he would then proclaim, there was a cure, which came
through Jesus Christ crucified on the Cross to cleanse us
from our sins and to reconcile us to God the Father.

His medical training, combined with biblical insight and
teaching, can be seen above all in his most successful book,
Spiritual Depression, a work which has sold hundreds of
thousands of copies worldwide. It brings his doctor's skills
together with those of the experienced pastor, to produce a
uniquely powerful result. (I elaborate on this in the chapter
on him in *Five Evangelical Leaders.*) Often someone would
come to see him in his study, saying that they were spiritually downcast. Using the diagnostic method acquired at
Barts, my grandfather would start to ask questions. Sometimes he would realise that there was no actual spiritual
problem at all—the Christian in question was simply over-
tired and needed sleep or a good rest. On other occasions he
would spot a mental illness, and recommend suitable
psychiatric help. But the problem presented often was spiritual in scope, and my grandfather would reason with the
depressed individual from Scripture. This was itself impor-

tant—so often today popular psychology has replaced the Bible at the centre of our Christian lives. The Doctor never made that mistake—God's Word to us was paramount in all things.

It has been said, and it is true in a way, that my grandfather never laid too much store by apologetics. But he was always reasonable in his preaching, and never declamatory. He would take his listeners carefully through the great themes of scripture. To him all preaching was expository, stemming from the Word of God. This was, of course, one of the keys to his uniqueness. He hated the frenetic search to be topical for its own sake. To him he was there to proclaim the eternal Word of God to a lost humanity. On his tombstone in Wales is a quotation from Paul's first epistle to the Corinthians: 'For I determined to know nothing among you save Jesus Christ and Him crucified.' That was the essence of the whole thing to the Doctor. To be biblical was what mattered above all else, which is why he would refer, as Peter Lewis so rightly points out in his chapter, to the 'primacy of preaching.' He eschewed other methods because he did not believe them to be biblically based. In the New Testament, he felt, the Holy Spirit saw fit to use what to the world often seemed to be the 'foolishness' of preaching. But if a man spoke with the power and anointing of the Holy Spirit upon him, then God would use and bless the results to His own glory. What we were called upon to be was obedient and faithful both in our lives and in our proclamation of the Good News.

At the same time it must be added that he never ceased to be contemporary. While he opposed over-academic speakers who paraded their learning, his sermons always showed how up to date he was in his reading matter—quotations from articles by scientists such as the Nobel prize-winners Sir Peter Medawar or Sir John Eccles, references to contemporary thinkers such as Arthur Koestler or novelists like V. S. Naipaul and Anthony Burgess, and allusions to reviews and books by a historian such as Arnold Toynbee. Just after President Kennedy was assassinated, the Doctor was able to show how while the tragic death of that man would not be able to bring the peace and unity which the world sought, the glorious death of Christ on the Cross was the only hope for a divided, fallen world.

Another area in which the Doctor demonstrated his considerable intellect was in the whole theological field. Although a medical doctor—or maybe *because* he was medically, not theologically, trained—his influence on the theological scene in both Britain and the USA was enormous. This can be seen at proper length in the two outstanding contributions in this book by J. I. Packer and Philip Edgcumbe Hughes respectively. There is no doubt that my grandfather was, in Britain at least, one of the people most responsible for the renewed interest in Reformed, and in particular Puritan, theology. (It should perhaps be said here that at the same time my grandfather reserved his special affection for the giants of the *18th* century revival—a picture of Whitefield preaching hung in the entrance hall of his London home.) But he always emphasised that he was a Bible Calvinist, not a system Calvinist. It is possible to take logic too far.

The Puritans lead one naturally on to the other half of the equation: 'fire!' As Hywel Jones points out, one of the Doctor's greatest concerns was that doctrine should never remain arid but should lead one to 'life' in the fullest and most Biblical sense. The Puritans, as Jim Packer so rightly shows, were not the dour people of popular mythology— they were profoundly joyous, as indeed all true Christians should be. To them, Christian faith should be 'experimental,' or, in 20th century English, doctrine ought to be experienced at the deepest levels of everyday Christian living as well as being simply known and believed in. One of the keys to my grandfather was the stress that he laid in knowing church history, and the lessons that the past have for us today. If one reads his works one sees the Puritans referred to either explicitly—as for example, in *Joy Unspeakable*—or implicitly, in a Puritan way of thinking, in his great series on Ephesians.

The Puritans were, in the main, English, but if it could be said that the Doctor had the 'logic' instilled into him at Barts, the 'fire' was in his veins through his Welsh birth and upbringing. It was perhaps appropriate that the day of his death—1 March, 1981—was not just a Sunday but also the national day of his beloved Wales. He never ceased to be patriotic, even though most of his life and ministry was outside his native land. He was called the 'last of the Calvinistic Methodists,' and that group was a uniquely Welsh combination of two usually separated strands in Christian history. For they brought together the logic and doctrine of Calvinism with the fire and emotion of the 18th-century Methodist revival.

Many of my grandfather's heroes came from the area in which he had been raised in South Wales, the leaders of the 18th-century revival in Wales, such as Daniel Rowlands and Howel Harris. Occasionally, from childhood on, I would be with him when he visited relations who still lived on the family farm at Llwyncadfor. We would go to Newcastle Emlyn, where his wife's grandfather, Evan Phillips, had played his part during the great Welsh Revival of 1904–5. There is a marvellous photograph of both of us, taken when I was two years old, standing together in front of the statue of Daniel Rowlands. (I have my hand in the air, imitating the preacher!) When he died my grandfather was buried in the cemetery not far away, near the river on the outskirts of the town.

The Doctor, as Leith Samuel has shown, had a lifelong passion for revival, one which he especially emphasised towards the end of his life. It was, as Jim Packer demonstrates, very much in the mould of that 18th-century American giant, Jonathan Edwards. But it was also very

Welsh, and it was more than fitting that my grandfather's funeral service should have taken place in Evan Phillips' old church. For it was not simply a Welsh service, with all the addresses in Welsh. It was also symbolic. This was where he belonged, not just nationally but spiritually—where God's Holy Spirit had poured out revival and where, my grandfather trusted, He would do so again. I was a pall-bearer at the funeral, and although the occasion was, for us, a sad one, nevertheless there was a great note of triumph of a faithful saint gone to his reward, highlighted by the power of a throng of Welsh voices singing with their special might.

It was his zeal to see revival that was in many ways, I think, a major factor in forming his views on the baptism with the Holy Spirit, an experience which he separated from conversion. By no means all of his friends and followers agreed with him on this, as is obvious from the different views on the subject contained in this book. On the one hand, as Henry Tyler points out, my grandfather encouraged many in the charismatic movement. On the other, he was always insistent on caution—phenomena, he preached, should never determine our beliefs, and we should test all things by Scripture. Furthermore, as Hywel Jones reminds us, the Doctor would tell ministers that whatever the problems that might arise, they were those created by 'life'— how many of those who condemned could be said to have an overabundance of spiritual life in their churches?

His views on all this reveal another key to the man—his profoundly biblical sense of balance. This can be seen in his treatment of the sealing of the Spirit in his Ephesians series, and in the two volumes which he edited in his lifetime but which were published posthumously, on John's Gospel: *Joy Unspeakable* and *Prove All Things*. On the one hand he believed in the baptism with the Holy Spirit—a view that pleased many of his more charismatic friends—but on the other he believed deeply in the sovereignty of the Holy Spirit, which meant that he opposed the idea that one could 'claim' a gift or teach that one had to evidence any particular gift in order to claim that one had been baptized. As time went on, he felt that a lot of Reformed doctrine had become in danger of turning theoretical or arid. We needed the power of the Holy Spirit to fill us anew and to revive us with power. But his perspective remained Reformed, in his stress on the sovereignty of the Giver and the need continuously to prove all things from Scripture to see whether or not they were from God. He rejected all man made systems or formulae and sought to return all those who listened to him to the Word of God. As Robert Horn has said, he defied all categorisers and remained bigger than those, on both sides, who tried to claim him exclusively for themselves.

Such attempts were often amusing to the family. I was once in the Far East and visited the minister of a church in Tsimshatsui. He was an Australian, who had been in Borneo. Friends of his in Canada had told him that my grandfather had become a Pentecostal—was this true? It was hard not to laugh, because not long before I had been in the north of England, where a minister whose sympathies were very different told me categorically that the Doctor was of the view that David Watson was the best of a bad bunch! As often happens with truly great men, followers and enthusiasts will impute their views to their hero, cheerfully regardless of what he actually thought. It was, perhaps fittingly, the Doctor's followers in Wales who best understood that one could believe in the baptism with the Holy Spirit without becoming Pentecostal and while remaining Reformed.

Another area where old friends disagreed was on the subject of ecclesiastical separation—his call, made in 1966, for Evangelicals to pull out of theologically mixed denominations such as the Church of England or Baptist Union into a purely evangelical affiliation. One can contrast the contributions in this book of John Stott and Jim Packer on the one hand with that of Hywel Jones on the other. (I

have dealt with this issue in chapters on Packer and Martyn
Lloyd Jones in *Five Evangelical Leaders*.) The call, which he
felt to be a prophetic one, did not meet with the response
that he might have expected, although that would never
have prevented him from making it. One of the keys to him
as a man was that he never compromised on what he felt to
be right. Partly, the reason was that people saw it as primarily negative—'come out'—rather than the positive
summons that he intended it to be—'come out so that you
may come in.' But the other reason was, perhaps, that the
Doctor's Welshness prevented him from appreciating fully
the deep loyalty to the Church of *England* that bound the
Anglicans to their denomination. They wanted to stay in it,
as they hoped, to rescue it. For his followers in mixed
denominations in Wales no such extra ties existed, and
several of them followed his call. Ironically, and we used to
tease him about this, his wife's cousin was the Anglican
Archbishop of Wales!

But, as John Stott points out, my grandfather always
distinguished between principles and personalities, and his
relations on an individual level with Anglican friends usually remained unaltered. He was, and this was another key
to his greatness, a profoundly humble man. Although never
afraid to proclaim his beliefs, he was generous in spirit. As a
young minister said of him, he was a lion in the pulpit but a
lamb in the vestry. He deplored the personality cult that
would surround distinguished Christian leaders—which is
why he allowed no biography of himself to appear in his
lifetime. He never sought to build ecclesiastical empires but
simply to proclaim the truth.

He has, however, left a considerable memorial, one that
owed a lot, in human terms, to his Welshness. This was the
International Fellowship of Evangelical Students—IFES.
Westminster Chapel had, through most of his time there, a
strongly multiracial congregation. Many of those from the
Third World were students. One of them, Daniel Arap Moi,

is now president of Kenya. Another, Gottfried Osei-Mensah, became executive head of the Lausanne Committee for World Evangelism, a body that arose out of the Congress which Billy Graham organised in 1974. A third, Chua Wee-hian, is now general secretary of IFES itself and a contributor to this book. As he points out, the Doctor's Welshness enabled him in a unique way to understand the feelings of Christians from the Third World. England had invaded and conquered his country too! Because of this the Doctor never had a patronising or colonial mentality towards them. They were his equals and the way in which he treated them caused them fully to reciprocate his warmth and respect. He saw, long before many Western Christians did, that the Third World church should be led as quickly as possible by its own nationals. Indeed, it is one of the unique features of IFES that this has been the case from early days. A national of his own country has none of the cultural problems that an outsider has, and, in an age in which many Governments ban foreign missionaries in any guise, he can continue the work of spreading the Gospel unhindered by such decrees.

Furthermore, the Welsh, perhaps unlike the more pragmatic English, are lovers of doctrine—whether Christian or political. One of the greatest strengths of the IFES has been its unashamedly Evangelical basis of faith, and the Doctor played a key part in its formulation. The words on his tombstone in Wales really sum up what he believed in most and what he saw his purpose to be—the proclamation of 'Jesus Christ and Him crucified.' The IFES has stood like a rock on the biblical foundation on which it was built. I remember being at an IFES gathering in Austria in 1971, which took place in Schloss Mittersill, the beautiful old castle that had been bought for them a few years earlier. My grandfather's addresses were on the continuing need to maintain the evangelical faith today. IFES still does so in over 77 countries around the world. All those of us who knew Dr Martyn Lloyd-Jones miss him more than we can say. We have not known anyone of such spiritual stature or personal qualities such as he possessed. We may never in our lifetimes see his like again. But whenever I go to the Austrian Alps and sit in the castle at Mittersill with Christian brothers and sisters from so many lands, separated by language or culture but united indissolubly in Jesus Christ, I know that all my grandfather taught and stood for lives on.

APPENDIX

The Books of Martyn Lloyd-Jones

Hodder and Stoughton
Preaching and Preachers
I Am Not Ashamed

Kingsway
Joy Unspeakable
Prove All Things
The Cross

Pickering and Inglis
The Plight of Man and the Power of God
Spiritual Depression (now co-published with STL)

Inter Varsity Press
From Fear to Faith
Studies in the Sermon on the Mount
Faith on Trial
(and many pamphlets—see below)

Christian Medical Fellowship
The Doctor Himself and the Human Condition
(many pamphlets are included in this volume)

Evangelical Press
(many pamphlets—see below)

Evangelical Press of Wales
Why Does God Allow War
Truth Unchanged, Unchanging

Banner of Truth
1) Ephesians:
God's Way of Reconciliation (2:1–22)
Life in the Spirit in Marriage, Home and Work (5:18–6:9)
The Christian Warfare (6:10–13)
The Christian Soldier (6:10–20)
God's Ultimate Purpose (1:1–23)
The Unsearchable Riches of Christ (3:1–21)
Christian Unity (4:1–16)
Darkness and Light (4:17–5:17)

2) Romans:
Atonement and Justification (3:20–4:25)
Assurance (Rom 5)
The New Man (Rom 6)
The Law—Its Functions and Limits (7:1–8:4)
The Sons of God (8:5–17)
The Final Perseverance of the Saints (8:17–39)
The Gospel of God (Rom 1)

3) Other titles:
Evangelistic Sermons at Aberavon
Expository Sermons on II Peter
Authority

Medical publication
Bacterial Endocarditis (ed. Charles B. Perry)

Pamphlets (various publishers)
The Presentation of the Gospel
Life's Preparatory School
The Mirage Shall Become A Pool
Christ Our Sanctification
Maintaining the Evangelical Faith Today
Sound An Alarm
Conversions: Psychological and Spiritual

The Basis of Christian Unity
1662–1962: From Puritanism to Nonconformity
The Approach to Truth: Scientific and Religious
The Weapons of Our Warfare
Roman Catholicism
Westminster Chapel 1865–1965
Luther and His Message for Today
What is the Church?
Will Hospice Replace the Church?
The State of the Nation
The Supernatural in Medicine [now in The Doctor Himself]
Inaugural Address of the London Theological Seminary.
Thanksgiving Address for David Leggett.

Some smaller pamphlets also came out, some of which were in Welsh. The Doctor has, of course, been translated into several languages, from Spanish to Korean.

Relevant publications
The First Forty Years by Iain Murray (Banner of Truth).
Five Evangelical Leaders by Christopher Catherwood (Hodder and Stoughton).
Memories of Sandfields by Bethan Lloyd-Jones (Banner of Truth).
The *Evangelical Times*, the *Evangelical Magazine of Wales* and the *Banner of Truth* all ran special obituary pieces on Martyn Lloyd-Jones in 1981.

Tapes
Most of Dr Lloyd-Jones post war sermons were recorded, and can easily be obtained from the Martyn Lloyd-Jones Recordings Trust, Crink House, Barcombe Mills, near Lewes, East Sussex (tel: 0273 400622).